C000116314

devon,
PL6 8BX,
UNITED KINGDOM

Bookbarn International Ltd

Unit 1 Hallatrow Business Park, Wells
Road, Hallatrow,
Bristol
Somerset, BS39 6EX,
UNITED KINGDOM

Packing Slip / Invoice
Price: £4.38

Standard

Order Date:	09/01/2020
BBI Order Number:	1073188
Website Order ID:	200109-50-1114

Customer Contact: Daniel Dilkes

NOS1

NOS2

SKU InvID	Locators	Item Information
3072972 10071697	A10-08-04 300082 Cream PAP ExLib - N U:G	**Partnership Agencies In British Urban Policy (The Natural and Built Environment)** Bailey, Nichola & Macdonald, Kelvin & Barker, Alison Published by UCL Press.

If you wish to contact us regarding this order, please email us via eCommerce quoting your order number.

webuk

Thanks for shopping with us

www.bookbarninternational.com

* 1 0 7 3 1 8 8 *

BOOKBARN
INTERNATIONAL

Greetings from Bookbarn International,

Thank you so much for placing an order with us, in doing so you've helped us grow as an independent bookseller.

We hope you're happy with your purchase, however if you have any issues or queries please do not hesitate to contact us.
Log into the website you bought from, locate your order in your order or purchase history and **Contact Seller.**
Our small and committed team provides a fast response to ensure you are fully satisfied.

Kind regards & happy reading!
The BBI Team

Bookbarn Internationalからのご挨拶、

この度はご注文していただきありがとうございます。
おかげさまで私たちはインディペンデント系書店として成長することができております。

ご注文いただいた商品に問題がある場合や質問がある場合は、どうかお気軽にお問い合わせください。

連絡方法は、お客様がご注文されたウェブサイトにログインしていただき、注文履歴のリストから出品者に連絡するボタンより直接ご連絡ください。

当社の小規模で献身的なチームは、お客様が完全に満足していただけることを確実にするために迅速な対応をいたします。

どうぞよろしくお願いいたします。

読書をお楽しみいただけますよう願っております！
BBI チーム

Salutations de Bookbarn International,

Merci beaucoup d'avoir passé une commande chez nous. Vous nous avez aidé à grandir en tant que libraire indépendant.

Nous espérons que vous êtes satisfait de votre achat. Si vous avez des questions ou des questions, n'hésitez pas à nous contacter.

Connectez-vous au site Web où vous avez commandé votre livre, trouvez votre commande dans votre historique d'achat et contactez le vendeur.

Notre équipe petite et engagée fournit une réponse rapide pour s'assurer que vous êtes pleinement satisfait.

Bonne lecture!

Cordialement,
L'équipe BBI

Saludos desde Bookbarn International,

Muchas gracias por hacer un pedido con nosotros. Nos ha ayudado a crecer como librería independiente.

Esperamos que esté satisfecho con su compra. Si tiene algún problema o consulta, no dude en contactarnos: Inicie sesión en el sitio web que utilizó para efectuar su compra, busque su pedido en su historial de compras y comuníquese con el vendedor.

Somos un equipo pequeño, comprometido con brindar una respuesta rápida para garantizar su completa satisfacción.

Saludos cordiales y feliz lectura!

El equipo de BBI

Grüße von Bookbarn International,

Vielen Dank für Ihre Bestellung. Sie haben uns dabei geholfen, ein unabhängiger Buchhändler zu werden.

Wir hoffen, dass Sie mit Ihrem Kauf zufrieden sind. Wenn Sie jedoch Probleme oder Fragen haben, zögern Sie bitte nicht, uns zu kontaktieren.

Gehen Sie auf Meine Bestellungen, suchen Sie Ihre Bestellung in der Liste und klicken Sie auf Verkäufer kontaktieren.

Unser kleines und engagiertes Team bietet eine schnelle Antwort, um sicherzustellen, dass Sie voll zufrieden sind.

Mit freundlichen Grüßen und viel Spaß beim Lesen!
Das BBI-Team

Partnership agencies
in British urban policy

Partnership agencies in British urban policy

Nick Bailey
University of Westminster

with Alison Barker and Kelvin MacDonald

UCL
PRESS

First published in 1995 by UCL Press.

UCL Press Limited
University College London
Gower Street
London WC1E 6BT

The name of University College London (UCL) is a registered trade mark
used by UCL Press with the consent of the owner.

ISBNs: 1-85728-069-5 HB
       1-85728-070-9 PB

British Library Cataloguing in Publication Data
A catalogue record for this book is available from the British Library.

Typeset in Times and Optima.
Printed and bound by Page Bros (Norwich) Ltd, England.

Contents

Acknowledgements

We would like to record our thanks to the many people who contributed so willingly to enabling us to complete this study. Naturally, any errors or oversights remain entirely the authors' responsibility.

We are particularly grateful to the many officers and members of the partnerships who agreed to be interviewed and the many others who met our requests for detailed information. For once it is possible to say genuinely that, without their openness and willingness to devote large amounts of time to us, this study would not have been possible. We were deeply impressed by their dedication and commitment, as well as the contribution of the many others to whom we spoke. We are especially indebted to Alan Bishop (Director of Planning and Development at Birmingham Heartlands Development Corporation), Roisin McDonough (Director of the Brownlow Community Trust), Antony Rifkin (formerly Co-ordinator of the Greenwich Waterfront Development Partnership), John Collier (Chief Executive of the Newcastle Initiative), Sorrel Brookes (formerly Director of the Wester Hailes Partnership), and Douglas Harrison (formerly Director of the Woodlands Community Development Trust).

Andy Thornley of Reading University and Mike Edwards of University College London generously agreed not only to assess the original proposal but also to read and comment on a final draft. Their support for the initial concept, and their valuable suggestions, were most gratefully received. We would also like to pay a special tribute to Roger Jones' sound editorial advice and continuing equanimity as several deadlines passed.

Financial assistance was gratefully received from the University of Westminster, which provided the salary of our researcher, Alison Barker. We would also like to pay tribute to our colleagues in the School of Urban Development and Planning for their direct and indirect assistance and intellectual stimulation. Bill Erickson kindly assisted with the preparation of the organizational diagrams. The university library responded cheerfully and promptly to our many requests for publications, and the planning subject librarian, Fiona Middleton, deserves special thanks.

Nick Bailey
University of Westminster, October 1994

Abbreviations

BCT   Brownlow Community Trust
BHDC   Birmingham Heartlands Development Corporation
BItC   Business in the Community
CAT   City Action Team
CBI   Confederation of British Industry
CCP   Comprehensive Community Project
CDP   Community Development Project
DLG   Derelict land grant
DoE   Department of the Environment
ERDF   European Regional Development Fund
EP   English Partnerships
ESF   European Social Fund
EU   European Union
FIG   Financial Institutions Group
GEAR   Glasgow Eastern Area Renewal project
GWDP   Greenwich Waterfront Development Partnership
GRO   Grants for rent and ownership (Scotland)
HAT   Housing Action Trust
LEC   Local Enterprise Company
MSC   Manpower Services Commission
PPA   Priority Partnership Areas (Scotland)
SDA   Scottish Development Agency
SE   Scottish Enterprise
RB   Single regeneration budget
TEC   Training and Enterprise Council
TNI   The Newcastle Initiative
UDC   Urban Development Corporation
UDW   Urban Development Wales
UP   Urban Programme
UPA   Urban priority area
WCDT   Woodlands Community Development Trust
WDA   Welsh Development Agency
WHP   Wester Hailes Partnership

CHAPTER 1
Introduction

Partnership has always been a concept associated with the inner cities and urban regeneration. It has been dismissed as "containing a high level of ambiguity" (Mackintosh 1992: 210) and "a meaningless concept" (Lawless 1991: 10) because of its application to a wide variety of policy initiatives by both advocates and critics. As Lawless rightly notes, "There is no legal definition of partnership, nor is there anything we can call the "typical" partnership (ibid.). Yet increasingly, the term is seen not only as an essential adjunct of policy but as the most important foundation of the government's strategy towards urban areas. It may not be overstating the case to say that there is now a broad consensus among the main political parties and practitioners that claims that partnership is now the *only* basis on which successful urban regeneration can be achieved. The extent of this transformation is indicated in the recent review of urban policy sponsored by the Department of the Environment (DoE), which puts the need to encourage long-term collaborative partnerships at the head of five policy conclusions (Robson et al. 1994: xiv). As we argue in the text, the reasons for the promotion of partnership to the top of the political agenda have much to do with the economic restructuring of local economies and deep-seated changes in the machinery of government at both local and national levels.

This book sets out to chart the origins and evolution of the concept throughout the past two and half decades of urban policy. Despite a long history of relatively close working relationships between public and private sectors (for example in the planning and construction of the new towns), the idea of partnership emerged in the late 1970s as part of an attempt to improve the co-ordination and delivery of central and local government services. From the 1980s onwards the incoming Conservative Government saw it as a means of transferring responsibility for urban regeneration to the private sector. More recently, policy has favoured closer collaboration between all local interests through initiatives such as City Challenge and the Single Regeneration Budget, in conjunction with a growing political accommodation between central and local government.

For the purposes of this book we have defined a partnership as a coalition of interests drawn from more than one sector in order to prepare and oversee an agreed strategy for the regeneration of a defined area. We use the term "partnership" throughout because it is used most frequently by government and practi-

1

tioners. The terms "coalition" and "urban regime" are more often used in the academic literature, but for our purposes these words are interchangeable. In Chapter 2 we attempt a typology of different kinds of partnership based on several variables. For completeness we include development partnerships, which normally refer to contracts or joint ventures between local authorities and private developers set up in order to promote a specific development where mutual benefits are intended. These joint working arrangements appear to us to open up a different set of questions about the development process and are therefore taken no further in this book. Our concern is those partnerships that involve longer-term relationships between the public, private and voluntary sectors, whereby the partners contribute to both strategy preparation and implementation in a defined urban area and over an extended period.

The ambiguity surrounding partnership largely derives from the different political positions adopted by commentators. Practitioners in particular often speak of "real partnerships", as though an ideal model existed if only all people of goodwill could be persuaded to adopt it. In our view there is no ideal model, but evidence suggests that different examples emerge through the political interaction of different interest groups in particular political contexts. It is the task of research to explore the perceptions of different actors and the extent to which the interaction between partners leads to the achievement of desired objectives.

Our approach has therefore been to explore the concept of partnership from three different directions. Chapter 2 examines the academic literature on the subject in a search for theoretical explanations for the rise of the partnership approach, to identify what institutional forms they take and what it is that partnership agencies actually do. Chapter 3 then goes on to explore how the concept has been applied in successive phases of urban policy and how central government has sought to use it as a vehicle for restructuring the boundaries between the public and private sectors. Chapters 4 and onwards examine six case studies of different partnership arrangements in England, Scotland and Northern Ireland. The conclusions draw on general themes emerging from the case studies, discuss the implications of a national policy based on partnerships, and identify directions for the future.

The examination of the changing definition of partnership over an extended period raises several practical and conceptual issues. First, it is possible to ask several straightforward questions about why partnerships emerge in some areas and not others, which interests are involved and what are they trying to achieve? A second set of questions is then raised about the role of government. Why has government adopted the concept and how has the idea been incorporated into national policy-making? In particular, why is partnership seen to be an essential ingredient of urban regeneration in deprived urban areas, when it is not a subject of debate in the mainstream delivery of government policy elsewhere? Moreover, if government genuinely wishes to integrate and co-ordinate the contributions of the public, private and voluntary sectors, what changes are needed in the structure and functions of government to achieve these aims? Finally, if the private sector is encouraged to play a larger role in urban regeneration, are we witnessing a wholesale transfer of powers and responsibilities to the corporate sector, or a fundamental transformation of the debate about what can and should be done to promote local economic development and to improve urban society?

We do not pretend to have answers to all these questions. What we hope to do is at least illustrate the diversity of approaches adopted in different parts of the country and to place these in a wider theoretical and historical context.

Carrying out research on complex organizations involves some methodological difficulties. By their nature, partnerships are dynamic organizations that operate on the basis of a complex interaction between the partners, as well as within different institutional and policy frameworks. They tend to be action-orientated, pragmatic, innovative and responsive to new opportunities, while maintaining few records of past achievements or having the time or resources to evaluate their activities fully. At the same time there is relatively little theoretical literature on carrying out such a research task. Our approach was influenced by the work of Smith & Cantley (1985) on pluralistic evaluation, which they applied in evaluating a new psychogeriatric day hospital. Through a series of interviews, with a variety of key actors and use of secondary sources, we have attempted to build up a narrative report on the origins, development and activities of each case. The conclusions to each example draw out the main issues for detailed examination later. In Chapter 10 we take a comparative approach according to several criteria in relation to the internal workings of the partnerships, as well as an examination of the external issues relating to partnership as an approach to urban regeneration.

The selection of case studies also produced methodological difficulties. First of all, we looked for examples that were reasonably well established, in the hope that there would be clear evidence of action "on the ground". Secondly, we wanted examples that illustrated the range of origins, whether genuinely local in the sense of being promoted by residents or the local authority, or inspired by public or private initiatives. Thirdly, we looked for examples in different urban and regional contexts. We thus chose Birmingham Heartlands because it had begun as a local public–private initiative and subsequently became a UDC, with half the board appointed by the city council. Greenwich Waterfront was selected for comparison with Birmingham Heartlands because of its interesting representative structure and the potential offered by large areas of derelict land. When first approached, a bid for the second round of City Challenge had been submitted for the Woolwich area, which would have added a further dimension to the study if it had been successful. The Newcastle Initiative is an example of a top-down partnership, promoted by the private sector and nearest to the American model, which was operating within a complex network of other developmental and promotional agencies in the region. Wester Hailes Partnership is one of the four "New Life" partnerships promoted by the Scottish Office, which we thought could offer some interesting comparisons with the English examples. Brownlow was selected because of its location in a former new town in Northern

Ireland and the fact that it was part of the European Poverty 3 programme. Finally, Woodlands appeared to be a good example of the growing movement of community-based development trusts, where local people were directly responsible for urban regeneration.

These six examples were selected from the growing array of possible organizations in order to illustrate the main dimensions of urban regeneration through partnership. Our intention is to describe in detail how each one has developed, their funding sources, organizational arrangements and implementation strategies, in order to draw out wider conclusions about good practice, to assist those setting up new partnership arrangements and to reflect more generally on the process of urban regeneration.

CHAPTER 2

The concept of partnership in urban regeneration

> The approach to urban policy I have described is not so very different from that which thousands of companies take in devising their business strategies and targets. Companies have to weigh the risks and opportunities of investments. They have to ensure that staleness and a loss of morale does not set in, even when times are hard. They have to spot and deploy talent and join with others to get results. They are accountable for the effective use of resources. My aim in our urban policy is to bring about an effective marriage of the private and public sectors in securing lasting regeneration. *Michael Howard MP, Secretary of State for the Environment, 25 January 1993*

Although cities have always grown and developed through a complex interaction of the public and private sectors, the current trend towards coalition-building in urban regeneration has only emerged in the past 30 years. During the post-war period, planning and urban development were carried out through a relatively clear division of responsibilities between central and local government. The dominant policies included the containment of urban growth, in part through the designation of green belts, the dispersal of population to new towns and a system of regional planning in order to prevent overdevelopment in the South East and to ensure an even distribution of employment. Local authorities had powers to guide and control development through statutory planning legislation, as well as the resources to carry out comprehensive redevelopment, which included house-building and the provision of community and leisure facilities. Central government retained strategic powers to operate the regional planning system, designate new and expanded towns and to appoint development corporations. A broad political consensus about the purpose of the planning system remained intact for the first three decades after the Second World War.

By the mid-1960s the continuing strategy of the dispersal of industry and population came under increasing scrutiny. The rate of growth of the national economy proved unable to sustain the ever-increasing cost of local-authority redevelopment programmes, and growing evidence of poverty, unemployment, educational disadvantage and poor housing was emerging in what became labelled the "inner city". Continuing economic restructuring and the movement of immigrants into the space left by population dispersal and relocation, which was exploited nationally by politicians on the Right, pushed Prime Minister Harold Wilson into launching a national Urban Programme directed by the Home Office. Indirectly, this invention of a new policy area also provided a means of support for the many community organizations that first raised the alarm about what was happening in the older urban areas.

From this point a series of urban initiatives explored a variety of strategies, structures and agencies, guided by an equally diverse set of political philosophies and problem definitions in order to come up with solutions to the "inner-city problem". In reality this was a problem that had far more to do with the results of structural changes in the economy as they impacted differentially on urban areas, than being related to any particular segment of the city. In the search for new solutions to growing problems, the roles and responsibilities of different levels of government, and the former certainties of the relationship between public and private sectors, became confused. Attention here is focused on the idea of partnership – just one of many to emerge from the complex arena of the politics of the inner city.

This chapter sets out to explore some of the key variables involved in the initiation and constitution of partnerships, looks at the processes by which they operate, examines the political science literature, which helps explain their growing importance, and sets out a framework for analyzing specific examples. It then goes on to identify the key variables that influence partnership formation, and a typology of different models of partnership is discussed. Finally, seven core processes are examined. In exploring the theoretical literature we hope to illustrate how partnerships need to be explained both in terms of their internal structure, powers and decision-making procedures, and as a response to external changes to the urban economy and the national policy context.

The rise of the partnership approach

The changing nature of the idea of partnership in urban policy must be seen against the backdrop of the fundamental changes in the political, economic and institutional context within which Britain was governed from the mid-1970s onwards. For almost 30 years the bi-partisan approach to Keynesian economics and full employment remained relatively intact, with an interventionist public sector operating a policy of demand management and a universalist approach towards consumption. The consensus towards policy-making included the direct involvement of business, trade unions and government in a series of corporatist national economic planning institutions. Local government received extensive powers and growing resources as the main agency for delivering national programmes such as education, social services and public housing.

From the mid-1970s the post-war consensus began to crumble and, partly as a consequence, the two main political parties moved towards opposite poles of the political spectrum. With the election of Mrs Thatcher as leader of the Conservative Party and her subsequent general election victory in 1979, a new political agenda was set for more than a decade. This was largely based on a free market philosophy, deregulation and privatization of State assets, which fundamentally altered the relationship between the State, business and the citizen. On the face of it, ideas about partnership might well have been thrown out with others to do with consensus government; in urban policy they remained intact at the local level and assumed all the characteristics of a new orthodoxy, despite being subjected to repeated redefinition. There are several reasons for this apparent contradiction.

Economic restructuring and deprivation

The extent to which the United Kingdom suffered a more rapid economic decline than it might otherwise have done as a result of the Conservative Government's economic policies in the 1980s is a matter of debate. However, the country suffered one of its worst recessions in 1980–3, causing growing unemployment that peaked at over 3 million in July 1986, and the decimation of manufacturing capacity in those regions where it had been a major source of employment. The subsequent boom, engineered through the deregulation of the City of London in 1986 and the expansion of credit, reduced unemployment to about 1.5 million in 1989 by the rapid expansion of service industries and property development. A further recession from 1990 onwards pushed unemployment back up to 3 million early in 1993, this time with both manufacturing and service industries being equally badly affected.

In the first recession of the period it was the major cities where economic restructuring was most apparent, through the closure of major manufacturing companies and branch plants. In cities such as Glasgow and Liverpool, unemployment levels exceeded 20 per cent, and in inner areas and peripheral estates went over 50 per cent. In the West Midlands, Birmingham lost 156 000 jobs between 1981 and 1983, of which 85 per cent were in manufacturing (Lawless 1991). Likewise, the steel town of Sheffield lost 42 000 jobs in metal goods, engineering and vehicle manufacture between 1971 and 1986.

In the early part of the decade, several cities experimented with alternative economic strategies, of which Sheffield and Liverpool were the best known examples (Judd & Parkinson 1990: 133), as a means of generating new economic sectors and creating jobs. Other cities, such as Newcastle and Birmingham, began to investigate the potential of closer links with the private sector. In Scotland, the Scottish Development Agency became the main agent of economic development in cities such as Glasgow, and experimented with initiatives, such as the Glasgow Eastern Area Renewal project, partnership agreements with local authorities in area projects such as Motherwell (Gilchrist 1985), initiatives dominated by the private sector in Inverclyde (Gulliver 1984), and through Glasgow Action (Boyle 1989) in the city centre. The Welsh Development Agency uses similar strategies in working closely with local authorities and the private sector through joint ventures, town development trusts or consortia (Pavitt 1990).

The centralization of power

Along with economic decline and growing levels of unemployment, the cities experienced a major political change in the 1980s, the gradual leaching of powers and finance away from local government, and, in the case of the Greater London Council and the metropolitan counties, outright abolition. Whereas in the 1970s local government had control of major services such as strategic planning, transport, education and housing, many of these have now been transferred to central government departments, quangos or special agencies, such as UDCs, Task Forces, City Action Teams and Housing Action Trusts, accountable only to central government. In 1988, Urban Development Grant was replaced by City Grant, and was allocated directly to private sector applicants without local authority involvement. The introduction of the Community Charge, and from 1993 the Council Tax, brought increased capping powers over total expenditure, and limitations on how particular budget heads might be spent. Income from the sale of council houses and other capital receipts was effectively frozen by Treasury regulations.

This dramatic shift of power to Whitehall meant that local authorities looked for new institutional arrangements at the local level in order to maximize both their influence and the leverage by which limited funds, or resources such as land, could be used to maximum advantage. Partnerships proved one way in which these two objectives could to some extent be achieved. In addition, local authorities began to realize that, by the mid-1980s, the balance of power between central and local government had shifted to such an extent that the possibility of launching and sustaining a high-cost publicly funded local economic strategy was extremely limited. Central government not only had full control of local government finance but could also use urban policy to remove large areas from local control by the designation of UDCs, Enterprise Zones and similar initiatives.

We examine in more detail below some of the theoretical explanations of why the idea of partnership has been so widely adopted.

The fragmentation of central government initiatives

In response to growing urban problems, central government launched a series of inner-city initiatives from 1968 onwards. These initiatives had several common characteristics. They tended to be relatively small in terms of the area covered and resources available, they tended to be sectoral or departmental in nature, and they focused on particular social groups, such as the educationally disadvantaged, ethnic minorities, the unemployed and those suffering multiple deprivation. Throughout the 1980s the Departments of Environment (DoE), Employment (DE) and Trade and Industry (DTI), the Home Office and the Department of Education competed for resources to be targeted on the inner city. The result was a struggle for competitive advantage, where narrow departmental objectives tended to override wider requirements to co-ordinate on an inter-departmental basis and to collaborate with other local interests.

City Action Teams were introduced in some urban areas in 1985 in order to co-ordinate the work of regional offices of the DoE, DE and DTI but the Audit Commission found their role "anomalous when UP funds are intended to serve a similar purpose" (Audit Commission 1989: 31).

Where evaluation did take place, it tended to adopt a departmental perspective to ensure the continuity of the programme, or where adverse recommendations were made they were often ignored by government (for example the report of the National Audit Office 1990). The impact of some of the major DoE initiatives, such as Inner City Partnerships, City Action Teams and the UDCs has rarely been collectively evaluated to assess their overall impact. Apart from the Audit Commission report (1989), no overall review of urban policy was published until 1994 (Robson et al. 1994). As a result, new initiatives have tended to be superimposed on existing programmes in a top-down fashion, making co-ordination more difficult and reducing the role of local authorities yet further.

The development of new alliances between local government, local businesses and the voluntary sector at the local level can therefore be seen as a partial response to the array of ill co-ordinated government initiatives. Adopting a partnership approach goes some way to fill the local policy vacuum where geographical areas or policy sectors have been removed from local influence, and has provided a new basis for promoting local regeneration. In many cases, such as Birmingham, Leeds and Sheffield, forming locally supported partnerships became a tactic to fend off (not always successfully) unwanted central government threats to impose UDCs.

Filling the leadership vacuum

Along with the increasing centralization of power and direct government control of urban regeneration in the 1980s has been an attempt to increase the role played by the private sector in managing and implementing urban policy. This objective was first set out in the inner cities White Paper (DOE 1977d) and has been repeated in subsequent documents such as Action for Cities (Cabinet Office 1988), and in the appointment of boards of management to UDCs, Task Forces, Training and Enterprise Councils and most recently City Challenge regeneration agencies. Likewise, partnerships in cities such as Sheffield, Birmingham and London have adopted a similar approach. There are several reasons for this.

In the first place, national organizations such as the Confederation of British Industry (CBI) and Business in the Community (BitC) set up working parties, promoted research to encourage companies to get more involved in community affairs, and disseminated ideas from the USA and Europe about corporate social responsibility. The setting up of business leadership teams in several major cities and a network of local enterprise agencies were two of the most significant outcomes of this process. In addition, central government actively promoted the greater involvement of the corporate sector through appointments by patronage to the boards of regeneration agencies and by the secondment of key staff into the DOE. The establishment of the Financial Institutions Group was just one of the more publicity-conscious responses to the civil disturbances of 1981. Although the response was patchy, some leading companies and individuals, particularly those in the contracting and building materials industries, or with a strong sense of local identity, began to see the financial benefits of direct involvement in policy-making and the potential to influence government from "within".

Local authorities and other public agencies have found that involving the private sector in urban regeneration gives their projects credibility with government and local employers and helps lever in new resources. This is particularly relevant when evidence of private sector involvement is needed to gain government funding for City Grant, City Challenge and the Urban Partnership Fund. As a result, local authorities have been keen to develop a variety of links with private sector interests, which in turn have assisted in lobbying for transport and infrastructure investment in places as diverse as Newcastle upon Tyne, Burnley, Camden and Park Royal in west London. In economically peripheral regions such as the North East, Wales and Scotland, there is a much longer history of the establishment of joint working parties and development agencies, of which local authorities are usually active members.

In Scotland, business representatives have for some years been involved in several different initiatives set up by the Scottish Development Agency. Glasgow Action and Aberdeen Beyond 2000 were both managed by a majority of industrialists with an interest in city centre development, and several area projects and partnership agreements included the private sector. With the merger of the Scottish Development Agency and the Training Agency in 1991, thirteen Local Enterprise Companies were formed, of which two thirds of their members are drawn from the senior ranks of the private sector (Hayton 1992: 270).

Although research is very limited on what real benefits business representatives bring to partnership arrangements, there is substantial evidence from all parts of the country that the private sector is now playing a much larger role in

10

urban regeneration than it was even five years ago (e.g. Whitney & Haughton 1990). This is largely a response to central government's intentions to give the private sector greater ownership of urban policy, but it also reflects both pressures from national bodies such as the CBI and a need to fill a vacuum left by the transfer of powers and the diminished resources of local government. An important motive for promoting ideas of partnership has been the unspoken expectation that the private sector will be less willing to disinvest from particular localities in which it is involved when restructuring is required.

Introducing synergy and new management skills

One of the arguments often presented in favour of partnerships is that they can lead to "synergy – pooling expertise and resources in complementary rather than purely competitive fashion can increase the total impact of a project, the whole being greater than the sum of the parts" (Haughton & Whitney 1989). Working together in developing and implementing a common strategy, it is claimed, can increase effort and effectiveness, utilize local knowledge and commitment to an area, and bring to bear the skills and expertise of all sectors (Haughton & Whitney 1989).

Although statements of this kind remain largely untested, there are several real benefits to central government in promoting this view. Perhaps most important, it implies a new role for the local authority as an "enabler", in assisting in setting up and jointly managing partnerships, but without having overall control. This relates closely to other aspects of partnership already noted, such as the centralization and privatization of urban policy.

Secondly, it is possible to argue that partnership will bring a new sense of urgency to local problems, in that it will, through private sector pressure, reduce delay and bureaucracy to a minimum and will encourage the use of private sector financial management and entrepreneurial skills. This can be seen as part of the growing use of managerialist terminology and processes in all levels of government.

Finally, there are substantial financial arguments in favour of partnership, which are close to the Conservative party's ideas about a suitable role for local government. Not only does partnership imply that public resources are used to lever private resources, but, proponents argue, that better value for money is achieved through priorities being influenced by the private sector. It is suggested that, through effective cost controls and the monitoring of contracts and the use of private sector-orientated management techniques in the initiation, the implementation and monitoring of contracts and projects is improved. Many of these management techniques accord closely with government initiatives already legislated for: contracting out of services, local management of schools, an emphasis on outputs and standards, the definition of performance indicators and the close monitoring of budgets and expenditure.

11

All of these factors have created a suitable climate for the mobilization of a wide range of local interests into coalitions or partnerships. Perhaps the most important has been the substantial changes in the balance of power between central and local government, which have given rise to a variety of experiments and new initiatives at the local level. Hence, it is necessary to examine some of the theoretical explanations for changes in the structuring of the local State in more detail.

The restructuring of the local State

The decline in local government autonomy

The local State remains an important focus of study in the political sciences because it has always retained an element of local autonomy in the delivery of local services and in influencing the initiation and control of local development. It is often the main contact between citizens and the delivery mechanisms for the provision of public services, and it plays a key role in mediating between public and private interests. Local government, which is one part of a wider array of local State interests, is closely defined by precise constitutional, statutory and legal powers creating "semi-autonomous concentrations of authority which can be used in the pursuit of a variety of interests" (Gurr & King 1987: 50). Although in most European countries local government has developed many similar characteristics of powers of revenue raising, electoral representation, appointed officers and a degree of influence over the local political environment, it has developed several different modes of operation and action (Goldsmith 1992: 395).

Gurr & King (1987: 56) focus specifically on the concept of the autonomy of the local State as the most significant variable, reflecting its historical formation, constitutional status, revenue base, power relations between national and local power elites and incorporation of social groups. They refine these down to two ideal types of local State autonomy:

- *Type I* The local State is autonomous to the extent that it can pursue its interests without being substantially constrained by local economic and social conditions.
- *Type II* The local State is autonomous to the extent that it can pursue its interests without substantial interference by the national State. (Gurr & King 1987: 57–62)

Both types of constraint on autonomy have the effect of limiting the ability of local government to influence community wellbeing. With Type I local economic circumstances affect the ability to raise local revenues so that the most deprived areas are least able to raise local taxes. High levels of urban deprivation, unemployment and declining economic activity will impose a growing burden on local budgets, whereas increased local taxes may stimulate the relocation of individuals and companies able to pay. Recent changes to local tax-raising powers have to some extent modified the relationship between income and expenditure between different localities in Britain. A rate equalization scheme used to operate between local authorities with different levels of prosperity. This was replaced by the Community Charge and subsequently the Council Tax, whereby a uniform business rate is levied nationally on all commercial premises and distributed according to complex criteria by central government. Britain therefore differs substantially from the USA, where pro-development growth coalition activity can significantly boost local tax revenues.

Secondly, dominant interests may exert a direct or indirect influence on the local political culture in order to influence decision-making or to remove issues from the political agenda. In Britain, it has been local, regional and national businesses that have had the greatest influence in promoting pro-growth, development strategies at the local level, aided by changes in central government policies. Influence may be brought to bear by direct pressure on local government decision-making, by creating a political environment that tends to promote business interests or by the appointment of representatives to key posts or election to local government. Likewise, and under particular circumstances, trade unions and community organizations can exert influence in a system of representative democracy that is responsive to local interests and public opinion.

Finally, the structure of local government can itself operate as a constraint on effective action. The fragmentation of powers and responsibilities between elected and non-elected elements of the local State and the transfer of powers to central government can significantly reduce the scope for action. For example, the abolition of the Greater London Council and the metropolitan county councils in 1986 affected the extent to which local government could operate effectively at a strategic level. The recent review of the future of county councils and districts has concentrated almost entirely on the delivery of local services through unitary authorities, with very little consideration given to how strategic functions might be carried out.

Type II constraints on autonomy – those imposed by changing central–local government relations – have been tightened over the past 15 years. In Britain, legislative powers and financial controls have been used consistently by central government, both to reduce the influence of local government and to transfer powers to other central and local agencies. British local government operates under the legal principle of *ultra vires*, where legal powers are prescribed by Parliament and no action can be taken beyond these limitations. In contrast, in the USA, local governments are the creatures of State governments and in some cases are given general competencies to act (Gurr & King 1987: 64). In some cases, central government has also been able to manipulate grant regimes without further legislation in order to bypass local government or to further certain national policy objectives.

Secondly, local autonomy may be limited by central government determining both levels of need and fixing the resources to be used to meet these needs. In Britain, Standard Spending Assessments are issued annually to each local authority prescribing the amount of resources to be spent each year: authorities wishing to spend more have to raise the additional sum from local (residential) tax payers. In addition, certain areas of expenditure such as housing cannot be cross-subsidized from general funds, and separate bids for expenditure on roads and transport and public housing need to be submitted and approved annually. Moreover, central government requires regular statistics and monitoring reports from local government to ensure that expenditure is made according to government-determined priorities and objectives.

Thirdly, central government issues advice and guidelines to local authority, some of which is mandatory, some discretionary. This has the effect of complicating the policy environment, since local authorities need to decide whether to conform, resist or oppose government directions, as well as to assess the implications of each kind of action. Central government's stance has been to reduce local autonomy as far as possible in order to increase local government's productivity, as well as to achieve ideological and financial objectives in line with national economic policy.

By assessing the extent of the two types of local autonomy it is possible to arrive at a residual estimate of the extent to which local government can have "an independent impact on the wellbeing of their citizens" (Goldsmith 1990: 31). By the end of the 1980s the autonomy of local government had reached a nadir as central government instituted several strategies to exert greater political, ideological and financial control on local government. Local government autonomy was at a low ebb but not entirely removed. The search for new forms of partnership at the local level was one significant response.

Changing central government strategies

Throughout the past 15 years the Conservative government has attempted to place a new political order on the inner cities, through a variety of policy initiatives, legislation and the setting up of new, non-elected agencies. The turning-point came in 1979 with the election of Mrs Thatcher's first administration, when the idea of partnership between central and local government was recast in the image of the evolving ideology of "the enterprise culture" (Deakin & Edwards 1993, Thornley 1993) and privatism (Barnekov et al. 1990).

Whereas the White Paper, *Policy for the inner cities* (DoE 1977d), described local authorities as "the natural agencies to tackle inner area problems" and found that new town development corporations were not a suitable model, because they lacked accountability to the local electorate, two years later Michael Heseltine was promoting the Urban Development Corporations (UDCs) as an alternative model. In doing so he argued that "there is a need for a single-minded determination not possible for the local authorities concerned with their much broader responsibilities" (DoE 1979).

In fact the designation of two UDCs in 1980, followed by a further 11 in subsequent years, soon came to typify the policy solutions favoured by the incoming government, and for some years they remained the "flagship" of urban policy in England. Instead of a concerted attack on inner-city problems by central and local government, new non-elected agencies were set up with sole powers to execute policies leading to market-led, property-based regeneration. As Parkinson noted in 1988:

> UDCs are the most important example of the current government's philosophy, presenting its distinctive view about urban regeneration, the way it should be organized and financed and the results it should achieve. The model assumes regeneration should be physically led by a single-purpose agency, free from the restraints of local democracy, which should establish at minimal public cost the conditions for private investment, which will generate wealth that will eventually flow back into the community. (Parkinson 1988: 110)

The assumptions built into the government's pro-market philosophy have been fully analyzed by commentators such as Thornley (1993), Deakin & Edwards (1993), Lawless (1990) and Robson (1988). In specifically examining the role of UDCs, Imrie & Thomas (1993) have suggested that most UDCs are becoming increasingly embedded in complex local policy networks and are choosing to adopt – or being forced into – new partnership arrangements with local authorities, community groups and business organizations in an "enabling" role not unlike some local authorities.

The rapid transformation of urban policy from a broadly public interventionist strategy in the early 1970s, to privatism in the 1980s and 1990s brought a dramatic curtailment of local authority autonomy in their ability to influence the local economy. Many of the authorities that experimented with interventionist enterprise boards and "alternative economic strategies" in places such as London, Liverpool and Sheffield are now operating within the policy parameters set by central government. Most notably, Sheffield shifted from radical intervention to partnership in a short period of time (Lawless 1990). Moore (1990), for example, suggests that the new urban Left had attempted to impose local State control on local companies in order to achieve policy objectives, but the lack of powers and central government support meant that no more than voluntary co-operation could be attained. This may have at least indirectly been a prerequisite for closer forms of partnership, once local policy had been redefined.

Moore (1990) identifies three basic processes underlying central–local relations, which cumulatively have reduced the role and autonomy of local government. The first, displacement, describes the systematic transfer of powers to other non-elected agencies, such as UDCs, Training and Enterprise Councils and Local Enterprise Companies in Scotland, inner-city Task Forces and Housing Action Trusts. In addition, some areas were subject to reduced local authority control, such as Enterprise Zones and Simplified Planning Zones designed to encourage property-led developments orientated towards private investment.

15

The second underlying process has been the encouragement of partnership. In this case central government has reinterpreted the 1977 formulation of partnership between central and local government as one between central government and the private sector. Here, local and national entrepreneurs have been encouraged to play a larger role by being nominated to the boards of UDCs and TECs, by having direct access to grant regimes such as City Grant and by redefining the role and board membership of development agencies in Scotland and Wales. In addition, private sector agencies such as enterprise agencies, business support groups and Business in the Community have been encouraged to play a larger role in the inner city on grounds of both self-interest and social responsibility (CBI 1988). Coulson (1993: 28) identifies patronage as an important element in the restructuring of urban policy, whereby "central government exerts its influence through the arbitrary dispensation of resources".

In the third process, privatization incorporates the other two processes as well as the legal requirement for central and local government departments to enter into service level agreements, to experiment with market testing and to contract out specified services and the management of buildings and facilities. The diversification of public sector housing to other tenures and the provisions for schools to opt out of local authority control are part of the same process.

Into the post-Fordist future?

A further area of analysis in this section throws a different light on the restructuring of the economy, the State and society. Stoker (1990) draws on the Parisian Regulation School, which is concerned with "the historically specific ways in which Western industrial economies are organized, how they cope with crises and how they change" (Stoker 1990: 243). The School distinguishes three broad stages in the development of industrial economies. The first is a period of "competitive" regulation stretching from the mid-nineteenth century to the 1920s. The second, from the 1930s to 1970s, is one of "Fordist" regulation; the third involves a shift to "flexible specialization". The latter period is characterized by the transition from mass production towards smaller, flexible and computer-aided companies orientated towards specific markets and consumer interests, and often primarily based in the service sector. Large corporations increasingly operate as a series of decentralized subunits, and management becomes less hierarchical, consumer-orientated and driven by quality of product and service. Likewise, employment practices change, so that there is an increasing differentiation between highly paid core teams of skilled workers and managers, and those on the periphery who are low paid, part-time and less skilled. The State is seen as having the role of facilitating the transition of the economy and society and absorbing many of the social costs involved.

Harvey has also written extensively on "the transformation in urban governance in late capitalism" (Harvey 1989). In reviewing trends in both Europe and the USA, he notes a transition from "managerialism to entrepreneurialism in urban governance" and that public–private partnership is a common element in very different political and legal contexts:

First, the new entrepreneurialism has, as its centrepiece, the notion of "public–private partnership" in which a traditional local boosterism is integrated with the use of local governmental powers to try and attract external sources of funding, new direct investments, or new employment sources . . . Secondly, the activity of that public–private partnership is entrepreneurial precisely because it is speculative in execution and design and therefore dogged by all the difficulties and dangers that attach to speculative as opposed to rationally planned and co-ordinated development. (Harvey 1989: 7)

Stoker goes on to suggest that local government has mirrored developments in the wider economy by adapting to its own purposes organizational principles and management practices from the private sector. Stewart (1989: 173) identifies three main organizing principles in local government from the 1930s to the early 1970s, broadly coincident with the Fordist period: functionalism (the division of the organization around particular tasks and responsibilities); uniformity (the provision of services to a common standard and on a common pattern); and hierarchy (organization through many tiers, with accountability running from the field officers, to the chief officer and eventually to the committee). In retrospect, it could be argued that a tendency towards fragmentation and increasing political turbulence led to the introduction of corporate management techniques imported from the private sector (see, for example, Benington 1975, Cockburn 1977). The close alliance between management practice in the public and private sectors should not be surprising, Stoker argues, in that it reflects "the economic and cultural domination of private capital" (Stoker 1989: 152).

Stoker goes on to predict that the current period of "post-Fordism" will lead to the restructuring of local government, including the introduction of new technology, internal restructuring, changing employment practices and the "opening up" of political processes to a different form of consumption politics. One key trend has been "the rise of new procedures for involving business groups in local decision-making" (Stoker 1990: 259), in both formal, unelected local political institutions and informal networks of influence.

Although regulation theory and propositions about a post-Fordist stage of development remain highly conjectural, they do provide a broader canvas on which to observe rapid developments in the economy, State and society. However, there are serious dangers of seeing current developments in the local State as inevitably dependent on wider socio-economic restructuring. Stoker maintains that the arena remains highly politically contested and that different political interests and commentators perceive very different roles for local government, although currently the Right wing perspective remains in the ascendant (Stoker 1989: 166). Others have argued that the local State is a key component in local

17

modes of regulation, but that local political and economic circumstances will produce an uneven pattern of neoliberal, neocorporatist or neostatist regimes. Goodwin et al. conclude that "the local State is both an object and an agent of regulation, which itself needs to be regulated so that its strategies and structures can be used to help forge a new social, political and economic settlement" (Goodwin et al. 1993: 67).

On the other hand, Harding (1990), who has written extensively on the rise of public–private partnerships, argues that "the restructuring of the State has been driven by political and ideological factors" and that changes in Britain have been sufficiently different from other advanced industrial countries not to support any theory that assumes a direct connection between economic and political/ institutional change. "It would be difficult to see . . . any hint of a conscious restructuring for a 'post-Fordist' society".

Harding (ibid.: 97) strongly takes the view that "the shift from radicalism to the local public–private partnership model by local authorities can be explained by a combination of external and internal stimuli among which the low level of significance granted to local autonomy in this particular unitary system is by far the most important".

Thus, local government has experienced a period of rapid change over the past 15 years for a variety of complex reasons. Although the decline in local autonomy and the growth of non-elected local State agencies based on patronage remain undisputed, the broader trends implied by the transition from Fordism are less easy to perceive and they continue to be subject to academic debate. What is clear is that central government has, through a variety of political and policy measures over an extended period, engineered the transition of local government from being the primary agency to tackle inner area problems to being one of many players in an increasingly fragmented local State, which "implies the need for councils more explicitly to find ways of reinforcing their democratic legitimacy, actively campaigning at the local level and setting out to build community support" (Cochrane 1993: 124). As a result, it is likely that local government will continue to build on the remaining autonomy available to it and, in order to resist the growing tendency of the centralization of urban policy, will increasingly collaborate with local State and other interests in a series of shifting coalitions. An understanding of local politics will in future depend on locating local government in the array of agencies, interests and forums that constitute the arena for local decision-making. The next section will examine how the three main sectors have responded to these deep-seated changes.

Local responses to the restructuring of the State and market

The main changes affecting the local management of urban regeneration include the restructuring of local economies requiring an entrepreneurial and competitive stance towards other localities, the shift towards central government in central–local relations, and a variety of policy measures by central government to infuse the enterprise culture at the local level. These changes have brought about a fundamental shift in power relations requiring each sector to reassess its role and relationships with other local interests. The outcome can broadly be described as a trend towards coalition formation. The responses of the three main sectors will be examined in turn.

The public sector

The government broadly favours the idea of partnership in promoting urban regeneration so long as this involves the private sector playing a greater role in decision-making and investment, and that it does not generate increased pressures on the public purse. Its attitude to local government and the voluntary sector is less consistent, but has reluctantly conceded that these interests have a legitimate role in urban regeneration. However, it has not been willing so far to make the resources available to enable these parties to achieve their full potential. Central government has also been inconsistent in that successive urban initiatives have been required to adopt very different attitudes to the idea of partnership. In the early 1980s, the UDCs and Enterprise Zones almost entirely bypassed local authorities and the voluntary sector, whereas more recent projects have given them a larger role. In Scotland and Wales greater latitude has been given the respective development agencies in setting up partnerships, so long as they achieve the required social and economic objectives, while financial controls are strictly retained by government.

Local government has fared less well and has suffered a diminution of local economic development powers under the Local Government and Housing Act (1989), whereas previously they could spend the product of two pence in the pound collected through local Rates in the interests of their area. Expenditure controls have also led to a reduction in funding available to the voluntary sector. The outcome has been that the leverage of public and private resources has taken on a new importance and particularly has gained access to central government and EU budgets allocated on a discretionary or competitive basis. Central government has encouraged the trend to local coalition formation by being more receptive to approaches from local authorities, which can clearly indicate that they have the support or involvement of chambers of commerce and local business interests.

The private sector

The response of the private sector towards the notion of greater involvement in urban regeneration can best be described as partial and fragmented, with only a few of the major companies adopting concerted corporate strategies by the 1990s. Government itself was a major influence in the early 1980s, for example in requesting that the CBI set up a Special Programmes Unit (SPU) to promote business participation in training programmes, such as the Youth Training Scheme. A series of studies were carried out in several cities, with local authorities and other interests, to see how far a collaborative approach could address to economic problems and training needs. After a conference convened by the Department of Environment in 1984, Business in the Community subsumed the work of the SPU (Moore & Richardson 1989: 49). In Scotland a similar organization (ScotBIC) took on a central co-ordinating role for the newly emerging enterprise trusts.

In several cases, local initiatives were taken by companies and representative bodies such as chambers of commerce; in others corporate executives were appointed through government patronage to agencies such as UDCs, TECs and LECs. At the national level, corporate sector agencies such as the CBI, Business in the Community and the Industrial Society promoted the idea of business leadership as being essential to "enlightened self-interest". Moreover, several national companies themselves took the lead in setting up private sector agencies such as the Phoenix Initiative in 1986 and British Urban Development Ltd (BUD) in 1988. BUD's membership was made up of 12 of the largest construction and civil engineering contractors, whereas Phoenix also included the British Property Federation, the Building Societies Association and the National Council of Building Material Producers. BUD and Phoenix were both concerned with lobbying government to provide direct or indirect subsidies to enable them to undertake profitable urban developments and to work closely with agencies such as the UDCs in undertaking such developments. By the early 1990s the Phoenix Initiative had been wound up, complaining of a lack of government support. BUD, whose Chief Executive was Hartley Booth, a former adviser to Mrs Thatcher on the inner cities, investigated sites in Middlesbrough, Swansea and Rainham Marshes, and for a time was associated with British Gas's Port Greenwich site in Greenwich. It eventually withdrew from all these projects and the company is now dormant. Hartley Booth was quoted in the press as saying "BUD was about leaving a legacy of ideas from which urban regeneration could happen. BUD was a catalyst during its short, high-profile life. It left an amazing number of grandchildren." (*The Guardian*, 15 February 1994).

An important national initiative occurred in 1987 when the CBI formed a task force to "identify what further steps business should be taking to assist in the process of urban regeneration" (CBI 1988). The conclusions from the study were that business must provide both the leadership and the vision to reverse social and economic decline, that the response from business needed to go beyond charity, that through partnership a common process should be established, particularly by establishing "early wins" through "flagship projects", and that an independent forum should be established to support local leadership teams. Existing examples commended by the report included The Newcastle Initiative, Sheffield Partnership in Action, Glasgow Action and Birmingham Heartlands.

In a wide-ranging investigation of corporate involvement in urban affairs the Policy Studies Institute (Christie et al. 1991) found that there were several motives for greater private sector involvement, which included a concern for growing unemployment and the impacts of industrial restructuring, changes in the political climate and lessons learnt from American companies about social responsibility. In a study of three cities, the PSI found that most corporate activity involved charitable donations, giving in kind, secondments, and involvement in training and educational initiatives. Direct involvement in local economic development tended to coalesce around chambers of commerce, business leadership teams and government initiatives such as UDCs and, more recently, City Challenge. A follow-up report prepared for the DOE Inner Cities Directorate presented the conclusions and recommendations for wider dissemination to business leaders (Christie 1991).

Following the CBI report, Business in the Community, the Phoenix Initiative and the CBI set up Business in the Cities to provide support to business leadership teams over a two-year period. Although the CBI is no longer directly involved in promoting business involvement in community affairs, Business in the Community continues to be active in support of business leadership teams, environmental initiatives and promoting business partnerships with local and central government, the voluntary sector and community groups. The CBI takes the view that the argument about the need for greater business involvement has been established and that it is now up to individual companies to identify local opportunities. It is thus hard to measure the extent of corporate activities at the local level, but it would appear that central government and, increasingly, local government are seeking closer collaboration with this sector. It also remains uncertain whether this is simply a response to the economic recession of the past four years or whether the trend towards greater corporate sector involvement will continue if the economy picks up.

The voluntary sector

The voluntary sector is made up of an increasingly complex network of community-based projects, ethnic minority organizations, not-for-profit trading companies and community development trusts, often based in the most deprived communities. Since as long ago as 1968, many have been directly funded by local authorities, from the Urban Programme or other initiatives such as inner-city Task Forces. This sector has expanded gradually over the past two decades and has sought to develop stronger relationships and sustainability by working in partnership with other local interests. City Challenge has been the most recent initiative that has recognized the contribution of community-based organizations in determining priorities and giving them access to resources.

The National Council for Voluntary Organizations (NCVO) estimated that about £55 million of the Urban Programme budget was allocated to voluntary organizations (Mabbott 1992). This represents a high-point of funding, since in November 1992 the government announced that the Urban Programme was to be wound down from a total central government contribution of £253 million in 1991–2 to £80 million in 1995–6. In partial replacement, an Urban Partnership Fund of £20 million was established in 1993–4 as one of four parts of the Capital Partnership fund, which is dependent on local authorities spending their capital receipts. The Urban Partnership Fund is allocated on the basis of competitive bidding, with preference being given to successful and unsuccessful City Challenge areas with partnership agencies in place. In addition, direct local authority funding is declining as resources are switched to protecting basic services.

The future for the voluntary sector currently looks bleak, as the Urban Programme is cut back and resources are transferred away from the 57 urban priority areas and allocated on a competitive basis to the narrowly defined City Challenge areas. In the latter, initial evidence suggests that there is a danger that the voluntary sector lacks the political or financial clout to exert real influence over decision-making (Macfarlane & Mabbott 1993). It is also likely that this sector will be increasingly forced into a contractual relationship with funding bodies and will no longer be able to meet a wide range of social needs, as was possible under the Urban Programme. The outcome may well be that the voluntary sector remains active only where funding is negotiated from partnership organizations such as City Challenge, Task Forces, Estates Action or Housing Action Trusts, or where community enterprises can become financially sustainable (see, for example, Pearce 1993).

Theories of partnership

Just as there has been a growing debate in political science on the restructuring of the State and the market, much has also been written on the institutional structures and arrangements for promoting development at the local level. In particular, several commentators have identified broadly similar trends in a variety of advanced economies, leading to the emergence of the "entrepreneurial city" (Harvey 1989, Judd & Parkinson 1990, Parkinson 1991). These cities, in both Europe and the USA, have all experienced extensive economic restructuring in the 1980s, the failure of regional policy and other centralist policy measures, and have undergone a "renaissance of interest in urban living" (Parkinson 1991: 299). One of the most common responses has been to develop innovative strategies for promoting economic development, which have necessitated a review of the institutional mechanisms required for effective implementation. Above all, it was the approach of the Single European Market in 1992 that was the primary catalyst for promoting consensus-based partnership arrangements in an increasingly competitive arena. Those cities that were able to create such alliances were more often associated with "the generation of dynamic development strategies" (Parkinson 1991: 301).

Initially, the debate in the UK was heavily influenced by literature from the

USA on urban growth coalitions (Molotch 1976, Logan & Molotch 1987). Logan & Molotch argued that the urban development process in many American cities was dominated by business-led coalitions of rentiers or "place entrepreneurs", whose main objective was to maximize exchange values in the form of rent or land values. These coalitions also have the tendency to manipulate the local democratic process by supplying funds to pro-growth parties or candidates. In addition, the promotion of place-marketing strategies would incorporate other local interests, such as large retailers, public utilities, universities and the local media, which would benefit from increased demand for their goods and services. In espousing exchange values in the form of "value-free development", it is argued, growth machines come into conflict with residents, whose primary interests are in use values, as well as with other growth coalitions pursuing similar strategies.

Although there is much of relevance to the UK in the urban growth machine thesis, and attempts have been made to apply it to the UK context (see, for example, Lloyd & Newlands 1990), it has several limitations that prevent its wholesale application to this country. For instance, it takes no account of the different systems of local administration and democratic representation and, perhaps more important, the limited impact that growth strategies have on local tax revenue in Britain. Indeed, it fits more appropriately into the history of "civic boosterism" in the USA. In contrast, in Britain such organizations have attempted to exert political influence over the development process through promotional activities and interlocking membership with development agencies.

The emphasis on the involvement of property interests in growth coalitions has also been questioned. Harding (1991: 308) found in a survey of 11 partnerships that in only one case did private property owners play a leading role in a property-based growth strategy, and this was Pilkingtons, which had a very special relationship with its home town, St Helens. In the majority of cases it was local authorities and other public agencies such as the Scottish Development Agency that which acted as both the triggers for setting up the coalition and as "key rentiers" in promoting growth strategies. From a similar perspective, in exploring the development of a new urban corporatism in the context of the North East of England, Shaw concludes that "within such coalitions it is often the public sector that provides a lead with local authorities continuing to play a role as coalition builders or mediators; and that, within the business sector itself, while property interests have become involved they have not been of special significance" (Shaw 1993: 252).

In a wide-ranging critique of Logan & Molotch, Cox & Mair (1989) argue that the relative mobility of company and property interests should be the starting point for examining local social relations. "It is local dependence, we would argue, rather than an interest in land-rent, that is the necessary condition for the formation of local business coalitions, including urban growth machines" (Cox & Mair 1989: 142). Local dependence is thus a precondition for coalition formation, but it does not necessarily apply to any particular type or size of firm, nor does it follow that the presence of local dependence means that a coalition

23

will inevitably be formed or remain in existence. These are contingent matters to be determined only by empirical investigation. However, local dependence will exist where companies perceive that involvement in a local coalition will assist in promoting their own self-interest, for example in securing a well trained local workforce or in improving the environment in which it is located, or in achieving a longer-term strategy of redevelopment, expansion, or improved infrastructure provision.

Perhaps more relevant to the British context is the debate about the significance of a "new urban corporatism" (Dunleavy & King 1990). It had generally been assumed that corporatism had been a phenomenon of the 1960s and 1970s that had largely withered away in response to the anti-statist policies of the 1980s. Yet several commentators have detected a growth in local forms of corporatism and find it a more relevant theoretical starting point than growth machines.

In reviewing the politics of urban regeneration in the North East of England, Shaw notes that the region has "since the 1930s, provided an almost classical illustration of corporatist political structures dominated by the labour movement, local/regional capital and representatives of regional government agencies" (Shaw 1993: 253). As a result, a fairly small but significant local elite has long been in existence to provide board members. Many of these can now be found in the multiple memberships of the boards of local development organizations such as UDCs, TECs, regional development and enterprise agencies, and two City Challenge agencies. Thus, "it is the continuity in structures, personalities and policies that need to be explained as well as the changes" (Shaw 1993: 258). This strongly suggests that local corporatist institutions run by business, professional and public sector elites have been operating more or less continuously for at least 30 years; what may have changed is the remit of the institutions and the extent to which the different sectoral interests have been able to maintain or expand their influence.

One local sectoral interest that has expanded its role in the past decade is the national network of chambers of commerce. Circumstantial evidence suggests that they are rapidly expanding their role, concentrating into larger and better funded units, and becoming far more closely involved in urban regeneration and in promotional agencies such as The Newcastle Initiative. In a review of the role of the Leeds Chamber of Commerce, King (1985) found that the Chamber was becoming increasingly involved in a series of economic policy issues in collaboration with the Labour-controlled city council. A notable change was the issuing of ministerial guidelines in 1981, requiring all chambers of commerce to vet bids from local authorities for Urban Programme funding before submission to the DoE. King concludes that although the viability of the local State is not directly dependent on the process of accumulation, economic recession and rising unemployment have created an interest in "promoting conditions conducive to capital accumulation". Since direct powers do not exist to do this, councils have sought the assistance of bodies, such as chambers of commerce, for help in encouraging businesses to improve their performance. He concludes that "these public–private initiatives may provide a more flexible form of interventionism, and are more finely tuned to the needs of local small capital, than would be provided by more direct statist or bureaucratic prescriptions" (King 1985: 226). Thus, although not strictly a partnership organization in themselves, chambers of commerce are becoming an increasingly important player in complex networks of corporatist institutions at the local level.

What broad conclusions can be drawn from the range of theoretical arguments available? Although it is clear that Logan & Molotch's arguments about urban growth machines are simplistic and of doubtful relevance to the UK, there are parallels between the relatively weak position of local government in the USA and more recent changes in the UK. However, we have a long history of "corporatist" State institutions largely composed of urban elites, particularly in economically peripheral regions such as Scotland and the North East. The continuity and change of these institutions is therefore as important as ideas imported from the USA as part of an anti-statist, deregulatory policy. Local dependence is an important starting point for identifying which public and private interests are most likely to seek closer collaboration with the remaining local State apparatus. In the end, local economies can best be seen as being created by local social and political relations formed through the uneven development of an increasingly global capitalist economy. Although fluctuating patterns of growth and decline will also give rise to institutional arrangements that may differ sharply between localities and regions, coalition-building has been identified as a common characteristic of those cities able to identify and exploit their competitive advantages. The relatively simple formulation of the urban regime perhaps best describes the ways in which the local State needs to be located within its constellation of intersectoral interests.

How that constellation is structured in any one instance cannot be predetermined, but must be the subject of empirical research. Stone (1987: 6) defines urban regimes as "the informal arrangements by which public bodies and private interests function together in order to be able to make and carry out governing decisions". In a later work, Stone et al. (1991) conclude that:

> . . . to understand policy-making we need to consider how the limited resources commanded by public officials are melded together with those of private actors to produce a capacity to govern. The arrangements by which such governing coalitions are created can be called regimes – in the case of localities, urban regimes. Governance rests less on formal authority than on arrangements through which public officials and private interests create a complex system of cooperation. (Stone et al. 1991: 223–4)

From this perspective, both the mobilization of adequate resources to meet the defined policy objectives and the role of urban leadership become crucial variables; for example, as to whether the regime is concerned with redevelopment or "opportunity expansion" (Stone et al. 1991: 236). Keating adopts a similar posi-

25

tion by suggesting that urban regimes consist of "constellations of public and private power within a structurally defined context. Public policy is seen as the outcome of both economic and political power, with the composition of each and the balance between them varying among cities" (Keating 1991: 7–8). The openness of urban politics to those without financial or property interests and the governing capacity of elected local authorities become the primary interests of research.

Keating concludes that because of limitations on the governing capacity of local government as a result of power exerted by external interests, there are three (ideal type) development strategies adopted at the local level: civic mercantilism, aimed at maximizing inward investment; planning and controlling development, the strategy adopted by several New Left authorities in the 1980s; and the partnership model.

> It is necessary, then, to examine individual urban regimes to see what the power balance is, and how this affects the development policies that emerge. (Keating 1991: 168)

Establishing a model of partnership

So far we have discussed some of the theoretical material advanced to explain the evolution of the partnership approach to urban regeneration and the ways in which the importance of coalition-building has developed. We will now examine in more detail the structural characteristics of partnerships, the ways in which they have evolved in different forms in a variety of contexts, and the core processes by which they operate. This should lead to a set of criteria by which different examples can be evaluated.

We have already noted that partnerships can best be perceived as urban regimes: "a set of arrangements through which policy decisions are made, encompassing formal structures and informal relationships among political and economic elites comprising the governing coalition" (Keating 1991: 7–8). They are thus adapted to reflect the social and political relations in a particular locality, tempered by their relationship to other local stakeholders, including central government. Moreover, they have evolved out of a long history of the interweaving of the State and the market as mediated by the planning process. Post-war reconstruction, central area redevelopment and the new towns have all involved varying working relationships between the public and private sectors, stretching back over at least 50 years (see, for example, Thornley 1993: Ch. 2).

As has already been established, partnerships evolved as a response to the loss of local government autonomy, which in turn was a direct result of the fracturing of the post-war consensus within which government played a major role in maintaining the Welfare State. It was the 1977 inner cities White Paper that advocated a partnership between State agencies in order to improve service delivery, only to be redefined by the incoming Thatcher government as an important mechanism for promoting the enterprise culture. In this context, conditions existed for the emergence of coalitions of local stakeholders, some of which were mobilized from below, in a direct response to local conditions, others from policy initiatives from above.

A working definition of partnership in the context under study might be the mobilization of a coalition of interests drawn from more than one sector in order to prepare and oversee an agreed strategy for the regeneration of a defined area. The crucial variables of partnership requiring further study are: the process of mobilization, the range and balance of power between the stakeholders, the nature and extent of the remit adopted, and the area of coverage.

The process of mobilization

Partnerships are normally created through a catalytic process of either a top-down or bottom-up nature. In the first case they are established as a response to a policy initiative by central government, in that they form part of a mechanism for delivering part of a national strategy. Urban Development Corporations, Training and Enterprise Councils, Local Enterprise Companies and City Challenge agencies are examples of the top-down model. In some cases appointments to management boards are made by the patronage of the relevant government department, in others the proportions of each form of representation are specified. In all cases there is clear national guidance on membership, funding and the agency's remit. In the second case, examples are more fluid and variable, and depend to a considerable extent on local circumstances and the views of key players involved in establishing the partnership. Local chambers of commerce (as in the case of Birmingham Heartlands), local authorities and community organizations have all acted as catalysts in coalition building. In the early days, shadow organizations (or steering groups) are often formed by the main stakeholders, and membership is then expanded, sometimes through elections, when a constitution has been drawn up and the organization is formally constituted. More recently, the availability of European Union Structural Funds has been an additional spur to the formation of urban or regional coalitions largely made up of local development agencies.

The range and balance of power between sectors

The second variable relates to the range of partners involved and the balance of power between sectors. This often reflects the process of establishment, in that top-down partnerships are often required to reflect national directives on membership. Bottom-up examples, on the other hand, aim for a wider spread of membership in order to stress consensus and common purpose. Although there is a

27

tendency for most partnerships to seek the involvement of local elites, bottom-up examples are more likely to include a wider range of voluntary and community sector representatives.

The balance of power between sectors is a reflection of the membership, the benefits, and access to resources and influence that each stakeholder brings, and the interaction between the membership.

The nature and extent of the remit adopted

The nature and extent of the remit adopted may be predetermined if the partnership is part of a wider governmental programme or it may evolve out of the perceptions of need and the priorities identified by the membership. In practice, the fact that partnerships can operate beyond the highly restricted powers of local government, and can pursue objectives either independently or through member organizations or third parties, is claimed as one of their main strengths. In reality there is considerable variation between those almost entirely involved in promotional activities and place-marketing – for example The Newcastle Initiative – and those involved in both property-related and social programmes, such as City Challenge agencies. The lifetime of the organization is also an important element of the remit, in that some are established for a limited time to oversee a particular task, others are time-limited to the length of the policy initiative, whereas a third category operate on a semi-permanent or open-ended basis.

The area of coverage

All partnerships identify clear boundaries that reflect indices of need and deprivation, local identity and political priority, or a combination of all three. Areas of coverage vary enormously from the single development site to one housing estate or neighbourhood, or the more usual sector or quarter of an urban area. Recent commentators have pointed to the apparent illogicality of identifying and targeting "inner-city economies" for special remedial measures, when the movement of capital and travel-to-work patterns have become increasingly complex (Deakin & Edwards 1993). However, the identification of boundaries has other benefits in terms of mobilizing local interests and the political necessity of targeting resources in relatively small areas, so that the impact is clearly visible.

A typology of partnership

An important aspect of the development of partnership in the 1980s and early 1990s has been the extent to which existing elements of the local State, such as local authorities and chambers of commerce, and some of the newer government agencies, such as UDCs and TECs, have been developing closer working relationships and coalition networks. In some cases this has given rise to newly constituted intersectoral partnerships. The current government appears to be willing to tolerate innovation and variety, so long as public resources and grant regimes are tightly controlled from the centre and the broad objective is achieved of involving the private sector in economic development. In Scotland and Wales a more structured system of partnership has emerged through the respective development agencies adopting innovative approaches at the local level, which bear all the hallmarks of local corporatism.

The fluid and ambiguous nature of partnership organizations does not make categorization easy. Table 2.1 sets out a typology of categories of partnership based on the previously identified variables. The categories are designed to indicate "ideal type" groupings of similar organizations; there may well be examples displaying characteristics that fit into more than one category. For example, City Challenge agencies can be seen as joint agreements and as agency partnerships. In addition, our research indicates that in some cases there may be a succession from smaller, local initiatives, such as development partnerships or development trusts, to larger and better financed coalitions, development companies or agency partnerships. For example, Birmingham Heartlands emerged out of previous partnership arrangements such as the Birmingham Science Park and National Exhibition Centre, and was subsequently designated a UDC in 1992. Likewise, in Lewisham a development trust and local coalition was succeeded by a City Challenge agency. Six types of partnership arrangements are identified:

- *Development partnership or joint ventures* These usually relate to a specific development site involving housing or commercial development, whereby a joint agreement is entered into by the local authority in order to ensure the successful completion of the development. The local authority often uses its powers of site preparation and infrastructure provision, and the developer brings the finance and project management skills. Profit-sharing arrangements may be entered into once the development is complete and third parties, such as housing associations, might be involved.
- *Development trusts* These usually operate at a local or neighbourhood level and are normally initiated by local community organizations, but often with local authority and private sector representation. Their purpose is to acquire land and buildings, and to carry out development in the interests of the local community, often involving cross-subsidy between commercial and not-for-profit activities. They may also be involved in local promotional activities such as increasing local participation in community affairs, training, sports and leisure provision and environmental improvements. Trusts are normally constituted as companies limited by guarantee and may also be charities. There are a growing number of examples across the UK, and the Development Trusts Association, has been formed as a national representative organization.

29

Table 2.1 A typology of partnerships.

Type	Mobilization	Area of coverage	Range of partners	Remit	Examples
Development	Locally	Single site or small area, e.g. town centre	Private developer, housing association, local authority	Joint development to mutual advantage	Commercial/non-profit development producing mutual benefits
Development trust	Locally	Neighbourhood	Community-based with LA & other representatives	Community-based regeneration	Coin Street, North Kensington Amenity Trust, Woodlands Trust
Joint agreement, coalition, company	Locally but may be in response to national policy	Clearly defined area for regeneration	Public, private, and sometimes voluntary	Preparation of formal/informal strategy. Implementation often through third parties.	City Challenge, Greenwich Waterfront, Birmingham Heartlands
Promotional	Locally, e.g. by Chamber of Commerce	District or city-wide.	Private sector-led. Sponsored by Chamber of Commerce or development agency.	Place marketing, promotion of growth and investment	The Newcastle Initiative, Glasgow Action, East London Partnership
Agency	Nationally based on legislative powers.	Urban, or subregional	Public sector sponsored with private sector appointees	Terms of reference from sponsoring agency	UDCs, TECs, LECs. Scottish Office "New Life" Partnerships
Strategic	Regional, county, local.	Subregional, metropolitan	All sectors	Determining broad strategy for growth & development & accessing EU funds	North Kent Forum, Western Development Partnership, London First

- *Joint agreements, coalitions and companies* This category includes a variety of mainly locally initiated partnerships where a variety of local stakeholders enter into an informal working agreement or formally constituted company in order to promote a local regeneration strategy in a clearly defined target area. Normally a strategy is prepared that forms the basis for implementation by either the partnership itself, through constituent members, or third parties. Examples include City Challenge agencies, which determine membership and their strategy locally (subject to DOE approval, and thus might also be defined as an agency partnership) and a wide range of coalitions often initiated by local authorities (for example, the Greenwich Waterfront Development Partnership, the Park Royal Partnership and the Drumchapel Initiative) or with the support of chambers of commerce (such as Birmingham Heartlands).

- *Promotional partnerships* This category includes those examples of partnership that are initiated largely by local business interests or in response to national initiatives such as the CBI's report, *Initiatives beyond charity* (CBI 1988). In Scotland, Glasgow Action (Boyle 1989) was the best known example until it was incorporated into the Glasgow Development Agency. The remit of this type is primarily promotional through place-marketing and by working through other partnership agencies, such as UDCs, City Challenge organizations and enterprise agencies. Membership is predominantly drawn from local business elites, although leading public sector representatives are often included. Examples include The Newcastle Initiative, Glasgow Action, Nottingham Development Enterprise and the East London Partnership.

- *Agency partnerships* These are locally based agencies that are part of a national network, with clear guidelines on their constitution and remit set out in national legislation. Membership is normally constituted on a patronage basis by the sponsoring government department, and funding comes largely from the public sector, with a limited amount from income. Examples include UDCs, TECs and LECs, all of which are required by statute to have a predominantly private sector board membership. Accountability operates through the sponsoring government department rather than locally.

- *Strategic partnerships* These are an emergent form of partnership, which operate at the metropolitan, county or subregional level. They usually include some local authority members, but also major landowners or industrialists. Their primary objective is to promote the development of the area and to attract infrastructural development and inward investment. Examples include London First, a body primarily initiated by government as a voice for London in the absence of an elected strategic body, and the North Kent Forum, which has been formed by Kent County Council, district councils and major landowners such as Blue Circle in order to exploit the potential of the Thames Gateway and the proposed rail link between London and the Channel Tunnel (see for example, Thompson 1993).

The rationale of partnership

Partnerships tend to rely heavily on promotional and marketing strategies, the identification of opportunities, and the negotiation of strategies between the partners involved and other interests in the area. Thus, objectives can evolve over time, particularly as market conditions change and new government funding mechanisms emerge. This contrasts with central or local government initiatives, which depend on statutory powers and procedures. It is possible to identify seven core processes that help to explain what partnerships do. These will naturally vary between organizations and they depend significantly on their membership, remit, funding and target area, as to which are most important in any particular case. The first three draw heavily on the work of Macintosh (1992).

Synergy

One of the fundamental principles of partnership is that it is claimed that more can be achieved by two or more sectors working together than separately. This normally implies a combination of profit-making and non-commercial interests, whereby all parties gain through a mutually agreed programme or development and none loses. From the private sector perspective, development may become feasible through partnership, in that some profit or commercial advantage is ceded to the non-profit sector in return for risk-minimization, capital subsidy or the provision at below market rates. Local authorities or other non-profit agencies may be keen to enter into partnership agreements in order to encourage development that would not otherwise occur, or to achieve additional social benefits such as affordable housing, community facilities or linked training projects.

Transformation

This process also reflects the fluid approach to decision-making within partnerships and the fact that each partner attempts to influence the values and objectives of the other parties. Mutual transformation may be the outcome in which both the methods of working and the objectives are modified through negotiation. Practitioners often comment on the difficulties of achieving a degree of consensus in the early days, as partners confront the stereotypical views they have of each other. Partnerships are arenas of bargaining and negotiation about purpose and objectives, and broad parameters of agreement need to be established quickly if results are to be achieved.

The public sector is often looked upon with suspicion by the private and voluntary sectors and is often accused of being inward-looking, overcautious and caught up in its own internal procedures. The private sector sees its role as bringing a commercial perspective and a task-orientated approach to highly bureau-

32

cratic organizations. The private sector is equally likely to be risk-averse, committed to short term profit-making and lacking in a wider social perspective. The voluntary and community sector, meanwhile, is often alienated from local government through the perception that it has been ignored and underfunded, and is suspicious of the commercial objectives of the private sector. Partnership thus becomes a "mutual struggle for transformation" by which:

> The private sector is seeking to bring private sector objectives into the public sector, to shake it up, get it to seek more market-orientated aims, to work more efficiently in its terms. The public justification offered is that this will be in the long-term public interest. The public sector, conversely, is trying to push the private sector towards more "social" and long term aims, justifying this in precisely the same terms. (Macintosh 1992: 216)

Budget enlargement

One of the most common justifications for entering into partnership is budget enlargement, whereby a public sector institution with limited resources, and a private company seeking subsidy or risk-reduction, construct a joint venture dependent on funding, in whole or in part, from a third party. This has been referred to as leverage planning (Brindley et al. 1989) and has been a common method of funding major developments within the private sector.

Negotiating for budget enlargement or leverage has now become increasingly common in the structuring of a wide range of development proposals and has recently spread into the provision of infrastructure and public transport, such as motorway construction and the proposed Jubilee Underground line extension. Central government has responded to the trend by increasingly linking capital expenditure, grants and loans to the need to obtain matching or partial funding for projects. Funding mechanisms, such as City Challenge and EU grants, now require evidence of matching public or private sector commitment.

In time of economic recession, one of the major opportunities for budget enlargement is to become adept at accessing resources from central government and other public sector sources by building commitment through leverage. There is also evidence that central government is increasingly allocating resources on a competitive basis to be available to those agencies best able to make a strong case for funding.

Unlocking land and development opportunities

An important motivation for the establishment of partnerships throughout the 1980s has been the need to unlock the complex patterns of ownership in inner-city areas and to prepare large parcels of land for redevelopment. This was one of the original purposes for establishing urban development corporations, which

33

were located in areas such as London Docklands, where large areas of derelict land were owned by public bodies such as the Port of London Authority, public utilities and local authorities. A similar rationale was followed in many of the partnership areas, such as the Victoria Dock, Hull, Birmingham Heartlands and Greenwich Waterfront.

Despite the resurgence of the commercial property market in the mid-1980s, and central government attempts to promote private sector development through the deregulation of planning controls and the reduction of local authority economic development powers, private developers proved unwilling or unable to venture much beyond the most favourable sites in or near city centres. Partnerships thus became one of the few options available to local authorities to assist in unlocking derelict or underused land, and to exert some influence over its subsequent use. Thus, contrary to much of the American growth coalition literature, Harding found that local authorities were the main agents of change:

> It is local authorities . . . which prove to be the key rentiers. This is consistent with (a) the historically more significant role of municipal property ownership in the UK, (b) the pressure to speculate with such assets that the 1980s has brought, (c) the fragmented, incoherent, often absentee (or simply unfathomable) urban private ownership patterns, particularly of land and (d) the failure of government policy to provide the incentives to private owners that they have, albeit in negative forms, in the public sectors. (Harding 1993: 229)

Lawless (1994) also identifies the dominance of the local authority in partnership arrangements in Sheffield.

Place-marketing and promotion

The extent to which public–private partnerships are associated with the rapid transition from the managerial approach to economic development to the entrepreneurial (Harvey 1989) has already been noted. In the UK, partnerships of various kinds have focused on attracting national and multinational capital, linked to an increasingly competitive system for allocating public sector investment.

Partnerships are well placed to exploit this trend, because flagship projects and marketing campaigns are a convenient way of launching initiatives where most parties foresee benefits additional to more traditional investment opportunities. By developing intersectoral consensus, the attributes of particular localities can be promoted and marketed in the form of flagship projects, urban villages, cultural centres, heritage developments, and the location of sports and leisure facilities. The underlying agenda for this kind of place-marketing are more mundane factors designed to attract the inward investor, such as labour supply, access to communications, housing availability and environmental quality.

From the early 1980s onwards, cities such as Glasgow, Birmingham, Sheffield and Manchester began to launch major image-building campaigns around cultural developments, garden festivals and sporting events, to exploit niche markets. More recently, coalitions based on UDCs, City Challenge and regional development agencies have entered the field. The extent to which the industrial and cultural history of cities and regions has been fiercely contested while exploited as cultural capital has been portrayed by several commentators (see, for example, Kearns & Philo 1993).

The limited research carried out on the growth of place-marketing has highlighted the drawbacks of the extent to which flagship projects create islands of affluence in seas of deprivation. In examining promotional activity in Newcastle upon Tyne, Wilkinson (1992) found at least four different agencies promoting different, and overlapping, segments of the North East in a constant campaign to attract a limited pool of investors. The outcome was competition, and duplication of effort, between the often publicly funded agencies and a fragmentation of the city of Newcastle into neatly packaged flagship projects:

> We would argue that as part of the image-management process, flagship projects represent the continuing fragmentation of the locality which has been a characteristic feature of urban regeneration efforts in the 1990s. They can be seen as isolated growth nodes within larger areas of decay, often dislocated in spatial and temporal terms from the localities which surround them. We would argue that flagships represent a marketing tool, a form of "branding" device aimed at boosting a city's image but in reality creating urban fragments which are floating free from the rest of the distressed urban area. It is an approach concerned with superimposing fragments on the city rather than with the comprehensive planning of urban areas. (Wilkinson 1992: 206)

In current economic circumstances, where investment decisions are frequently made on a global or pan-European basis, many cities have discovered the need to compete by devising a marketing strategy and that setting up partnerships has become the most effective way to access central government co-operation and infrastructural investment. Flagship projects may assist in developing an appropriate marketing strategy, but city centre developments have a negligible impact on deprived and spatially segregated localities, as is well illustrated in the case of Glasgow. As Bianchini et al. (1992: 255) conclude "they [flagship projects] are useful, and maybe even necessary, elements of an urban economic regeneration strategy, but they are by no means sufficient".

The co-ordination of infrastructure and development

An important and often unacknowledged role of partnerships is to take on the functions previously performed by metropolitan authorities of co-ordinating the

35

provision of infrastructure and the planning of new transportation linkages. In large cities such as London and Birmingham partnerships have entered the vacuum left by the abolition of metropolitan councils such as the Greater London Council and the West Midlands County Council. In the Greenwich Waterfront area, the partnership is liaising between the borough council and the Department of Transport in planning a third river crossing at the Blackwall Tunnel, and with London Underground over the extension of the Jubilee line. British Gas, which is a leading player in the Waterfront partnership, is awaiting a satisfactory outcome to these two proposals before proceeding with the development of its 120 ha site at the Greenwich Peninsula. A senior civil servant in the Department of Environment's London regional office is chairing a task force of local business interests on transport issues. Birmingham Heartlands, and subsequently the urban development corporation, is promoting a new spine road at a cost of £113 million in order to open up several derelict sites capable of sustaining up to 11 000 jobs.

This aspect of the work of partnerships reflects the increasing centralization of urban policy and the need for local agencies to take a comprehensive view towards the co-ordination of local development. Partnerships aim to bring together public and private partners with an interest in promoting and co-ordinating development, which in turn are able to project a sense of urgency towards political and administrative decision-makers.

The East London Partnership was founded in 1989 and now has 65 private and public sector members, including representatives from the police, two local universities and two local Training and Enterprise Councils. It operates in the boroughs of Hackney, Newham and Tower Hamlets and has assisted all three boroughs in winning City Challenge funding. Not only does it promote and raise funds for 80 local projects, but is also heavily involved in lobbying for strategic improvements to, and investment in, East London. The Chief Executive, Tony Hawkhead, is also chair of the Stratford Development Partnership:

> We (the East London Partnership) are founding members of the East London Line Group, which this year succeeded in persuading the London Underground board to press on with the line's extension north into Hackney and Islington, and south into the Peckham area of Southwark. We are also strong supporters of the campaign for the Jubilee line, with member chairmen such as Neil Shaw of Tate and Lyle writing to John MacGregor at the Department of Transport in support of the extension. (Barker & Bailey 1992: 10)

In the absence of a comprehensive strategy towards infrastructure and transportation, it is evident that partnerships are filling the vacuum left by local government, and are using private sector members to lobby ministers. As with place-marketing, those areas with the institutions best able to exploit these opportunities are most likely to attract additional public resources to provide a foundation for private investment.

Confidence-building and risk minimization

In current circumstances, when the public sector is severely restricted in its development capacity and the development industry is in recession, confidence-building and risk minimization become important tasks for partnerships. In all but the strongest market locations, confidence is lacking and development finance hard to obtain.

In this context, partnerships can play an important role in evolving growth strategies that provide a sense of stability and continuity in order to secure both public and private investment. Evidence from many inner-city locations suggests that the normal response is to await an upturn in the market and to leave buildings and land derelict and underused. Private developers are often wary of local authority advances and they perceive planning initiatives such as development plans as discouraging or even hostile.

Collaboration between sectors, together with the direct involvement of local communities, can be used to build confidence in long-term planning, especially when flagship projects are closely linked to redistributive strategies for training, childcare, crime prevention and environmental improvement. Additional benefits can be achieved by streamlining decision-making procedures within and between central and local government and by preparing a clear strategy that extends well beyond normal political or budgetary horizons.

Conclusions

In this chapter we have reviewed the main factors leading to the adoption of partnership as a mechanism for delivering urban regeneration strategies. We have examined several theories put forward to explain the trend towards urban coalitions, which operate over and above traditional delivery mechanisms. We have also set out a typology of partnerships and identified the core processes employed.

It has been established that partnerships operate as urban regimes in representing coalitions of significant local elites and agencies, with varying degrees of local dependence, in order to exert influence over growth-related and redistributive strategies in defined areas. The strategies deployed vary according to local circumstances, national and local policy, and the interplay of the different interests in the coalition. These may vary from promotional and place-marketing strategies, to property-led flagship projects, to a combination of growth-related economic and redistributive social policies. Seven core processes of implementation have been identified.

In the next chapter we review the ways in which the concept of partnership has been an increasingly important element of urban policy, while being subject to different definitions and interpretations in a succession of government policy initiatives.

CHAPTER 3

The evolution of government policy towards partnership

> The Government is committed to take a radical look at the way in which bureaucratic institutions affect our industrial and economic performance. We see the need to redefine the frontier between the public and private sector.   Michael Heseltine MP, Secretary of State for the Environment (*Hansard*, 13 September 1979)

For more than 25 years the State has been experimenting with different formulations of urban policy. In all cases the targets, agencies and mechanisms for policy delivery have varied according to current conceptions of the nature of the problems to be tackled, the geographical location of the problems and which form of delivery mechanism is most appropriate to achieve the desired objectives. Throughout this period of experimentation there have been several fixed points that have defined the focus of policy. In the first place the target was the inner city: what were assumed to be definable areas near the heart of the major urban centres, where indices of deprivation indicated economic failure and social distress defined by out-migration, poor housing conditions, poverty and unemployment. Secondly, it was assumed that special programmes were needed to target areas of deprivation in order to eradicate or ameliorate aspects of deprivation. Thirdly, it was assumed that special delivery mechanisms, and in some cases new agencies, were needed to ensure that programmes and policies were co-ordinated and effectively delivered.

Whereas in the early days emphasis was placed on the need to improve the co-ordination and delivery of services to identified "pockets of deprivation", more recent initiatives accentuated the need for existing State agencies, and increasingly State agencies working closely with other local interests, to formulate collaborative strategies in "partnership". Thus, an integral element of British urban policy since 1968 has been the growing realization that no single agency or level of government has the resources or capacity to deliver a programme by itself. Success would come only through the effective co-ordination of all those with an interest in regenerating the inner city.

The concept of partnership contains a high level of ambiguity and is relatively neutral, in that it refers to a mode of working rather than implying means or ends. It is relatively easily assimilated by a wide range of political interests in that it implies pooling resources for mutual gain, particularly when the nature of the problems to be tackled is not easily defined or when the level of commitment cannot be easily predicted. Furthermore, partnership is an attractive concept to government, because it commits other interests to regeneration, such as the private sector and the local community, it diffuses responsibility for success or failure, and ensures that relatively low levels of public expenditure can be used to lever large amounts of private investment. Finally, the debate and potential conflict about means and ends normally associated with such programmes is largely transferred to the agencies within the partnership and thus is relatively excluded from wider public debate.

One of our central arguments is that the concept of partnership has evolved over the past 25 years through a series of experiments in urban policy. The idea has developed not so much through detailed evaluation of these experiments but more as a reflection of changing national economic priorities and the political ideologies of successive governments. Hence, initiatives from different stages of development have often been retained and managed as relatively discrete programmes, and they often overlay each other in the same geographical locations.

Until the early 1990s, government-sponsored policy evaluation focused largely on levels of expenditure and the impact of particular policies and programmes, thus reaffirming the compartmentalism of central government policy-making. The first study of the impact of urban policy at the national, regional and local levels was commissioned by the DoE after the 1991 General Election and published in 1994. It is reported on in more detail later in this chapter (Robson et al. 1994).

This chapter sets out to chart the development of the concept of partnership in relation to a series of policy measures and changing perceptions of the role of the central and local State, to explore the reasons why partnership is now heavily promoted as a vehicle for urban regeneration, and to identify the dimensions of current practice that have proved most attractive in a series of central and local government initiatives.

The role of the State in urban regeneration

For almost 30 years after the end of the Second World War the UK was governed by administrations broadly committed to a consensus based on full employment through a Keynesian management of the economy, an active public sector intervening to provide a range of public goods, such as universal healthcare, public education and social security, and responsibility for post-war reconstruction, planning and housing delegated to local government.

During this period much was achieved through post-war reconstruction of bomb-damaged cities, the establishment of the foundations of the wartime vision of the Welfare State, the nationalization of key public utilities and periods of economic prosperity. Yet, from the mid-1970s, fissures and fault-lines began to appear in the post-war consensus. Worsening economic circumstances, growing unemployment and evidence of public resistance to the paternalistic approaches of the public sector, most evident in areas of clearance and the development of high-rise housing, produced a fundamental rift between the two main political parties, leading to the electoral defeat of the Labour Party in 1979 and the rise of Thatcherism.

The views of government on appropriate mechanisms for urban regeneration closely match current thinking about the wider role of State intervention through the planning system. In his study of urban planning under Thatcherism, Thornley (1993: 31) identifies three main phases in the evolution of post-war planning up until the election of the Thatcher Government in 1979.

The first phase lasted for about a decade after the end of the Second World War and represented both a continuation of the wartime consensus to rebuild war-torn cities and the battered national economy, as well as a determination to remove the worst aspects of squalor and want represented by the 1930s. The broad political consensus was based on what proved to be weak foundations and poorly defined objectives, and was largely executed "in an elitist fashion by a small number of politicians, civil servants and experts" (Thornley 1993: 31). State intervention on a large scale was tolerated in both the production and consumption sectors, on grounds of urgency and the "public interest". During this period the private development industry played a modest role in reconstruction and private housebuilding; the first phase of the New Towns programme and industrial redevelopment was almost entirely funded and managed by the public sector. However, several of the leading players in a series of subsequent phases of commercial property development began in this period by acquiring sites and property in what later became prime locations (see Marriott 1989).

In the second phase, from the mid-1950s to the late 1960s, a reaction to shortages and State intervention set in and a series of Conservative governments set about relaxing planning controls over land and development, in order to encourage an emergent private sector. Towns and cities were undergoing comprehensive redevelopment and a major roadbuilding programme was under way to meet the demands of a rapid growth in the car and commercial vehicle industry. In a period of growing economic prosperity and with the increasing availability of credit, there was an increasing demand for private housing, particularly in the urban fringe.

With the lifting of restrictions on development and building, the role of planning changed towards accommodating and mediating between the conflicting demands of the private sector. Partnership and negotiation, rather than reliance on regulatory powers, began to make their appearance in the professional literature. One such example is the Ministry of Housing and Local Government publication, *Town centres; approach to renewal*, issued in1962, to inform local authorities about how to approach city centre development. In it, local authorities were urged to be flexible and responsive and willing to enter into agreements with developers:

> Renewal cannot be undertaken without public support and it cannot be carried through without private enterprise. There is increasing evidence of readiness by private developers to collaborate with local authorities in this field and it is the Minister's policy to encourage this. In many towns today the initiative in redevelopment is coming from private developers and the local authority has to move fast to keep pace with them. (MHLG 1962: 6)

As a result, many local authorities began to negotiate both increasingly complex joint ventures and "planning gain" deals with private developers. As the private sector expanded, with the support of City banks and financial institutions, the Labour governments of the mid-1960s began to adopt an increasingly corporatist approach to national economic planning. New tripartite arrangements such as the National Plan, the National Economic Development Organization and the Department of Economic Affairs drew the private sector and trade unions more closely into planning for economic prosperity. As a result, the role of the State changed from one of owning and controlling major elements of the national economy to one of setting a strategic framework in which the private sector could achieve agreed targets through negotiation and consensus. Thus, partnership between government, private industry and the trade unions became a major theme of the decade.

In Thornley's "third phase", from the late 1960s to 1979, the poorly integrated and increasingly ineffective structures of corporatism at the national level began to disintegrate or proved unworkable. A worsening economy, through a series of balance of payments crises, increasing unemployment and growing social tensions, coincided with the "rediscovery of poverty" (Abel-Smith & Townsend 1965) and a recognition that certain regions and "the inner cities" were suffering disproportionately the adverse consequences of economic restructuring and the fiscal crisis of the State. The corporatist, and generally elitist, system of planning remained in place, but its ability to operate in the public interest was increasingly questioned and subjected to demands for more participation. As circumstances worsened, governments looked increasingly for explanations of deprivation and appropriate policy solutions.

The origins of British urban policy

From the mid-1960s onwards, both Wilson's Labour Government and Heath's 1970–74 Conservative Government launched a series of urban initiatives that explored different aspects of the inner-city problem, and were to have a significant influence on both perceptions and policy solutions in the future. At first, some of the early policy prescriptions focused on discrete policy areas. The Milner Holland Report (1965) examined housing stress, the Plowden Report (1967) educational disadvantage and Seebohm (1968) social services – all recommending the targeting of additional resources on defined areas of need. The Urban Programme, then called Urban Aid, was launched by Harold Wilson in direct response to Enoch Powell's anti-immigration speech in 1968. This provided additional resources to areas of high immigration and it sought bids from local authorities and voluntary groups for projects to alleviate inter-racial tension and inner-city stress. Academic evaluation suggests that it lacked clear objectives, was poorly monitored and was often used by local authorities to fund projects not otherwise affordable (Edwards & Batley 1978).

Of more lasting significance were three initiatives designed broadly to investigate issues of strategy, co-ordination and service delivery. The Comprehensive Community Programmes (CCPs) were launched in 1974 and were designed to apply current management techniques to the identification of the nature of deprivation in a local authority area, the development of policy towards subareas and client groups, and the specification of projects to be funded jointly by central and local government.

The initiative held out the promise of systematically identifying and targeting issues and resources in order to reduce urban deprivation. In the event, only two authorities were designated – Gateshead and Bradford – and since both were largely marginalized within local councils experiencing increasing financial restraint, the programme was wound up in 1980 (Spencer 1980, 1981).

A total of twelve Community Development Projects (CDPs) were launched by the Home Office between 1969 and 1972, combining community action projects with an extensive programme of research. Their initial brief had been a modest and reformist one: to identify through action projects how resources could be better co-ordinated and targeted on those suffering urban deprivation.

Through a series of increasingly innovative redefinitions of their brief, they successfully undermined current nostrums, such as the "culture of poverty" thesis, and published a set of research reports that argued that poverty arose from the political economy of society (NCDP 1974, 1975). Although this approach was never officially accepted by government, the CDPs had a significant impact on the growing emphasis on the urban economy in the 1977 White Paper and beyond.

The three Inner Area Studies (IAS) were commissioned in 1972 from consultants by Peter Walker, Secretary of State for the Environment. Their task was to investigate the causes and possible solutions to urban deprivation in parts of Birmingham, Liverpool and Lambeth. When the final reports were published in 1977 (DoE 1977a,b,c), their main contribution was to highlight the individual and collective deprivation caused by a combination of economic restructuring, environmental dereliction, poor housing conditions and inadequate social services. Conditions could be improved largely through existing agencies, they

42

argued, so long as sufficient resources were available and the political will existed.

All the urban initiatives originating in this period have some common characteristics that broadly defined the nature of the debate and determined what constituted an appropriate response in subsequent decades. In the first place, they were all predicated, at least in the early stages, on the assumption that urban deprivation existed in defined inner-city locations that were abnormal in the sense that they were surrounded by areas of greater prosperity. This then led to the view that additional resources, co-ordination and targeting could ameliorate the dysfunctional nature of the inner city. Secondly, drawing heavily on the contemporary USA poverty programme, special, often innovatory, programmes were devised by which central and/or local government would deliver remedial measures with (in some cases) the participation of the recipients. Third, extensive and linked action research was needed to enable the experiment to be fully monitored and evaluated. Fourthly, since many of these programmes were experimental, it was generally assumed that they should only run for a limited period, after which the lessons learnt would be absorbed by existing agencies. Finally, it should be noted that concepts of partnership had not entered into the debate about delivery mechanisms. Reform, it was argued, would come about through improved planning, co-ordination by local authorities and the targeting of resources on the schools, client groups, voluntary organizations and areas in greatest need.

In practice, there may be more practical and pragmatic reasons for these characteristics, which in later periods became essential aspects of a permanent urban policy. Perhaps most important, there were substantial benefits to Secretaries of State and their civil servants in being seen to instigate and manage innovatory urban projects, albeit of a limited nature and at modest cost. Central government departments were able to achieve a high political profile and could be seen to be playing a role in funding initiatives that were designed to have a direct impact on urban disadvantage. From this may well have arisen the general presumption, which later suited other political objectives, that local authorities were relatively inefficient and lacked the motivation to launch effective urban strategies. Nevertheless, whereas central government often gave the impression that it was launching rational and comprehensive strategies, observers of the early phases of experimentation noted that many initiatives were *ad hoc* and politically driven (Edwards & Batley 1978).

The origins of partnership 1977–9

By the mid-1970s several significant administrative and conceptual changes were contemplated with far-reaching implications. On the economic front, the intervention of the International Monetary Fund caused the Labour Government considerable alarm and led to a series of warnings to local government about future funding. At the same time, the general presumption that the decentralization of population from the main urban conurbations through the New Towns programme and related measures began to be seriously questioned. The Government decided that no more new towns were to be designated from 1977 and the previous year the Scottish Office abruptly cancelled the commissioning of Stonehouse New Town and transferred the staff and resources to a major regeneration project in the East End of Glasgow. A full review of urban policy in England had already been announced in September 1976.

The outcome of the review was the publication of the White Paper, *Policy for the inner cities* (DoE 1977d), which marked a turning point in policy-making towards the inner city and committed both central and local government to work in partnership towards the regeneration of the inner cities. Although drawing on the experience of at least six initiatives discussed earlier in this book, it was also the government's formal response to the recommendations of the Inner Area Studies.

The White Paper proposed to recast the Urban Programme and to increase funding from £30 million to £125 million in 1979/80 and to designate several partnership areas –initially identified as Liverpool, Birmingham, Manchester/ Salford, Lambeth and the London Docklands authorities. The partnerships would be between central and local government, including the Manpower Services Commission and health authorities, and each would prepare an inner area programme funded by Urban Programme grants. It was made clear that a concerted and co-ordinated effort was needed by all the agencies involved focusing particularly on the areas of greatest need:

> The Government consider that if real progress is to be made in tackling some of the major concentrations of problems, special efforts must be focused on a few cities in the next few years. Inner area problems are interdependent and complex. There is much fuller understanding of their character now, but they remain to be tackled successfully. The powers and finances of central and local government will need to be used in a unified and coherent way. New forms of organization and new methods of working may need to be tried. In the Government's view, success is more likely to be achieved by concentrating special attention and the major part of urban aid on a few major areas initially. Spread too thinly, any special efforts will achieve much less. (DoE 1977d: 16)

While asserting that "local authorities are the natural agencies to tackle inner area problems", the White Paper made clear that other interests had a role to play:

> The regeneration of the inner cities is not, however, a job for central or local government alone. A new and closer form of collaboration is required between government and the private sector, between government and the community including the various representative organizations in

44

the cities and larger towns, with the voluntary bodies, and above all with the people living in the inner areas. It is their welfare, immediate and long term, which must be the ultimate touchstone for success. (DOE 1977d: 25)

Most of the recommendations were implemented under legislation already in place to provide for the Urban Programme (Local Government (Social Need) Act 1969) and additional powers to make grants and loans to private firms, including the declaration of Industrial Improvement Areas, were included in the Inner Urban Areas Act, 1978. This Act also confirmed that the Urban Programme would be divided between three categories of urban deprivation: 7 partnership, 15 programme and 19 designated local authorities. In retrospect, the partnership provisions lacked both the resources and the organizational weight to make a significant impact on the target areas. The resources appeared to be arbitrarily divided between the target authorities and there was little evidence that either government agencies or local government departments were willing to bend their mainstream budgets. In addition, local government capital and revenue budgets were under pressure. For example, Liverpool suffered a reduction from almost £60 million to less than £40 million in its capital programme between 1974 and 1979 (Lawless 1989: 42). It is not surprising, therefore, that local authorities skilfully used the inner area programme for schemes that were not otherwise fundable. Likewise, there is little evidence that the partnership authorities were able to develop coherent strategies towards their areas or that a consensus was achieved between the partners. Decision-making was highly centralized and bureaucratic, and, while the voluntary sector in particular benefited from additional funding, it and the private sector were afforded few opportunities to contribute to long-term planning or the identification of local needs.

Thus, despite the commitment to collaboration, all the new policy measures to be implemented remained firmly in the control of civil servants in Whitehall, the government ministers who chaired the partnership committees, and town hall officials. As Barnekov et al. said:

Neither the central nor local government officials had direct experience with promoting local industry or commerce; business and the trade unions were not invited to be formal members of the partnerships; and representatives of the private sector had only peripheral involvement in the new economic programmes. (Barnekov et al. 1989: 157)

Thus, as the decade came to an end, there was already growing evidence that the policy measures instituted by one of the most far-sighted policy reviews in the post-war period had failed to establish an adequate mechanism for dealing with the growing problems of the inner city. Economic and social conditions were worsening, local government spending was under attack and the newly established inner-city partnerships were overcautious and lacking in the political clout to bend mainstream programmes or to involve wider local interests. It could only be a matter of time before an incoming government would institute a further review.

45

Privatism and the enterprise culture

The fourth phase of urban policy began with the election of Mrs Thatcher's Conservative Government in 1979, and subsequent victories in 1983, and 1987. Succeeding Secretaries of State for the Environment have introduced a flurry of policy initiatives, White Papers and deregulatory measures to reflect changing ideological perceptions of the problems to be tackled and agencies best able to deliver solutions. Within this context, the broad thrust of government policy "is not the regeneration of cities but rather the adaptation of the urban landscape to the spatial requirements of a post-industrial society" (Barnekov et al. 1989: 230). The underlying philosophy that underpins the changes in urban policy since 1979 has been variously described as Thatcherism (Thornley 1993), privatism (Barnekov et al. 1989) and the enterprise culture (Edwards & Deakin 1992).

In drawing comparisons between policy developments in the USA and Britain, Barnekov et al. define privatism as:

a tradition that encourages a reliance on the private sector as the principal agent of urban change . . . Privatism stresses the social as well as economic importance of private initiative and competition, and it legitimizes the public consequences of private action. Its legacy is that both personal and community wellbeing are evaluated largely in terms of the fulfilment of private aspirations and the achievements of private institutions. (Barnekov et al. 1989: 1)

Thornley describes the underlying elements of Thatcherism as a combination of economic liberalism, authoritarianism and popularism and "as a result of these changes it is argued that the scope and purpose of planning has undergone a major shift since 1979" (Thornley 1993: 219). He defines the main goals as deregulation, bypassing the planning system and simplification. He concludes:

During the post-war period planning was fulfilling three different purposes, although often in a confused or veiled fashion. These purposes covered the promotion of economic efficiency, the protection of the environment and the fulfilment of community needs. Since 1979 the first of these has become paramount, the second important only in specific geographical areas and the third no longer seen as the remit of planning. (Thornley 1993: 219)

The increasing emphasis on economic efficiency was also reflected in several changes to urban policy, but the commitment to partnership first articulated in the 1977 White Paper remained intact, albeit with a greater emphasis on employment-related projects.

In the early years of the Conservative regime, the urban riots that broke out in several inner-city areas were an important influence on policy. In 1980 major civil disturbances occurred in Bristol, in 1981 more than 4000 arrests for public disorder were made in areas such as Brixton (London), Toxteth (Liverpool) and

Handsworth (Birmingham), and in 1985 further incidents occurred at Broadwater Farm, Tottenham (London), and again in Birmingham. Although many commentators drew comparisons with similar events in the USA in the 1960s, there was little consensus about the causes. Growing unemployment as a result of economic restructuring, declining local authority expenditure, immigration and the role of the police were all questioned. Lord Scarman's inquiry favoured centrist and reformist improvements through existing institutions and policies (Scarman 1981). The government's response was to institute several policy changes designed to reaffirm the need for a much greater role for the private sector in policy-making and implementation.

Michael Heseltine, Secretary of State for the Environment from 1979 to 1983, decided to take the initiative and promote several policy changes set out in his report to Cabinet, "It took a riot". These involved increases in public expenditure as well as moves to involve the private sector. The setting up of the Financial Institutions Group (FIG), the drafting into the Environment Department of private sector advisors, and Heseltine's personal direction of government policy towards Merseyside complemented other legislative changes already in place, such as urban development corporations, Enterprise Zones and Urban Regeneration Grants (Heseltine 1987), together with a redirection of the Urban Programme towards economic priorities.

While the FIG brought little in the way of tangible new investment to the inner cities, in a report to the House of Commons Environment Committee the DOE portrayed the move as a beneficial learning process for both sides. Although the financial institutions were exposed "to the idea of working together with the Government, and to urban problems hitherto regarded as exclusively for the public sector", there were also benefits in the other direction:

> Civil servants (had) worked for a year very closely with people from the major financial institutions who in most cases had remained based in these institutions and had a direct link to top management. Thus, the Department was given an unprecedented opportunity to see how the institutions reacted to proposals affecting them, and what their working methods, attitudes and capabilities were; and . . . how managers with a training in various private sector disciplines approached social or policy problems. In the context of an overall policy aimed at increasing private sector involvement on urban questions, the exercise was very useful. (House of Commons Environment Committee 1982–3, Minutes of Evidence 507, quoted in Deakin & Edwards 1993: 30).

Throughout the 1980s the emphasis on involving the private sector in urban regeneration was closely coupled with the increasing centralization of urban policy. The partnership between central and local government, established by the previous Labour Government, was reinterpreted as a partnership between what were presumed to be like-minded interests: central government and the private sector. New initiatives, such as urban development corporations, City Action

47

Teams and Inner City Task Forces were increasingly staffed and managed by civil servants and private sector appointees, with strategic policy being determined by Westminster. Although the voluntary sector benefited to some degree from funding under the Urban Programme, it played no role in the management of, and was rarely consulted about, the individual initiatives or the broad direction of policy. In essence the voluntary and community sectors were seen as wedded to the outdated dependency culture and thus were largely bypassed along with local government.

Redirecting the Urban Programme

Closer examination of the workings of the inner-city partnership and programme authorities was beginning to reveal serious limitations to the approach. Birmingham was one of the largest and most successful of the partnership programmes and was consuming an eighth of total Urban Programme expenditure. A five-year review of the Birmingham Inner City Partnership, commissioned by the DoE and published in 1985, found that it was making an impact at the individual project level, but "there is no clear linkage between the Partnership's aspirations, and the operational objectives of the topic groups" (Public Sector Management Research Unit 1985: 196). Moreover, there was a lack of innovation or linkage between topic groups, little evidence that public sector agencies had bent their programmes to meet the needs of the target area, and that, where private sector involvement had occurred, it was largely independent of the activities of the Partnership:

> Our review indicates that collaboration with central government departments has been most effective in the context of the evaluation of project appraisals. The DoE, in a lead department capacity, has conducted bilateral negotiations with other departments in respect of specific project proposals. Departments have advised to the best of their ability, given that most have no inner city focus to their activity. For example, the Department of Industry is concerned mainly with individual firms, primarily in manufacturing industry, and does not take a spatial interest other than in regional policy, which was not acceptable to the West Midlands Region in the review period. Other departments, through their representation on Partnership committees, admitted to a "vague" role in Partnership. It is not uncommon for some central government departments to embark on substantial initiatives within Partnership boundaries without consultation with the local authority partners. The Partnership has not been the forum for review of central government policies as they impinge on it. (Public Sector Management Research Unit 1985: 200)

Although the total expenditure of the Birmingham Partnership was nearly

£100 million between 1978–9 and 1983–4, the review was clearly aware of the political sensitivities and concluded that the Partnership "should be retained and strengthened". Serious doubts were expressed about the extent to which it was operating as a genuine partnership, even within the public sector, and there is no evidence to suggest that this did not apply equally to others of its kind.

As early as 1981, Urban Programme authorities had been required to consult local chambers of commerce before submitting projects for departmental approval, but this was little more than a token gesture towards private sector involvement. In May 1985 the Urban Programme Management Initiative was introduced using 53 standard output measures to provide strategic direction to the programme. In addition, further guidelines were issued to stress economic priorities:

> The unemployment, physical dereliction and social stress in the inner cities cannot be tackled by the public sector alone. Involvement of the private sector and the community is essential . . . Ministers expect a continued presumption in favour of economic projects; those that stimulate wealth creation, increase economic activity and employment opportunities, bring idle assets of land and buildings back into use, remove obstacles to development and investment, and improve business confidence. (DoE 1985)

However, a report of the House of Commons Public Accounts Committee towards the end of the year remained unconvinced that ". . . the UP yet represents a well designed policy instrument based on a clear understanding of the problems and what needs to be done to solve them" (House of Commons Public Accounts Committee 1986). Other commentators were equally critical of both the fragmented nature of the policy and the weaknesses that were exposed in the delivery mechanism. As Parkinson & Wilks observed (1986: 302):

> Our study of Partnership has identified some damaging characteristics which are widely experienced in English central–local relations, but which appear in a particularly clear or virulent form in the Partnership case. Such characteristics include: The departmentalism of central government; the ignorance of local circumstances; the disinterest of the centre in the local impact of policy; its insulation of national politicians from local pressures.

One of the major themes of this period was the increasing centralization of all aspects of government, and the converse, the struggle to restrain the expanding cost of local government, not least because almost all the large city authorities were under the control of the Labour party. "Reducing the issue to the barest essentials, the Treasury and the DoE had two main priorities: to keep local authority expenditure within overall public expenditure targets and to keep down local authority Rates as part of their counter-inflationary policy" (Barnekov et al. 1989: 174).

The outcome of the imposition of these priorities was that local authorities were severely penalized for "overspending" through Rate-capping and other financial penalties, and outright abolition was the final solution in the case of the Greater London Council and metropolitan counties. Meanwhile, central government was able to instigate detailed control over the priorities and levels of local expenditure, as well as removing local powers over the control of development through the designation of UDCs, enterprise zones and other financial incentives offered directly to private developers.

As the financial stringencies of the mid-1980s bit more deeply into the budgets of local authorities and as central government departments were failing to target even the officially recognized partnership areas, it was the inner city that suffered most. The Archbishop of Canterbury's Commission on Urban Priority Areas found that between 1981–2 and 1984–5 the seven designated partnership authorities suffered a 22 per cent cut in Rate Support Grant (RSG) and the 23 programme authorities an equivalent 13 per cent cut. In addition, the complex formulae used to allocate Rate Support Grant tended to work against the interests of inner-city authorities, which also suffered penalties for taking on commitments arising from the Urban Programme (Archbishop of Canterbury's Commission 1985: 177–85). The TCPA computed that the inner London boroughs received £261 million through the Urban Programme between 1979–80 and 1983–4, while losing £865 million in RSG and reduced housing subsidies (TCPA 1986). Meanwhile, the amount allocated to urban development corporations increased from £255 million to £602 million between 1988–9 and 1991–2, and total DOE spending on urban policy measures increased from £598 million to £980 million in the same period (DOE 1993a).

The changes between the different budget heads are set out in the expenditure programmes within the urban block of the Department's current spending plans (Table 3.1).

Table 3.1 Urban expenditure 1988–9 to 1995–6 (£m, current prices).

	88–9	89–90	90–1	91–2	92–3	93–4	94–5	95–6
Urban Programme	224	223	226	237	243	176	91	80
City Challenge	–	–	–	–	64	214	2144	214
City Grant	28	39	45	41	60	71	71	83
Derelict Land Grant	68	54	62	77	95	93	93	120
URA	–	–	–	–	–	2	2	2
UDCs and DLR	255	477	607	602	514	337	293	284
Task Forces	23	20	21	20	23	18	16	15
City Action Teams	–	4	8	8	4	3	1	1
Manchester Olympics	–	–	–	1	13	35	25	–
Other	–	–	–	–	–	3	8	1
CF extra receipts	–	–2	–4	–7	–2	–	–	–
Inner cities total	598	815	964	980	1014	952	813	800
New Towns Commission	–558	–463	–333	–371	–129	–117	–203	–254
ERDF	27	8	2	3	16	176	199	174
TOTAL	67	360	633	611	901	1011	809	720

Source: Department of Environment Annual Report 1993.

Single-minded regeneration agencies

Although local authorities have traditionally had the role of overseeing and co-ordinating urban development, with assistance from central government, there have been occasions when single-purpose agencies have been established to take on special tasks. The early new towns had initially been promoted by private companies, although, as part of the commitment to post-war reconstruction from 1946 onwards, new town development corporations were established by central government appointment. Their ability to acquire land at agricultural-use value and to promote public and private development in order to relocate large populations from the overcrowded metropolitan areas was often presented as a model for similar agencies to work within urban areas with extensive derelict land. However, the approach was rejected in the 1977 White Paper because of the importance of preserving accountability to the local electorate (DOE 1977d: 8). By the mid-1970s, it was becoming clear that the relocation of urban populations to new towns was in itself exacerbating many of the problems, and that new forms of partnership arrangement might be needed. Several experiments followed in England, Wales and Scotland. In Scotland, the Labour Government of the time promoted what was claimed to be Europe's largest urban regeneration project in the East End of Glasgow, and in England the incoming Conservative Government launched the urban development corporations (UDCs) – with few qualms about local accountability. England also witnessed some smaller and less costly initiatives, such as Task Forces, City Action Teams and Housing Action Trusts, which to varying degrees applied different interpretations of the partnership concept.

The introduction of the UDCs as part of a broader set of measures in the 1980 Local Government, Planning and Land Act is largely attributed to Michael Heseltine. The previous year he had suggested that "there is a need for a single minded determination not possible for the local authorities concerned with their much broader responsibilities" (DOE 1979). In economic terms, the UDCs are required by Section 136 of the Act "to secure the regeneration of its area, by bringing land and buildings into effective use, encouraging the development of existing and new industry and commerce". Although extensive powers were made available to acquire land in addition to that owned by the public sector, which was vested in the UDC on designation, they had very limited powers to assist in the provision of affordable housing, or to support community initiatives. Politically, they embodied the New Right philosophy of a streamlined bureaucracy able to bypass the supposed rigidities of local authorities and to enable the private sector to play a primary role in property-led regeneration. By 1993, 13 UDCs had been designated in five phases. The first two, London Docklands (LDDC) and Merseyside (MDC), were designated in 1981; the last two, Birmingham Heartlands and Plymouth, were announced in March 1992. The remainder were launched in 1987 and 1988.

Although the UDCs varied considerably in size and population, they tended to

51

be located in either city centre locations, such as Bristol, Merseyside and Manchester, or in areas of derelict industrial land, such as Teesside, Cardiff Bay and Birmingham Heartlands. As Imrie & Thomas (1993: 13) note, there are some features common to all UDCs. They are exclusively accountable to the Secretary of State for the Environment and hence to Parliament. It is the Secretary of State who makes the designation, defines the area, appoints the board and its Chair, and approves its annual corporate plan and budget. All UDCs are required to have regard to local planning policies, although in practice these are often interpreted flexibly. Development control powers are either retained by the UDC or carried out by the local authority under an agency agreement. In addition, both Imrie & Thomas (ibid.) and Healey (1991) note the relative importance of place-marketing as a means to build confidence in the local property market and to restore faith in the older industrial cities. Since 1981, the LDDC alone has spent £20 million on promotion and marketing (Colenutt 1992).

In the decade from 1981, the UDCs gained both from being promoted as the flagship of the government's urban policy, as well as benefiting from a booming property market resulting from an expansion of credit and the growth of the service sector. Funding came from three sources: an annual budget from central government, finance borrowed from the national loan fund and income derived from land sales. The LDDC had by far the largest allocation, receiving £1800 million between 1981 and 1990 (Imrie & Thomas op. cit.: 15). This exceeded the total allocation to the 57 urban programme priority areas.

Commentators on the role of UDCs in promoting flagship projects and in pursuing property-led regeneration have been universally critical (Lawless 1989, Imrie & Thomas op. cit., Thornley 1993). Particularly in the early days, UDCs were required to adopt an aggressive stance towards acquiring land, promoting commercially orientated development, overriding local planning policies, and ignoring local democratic accountability. However, as Imrie & Thomas (op. cit.) note, the 13 UDCs have adopted very different strategies towards their areas, some operating in isolation, whereas others have developed complex working relationships with elements of the local State and other local interests. As the case studies presented by Imrie & Thomas (op. cit.) indicate, defining UDCs as single-minded institutions operating in a vacuum, as government rhetoric has in the past suggested, ignores the complexities of very different local contexts:

> Indeed, the range of institutional networks, between the UDCs and local actors and agencies, are much greater than is supposed, while it is increasingly clear that the property-led objectives of the UDCs do not remain unaffected by alternative, competing goals, which emanate from local sources (Clavel & Kleniewski 1990) . . . yet there is still an issue of how far, and in what ways, a pluralist policy system is able to emerge and operate under conditions largely set by the central State. (Imrie & Thomas op. cit.: 20)

Far less has been written about UDCs as an example of the partnership approach to urban regeneration. In many ways they appear to negate all the principles normally associated with the term. They are managed by boards appointed directly by the patronage of the Secretary of State for the Environment; they are directly funded by central government and have extensive powers to take over or acquire derelict land; and there is no requirement to involve or be accountable to local interests. However, they do represent a close alliance between central government and major national property-owning and -developing interests. In this sense they embody a particular phase of New Right ideological thinking about how best to institutionalize processes of urban regeneration, the interests to be included and supported, as well as those to be excluded and bypassed.

Yet, even in this respect, membership of the UDC boards varies considerably across the country. Whereas the LDDC, for example, had Chairs such as Nigel Broackes from Trafalgar House, followed by Christopher Benson from MEPC, together with some other representatives of major companies with few local connections, other boards were largely made up of local business executives, often with overlapping interests. In Sheffield there was considerable overlap between the UDC and other partnership organizations: Sheffield TEC, Sheffield Partnerships Ltd, Universiade GB Ltd, Sheffield Science and Technology Park, Sheffield 2000 and Sheffield Economic Regeneration Committee (SERC). For example, in 1989, Richard Field, who was chairman of a local mining company, was a member of SERC, Chair of Sheffield TEC, a director of Sheffield UDC, a past president of the Chamber of Commerce, a director of Sheffield Polytechnic and a governor of a local school (Bennett et al. 1990: 49). Similar interlocking memberships occur in Newcastle between the Tyne & Wear UDC, the two City Challenge agencies and The Newcastle Initiative. In almost all UDCs, the relevant local authorities also have representation. The gradual trend towards closer integration of UDCs into the constellation of local partnership agencies is perhaps best illustrated in Birmingham Heartlands, where, exceptionally, half the board is appointed by the local authority and half by the Secretary of State. Sir Reginald Eyre continues his role as Chair, whereas the representatives of the five development contractors have been replaced because of a potential conflict of interest.

The Scottish approach to urban regeneration

The origins of the concept of partnership in Scotland emerged in the mid-1970s from a different institutional and political background to that in England. For example, Boyle (1993) notes that, because of structural weaknesses in the Scottish economy and the rise of nationalism as a significant political force, there has been a long history of public–private sector collaboration since at least 1936. Unlike England, Scotland already had a strong regional co-ordinating body in the form of the Scottish Office, and in response to political pressures the Wilson Government had established the Scottish Development Agency (SDA) in 1975. This was given extensive powers to restructure the Scottish economy, along the lines of the National Enterprise Board in England, but in addition had powers of land reclamation and urban renewal. For these reasons, provisions for inner-city partnerships and UDCs were felt to be superfluous in Scotland. Instead, together with several other public sector partners the SDA embarked on the Glasgow Eastern Area Renewal (GEAR) project in 1976.

Several commentators have recorded the background to the launch of GEAR (Leclerc & Draffan 1984, Wannop & Leclerc 1987a). Growing concern about rising levels of deprivation and environmental decay in the major cities, while dispersal to new towns continued; a perception in the Scottish Office that Glasgow Corporation was unable to cope with one of the largest rehousing programmes in Europe; and a series of reports from organizations, such as the West central Scotland Plan team – all contributed to the major sea change in policy in the mid-1970s. After protracted negotiations between the Scottish Office and other public sector bodies, the newly designated Stonehouse New Town was cancelled in 1976 and the SDA was given the task of co-ordinating a major programme of urban renewal in Glasgow's East End. The GEAR project, covering 1600 ha (of which 18% was derelict) and an initial population of about 45 000, was to take ten years and to absorb £383 million of public expenditure (based on an unpublished report quoted by McCrone 1991: 927).

The initial partners in GEAR were the SDA, Strathclyde Regional Council, Glasgow District Council and the Scottish Special Housing Association. Four other public sector agencies joined the partnership over the next year: the Housing Corporation, Greater Glasgow Health Board and the Manpower Services Commission, making a total of eight in all. After extensive discussions, the Scottish Office set out the working arrangements in the Working Document on Organization (unpublished, quoted in Leclerc & Draffan 1984: 338). The objective of GEAR was the "comprehensive social, economic and environmental regeneration of the East End and the creation of conditions for the development of a balanced and thriving community". A governing committee of senior officials from all the partners, chaired by a Scottish Office minister, had general oversight over the project. A consultative group of officials co-ordinated and reviewed joint working arrangements. Although the SDA acted as lead, co-ordinating agency, each participant was expected to "retain its full statutory powers and responsibilities, but would act in full consultation with each other and . . . with the Agency as co-ordinator" (ibid.: 340). In addition, there was a "clear recognition of the fundamental importance of the involvement of existing communities within the area in the planning and regeneration of the area." (ibid.).

Wannop & Leclerc (1987b), McCrone (1991) and other evaluations generally agree that over the ten-year funding period much was achieved by GEAR. The area was transformed environmentally and a large proportion of the housing was renovated. Towards the end, the area became attractive to private housebuilders, which was itself seen as an indicator of success. However, in an unpublished report commissioned by the Scottish Office in 1988, the consultants PIEDA found that unemployment rates remained consistently high and that only 450 jobs were retained or created by financial incentives and a further 1000–2000 jobs were created or retained by the construction of factory units (quoted in McCrone 1991: 927). Without question, GEAR successfully bent mainstream programmes in its favour and achieved a higher level of public, and most likely private, expenditure than in the absence of the project (Wannop & Leclerc 1987b: 220–22).

Organizationally, GEAR faced some real difficulties, particularly in the early years, in having a top-heavy and complex management structure. It also lacked both clear objectives and a strategy against which performance could be measured, despite the preparation of a strategy and programme in 1980. Much therefore depended on the skills of the GEAR team in maintaining the commitment of the wide variety of partners and in ensuring their separate contributions were fully co-ordinated. As the project progressed, project staff developed some innovatory approaches, particularly in using SDA resources to promote imaginative projects, such as a major sports facility, and to levering in other resources. Considerable efforts went into maintaining public interest in the project, for example through publicity material and in the opening of local information and advice centres, but neither the local community nor the private sector were effectively involved in policy-making.

Throughout the lifetime of GEAR, the SDA set up several area projects in areas of central Scotland suffering most severely from plant closure and economic restructuring. Gulliver (1984) identifies at least four phases involving SDA Task Forces working in areas of major plant closure, integrated projects where project agreements were normally signed with other partners, and self-help projects, where, largely because of pressure from the Scottish Office, the SDA remained in the wings, whereas the lead was nominally taken by a local enterprise trust or private sector interests. The political imperative to involve the private sector increased in the early 1980s and the SDA quickly adapted to the changing climate. As a result, its primary objective became one of intervening only where market failure was self-evident and in stressing its economic remit. As the 1986 Treasury review of the SDA asserted:

> The continued rationale for the Agency and its activities must reflect the Government's general approach to intervention in the economy. In brief, the public sector should only be involved where the market alone will not produce the outcome desired by policy; and its intervention should wherever possible seek to achieve its ends by improving the workings of the market and not create dependency. (Industry Department for Scotland 1986: 2)

One response to growing political direction was to set up a project where the private sector could clearly demonstrate its leadership potential at minimal cost to public funds. In 1984 the SDA commissioned McKinsey and Associates to carry out a major study of Glasgow city centre. The result was the launch of Glasgow Action, whereby a board of prominent city businessmen, chaired by Sir

Norman Macfarlane, himself an SDA board member, promoted a strategy "unashamedly based on civic 'boosterism' " (Boyle 1989: 21). Although its objectives were similar to those of its American equivalents – promoting the relocation of company headquarters, software and service industries, tourism and culture – it was underpinned by both staff and at least £300 000 from the SDA (Boyle 1989).

Glasgow Action was perhaps most successful in its ability to work pragmatically with other organizations involved in promotional activities, such as the district and regional councils, which were also represented on the board. Given the close-knit nature of such organizations in Scotland many (including Glasgow Action) laid claim, for example, to securing Glasgow as the European City of Culture in 1990. By the end of the 1980s, Glasgow's negative image had been reversed and there was growing evidence that it was attracting commercial relocations from the south and was competing effectively with Edinburgh as a tourist and cultural destination. However, the economic justification was one of trickle-down of economic benefits, but all the indicators suggested that the impact on those living in the peripheral estates in particular was negligible. Nevertheless, the commitment of the private sector to initiatives such as Glasgow Action strengthened the hand of government in carrying out a major reorganization of the SDA and a review of urban policy.

Engaging the private sector

Throughout the 1980s, central government used several new initiatives to achieve urban regeneration objectives through the promotion of the enterprise culture. These initiatives focused particularly on the improvement of public sector housing, training and economic development. They have several characteristics in common:

- they involve central government identifying priorities and allocating resources directly to areas of need, whereas previously these resources had gone directly to local authorities
- in varying degrees they promote the idea of integration and co-ordination of policy delivery
- they involved the principle of partnership, but with local authorities either excluded or playing only a supporting role
- and they are predicated on the assumption that the private sector would be involved either through patronage or as a commercial partner in policy delivery.

Moreover, as unelected local agencies of government, they contribute substantially to the growth of unaccountable quangos.

Whereas, in the past, local authorities had received an annual allocation for the management and development of their housing stock, the Estate Action programme began from 1985 onwards to allocate increasing levels of resources towards problem estates on a competitive basis. In 1986–7 approximately £50 million was allocated for this purpose, but by 1992–3 this had reached £348 million. In submitting bids for Estate Action, local authorities are required to demonstrate their own level of commitment to the project and are increasingly required to lever in private sector contributions. This programme also requires the diversification of the tenure of the estate into owner-occupation and housing association management. Between 1985 and 1993, over 1000 schemes had been approved at a total cost of over £1000 million (DOE 1993c). Some of the larger projects are designated Comprehensive Regeneration Schemes or Community Refurbishment Schemes. The latter involve partnerships with the local TEC in providing linked training in construction skills.

Whereas properties improved through Estates Action remain in the ownership of local authorities, Housing Action Trusts (HATs) involve a transfer of ownership to a board of management appointed by the Secretary of State, subject to a vote by the tenants. HATs were introduced by the Housing Act (1988) and involve more drastic action where physical, social and economic regeneration is required. They initially proved unpopular, but when it became clear that resources for the improvement of designated estates would not be forthcoming, the number of HATs has increased. North Hull (made up of 2084 properties) and Waltham Forest (2500 properties) HATs were the first to be established in 1991. Tenants in 67 tower blocks on 35 sites in Liverpool voted to become a HAT in 1992. Two more are being established in Castle Vale, Birmingham, and Tower Hamlets (London) after votes in 1993. In both North Hull and Waltham Forest, partnership steering groups have been established to represent tenants' interests, and steps are being taken to develop appropriate training facilities with the local TEC. At the end of the funding period, tenants are able to decide on the future tenure of their property, remaining with the local authority being one of several options.

Government concern about the lack of co-ordination between the major departments with an inner-city remit led to the establishment from 1985 of a series of regional City Action Teams (CATs). These involved regional officials from the Departments of Employment, Environment, and Trade and Industry. working in eight regional centres in co-ordinating action at the local level. Each office has a small budget, but primarily operates through influence and negotiation. Since 1991 the CATs have acted as a conduit between Whitehall and other local agencies in managing the two rounds of City Challenge. Although the CATs have no doubt played an important part in liaising between the major Whitehall departments, criticisms of poor communications and limited co-ordination remain. In 1994 they were replaced by integrated regional offices of the Departments of Environment, Transport, Employment, and Trade and Industry.

Like the CATs, the Inner City Task Forces first came into operation in 1986, initially in eight areas but subsequently extended to a rolling programme of 16. They are targeted on small inner-city areas of three local authority wards, usually in locations subject to industrial restructuring, with populations suffering

high levels of unemployment, inappropriate skills and often with high proportions of ethnic minorities. Their task is to encourage "enterprise", enhance the
employability of the local population, and to support education initiatives to
improve access to employment opportunities. Although currently sponsored by
the DoE, they employ a staff of five or six civil servants from different departments, together with secondees from private industry or local authorities. Task
Forces operate through annual action plans over a period of about five years.
Because of their temporary nature, emphasis is placed on working in partnership
with other organizations and in devising an appropriate exit strategy. Since the
programme was launched in 1986, Task Forces have proved project funding
totalling almost £120 million. The DoE claims that Task Forces have helped to
create over 21 000 jobs and to provide 124 000 training places in their areas;
29 000 businesses have been supported and over 600 community projects have
been helped (DoE 1993d: 4).

Perhaps the most far-reaching attempt to involve the private sector in developing local economies was the review carried by the Department of Employment
in 1988 relating to the delivery of the government's training policies. As a result,
82 Training and Enterprise Councils (TECs) were established in England and
Wales from 1990, and by 1993-4 these were responsible for a total budget of
£2.4 billion (Bennett et al 1994).

The broad direction of training policy is overseen by a National Training Task
Force, made up largely of appointed industrialists. About the same time, similar
proposals, said to have come from within the Scottish Conservative Party,
resulted in the disbandment of the Scottish Development Agency and the amal-
gamation of its functions with the Training Agency in Scotland. From April
1991, 21 Local Enterprise Companies (LECs) were established under the strategic guidance of Scottish Enterprise in eastern and central Scotland, and Highlands Enterprise for the area formerly covered by the Highlands and Islands
Development Board. The primary responsibilities of the TECs are the delivery of
training programmes, skills development and the promotion of enterprise,
whereas the LECs have a wider remit that includes the promotion of development,
land reclamation and the environmental improvement. Annual budgets are negotiated by the TECs from the Department of Employment, and in Scotland annual
contracts are awarded to each LEC by Scottish Enterprise.

In both cases it was the government's view that the private sector should have
at least two thirds of the places on each board, in order to encourage local ownership of training strategies and to lever in additional resources. The intention
was that the responsibility for training and enterprise development should be
transferred to private companies able to exploit opportunities for innovation
while avoiding the bureaucracy of agencies such as the Manpower Services
Commission and Training Agency. The appointment to the boards of a relatively
narrow band of White, male, middle-class industrialists – and the consequent
exclusion of women, members of ethnic minorities, trade unionists and public
sector representatives – has been extensively criticized. Emmerich & Peck

(1992) note that, in 1991, TEC boards were composed of 89 per cent of male directors, with 71 per cent coming from the private sector. Only 3.5 per cent were from an ethnic minority background, 8.5 per cent were from local authorities and 5 per cent from the trade unions. Comparable research by Hayton & Mearns (1991) found that, in the Scottish LECs, 73 per cent were from the private sector, whereas 15 per cent were local authority councillors and only 3 per cent from the unions. There was 3.7 per cent and 1 per cent representation by the voluntary sector in England and Scotland respectively.

Whereas central government has tended to see the role of the TECs as a relatively specific one of the effective local delivery of training programmes within a fixed budget, some have sought a wider and more strategic role in working with other local agencies. Performance across the country has therefore been variable, with some adhering to their training remit, whereas others have adopted more innovative partnership-based strategies (see the case studies in Emmerich & Peck 1992). For example, the TECs have worked closely with UDCs, City Challenge agencies and partnerships based in local authorities, in developing complementary targeted training strategies. Emmerich & Peck (ibid.) suggest that greater effectiveness could be achieved by increasing local accountability, allocating core funding for three years rather than annually, and setting the TECs' local and sectoral policy within the context of an overall regional strategy. Christie & Rolfe (1992) also argue that the TECs' role could be strengthened, particularly in inner-city areas, by improved accountability and by developing a clear strategic context. In a more recent article, Peck (1993) finds the assumptions behind the market-driven skills revolution, which the TECs were designed to usher in, fundamentally flawed, not least by the dramatic reversal in the late 1980s, when a period of skills shortage was rapidly transformed into one of growing structural unemployment.

It is apparent that throughout the 1980s several new departmental initiatives were established that were designed to promote enterprise, increase the direct involvement of the private sector, and bypass local authorities and long-standing mechanisms of local accountability. In housing, the initiatives examined above have the effect of centralizing resource allocation and diversifying housing tenure away from the public sector. With economic development, the Task Forces and TECs provide additional resources over and above other inner-city initiatives and local authorities, whereas all lack a clear division of responsibilities and a strategic context within which to achieve maximum impact. Successful partnership arrangements have emerged in places at the local level, but distortions introduced by centralized policy-making, the competitive allocation of resources, the lack of clear metropolitan or regional strategies and patronage, rather than accountability, have led to fragmentation and duplication of effort. In Scotland, the absence of agencies such as HATs, Task Forces and UDCs, and the presence of co-ordinating agencies such as Scottish Enterprise and the Scottish Office, have has meant that a greater sense of strategy through partnership could begin to emerge.

Consolidation and review of urban policy: 1987–91

After her election to a third term in 1987, Mrs Thatcher committed her government to a further onslaught on "those inner cities". Britain had already experienced a decade of urban policy in which a commitment to the enterprise culture had been superimposed on more traditional administrative requirements to achieve intersectoral collaboration and closer co-ordination between government departments. Whereas the UDCs remained the government's flagships in the inner city, local authorities were increasingly circumscribed by reduced powers and spending restrictions, and there was growing evidence that central government initiatives were leading to duplication of effort, displacement and deadweight. It was during this period that the government's vision: of the private sector taking the leading role among the cast of inner-city actors reached its zenith.

In 1987, Kenneth Clarke was appointed Cabinet Minister with special responsibility for the inner cities. At a series of breakfast meetings with business leaders, he portrayed new and existing central government initiatives as forming the basis for a new alliance with the private sector in the inner cities. The government, he claimed, was willing to work with local authorities ". . . but where – perhaps for ideological reasons – they try to obstruct us, they will not be allowed to get in the way" (*British Business* 1987: 18). It was also not simply a matter of funding:

> It is not now primarily a question of new government expenditure and new initiatives, although there will be both if and where necessary. It is a case of getting maximum impact from all the various programmes that government now has or is creating. I believe that we need to see a pooling and concentration of effort in the localized areas where the worst problems are all found. We need to take a sledgehammer to crack a nut. If we identify our target carefully, and then swing the whole sledgehammer at it, I believe that we can achieve the transformation we seek. (*British Business* 1987: 19)

One of the main outcomes was glossy brochures aimed largely at its political supporters, where the government attempted several contradictory aims: to claim success for previous policy initiatives, to set out several one-off developments, road proposals and new UDCs in order to inflate the total inner-city budget, and to stress the need for collaborative action without the institutional mechanisms to achieve it (Cabinet Office 1988, DoE 1989). The role of local authorities continued to be sidelined, a move that was reinforced by measures such as the consolidation of City Grant, which was allocated and paid for by central government as a subsidy towards marginal commercial developments in priority areas. Yet the Action for Cities initiative argued that a "pooling of resources of the private and public sectors is the way to achieve real success in the inner cities" (Cabinet Office 1988: 4). The subsequent review the following year urged that "the energy, commitment and talent of local people of all backgrounds and origins – in business, local authorities, voluntary bodies and throughout the community – are essential to inner city revival" (DOE 1989: 6).

As the decade came to a close, an increasing proportion of the urban block was being allocated to property-related development activities under the direct control of central government. Although the government's confidence was boosted by an expanding economy – best illustrated by the rapid pace of development in London Docklands – its strategy could equally be undermined by a rapid economic downturn. Local authorities fared less well, and by 1988–9 retained some influence over only about one tenth of the £3000 million government claimed was being spent on the inner cities (Lawless 1991: 25).

Local residents also gained little, in that consultative arrangements and public accountability were broadly precluded by the terms of reference of all the main partnership initiatives. The primacy given to the private sector to stimulate investment meant that residents and community organizations were excluded from involvement in policy-making, and rarely benefited from new jobs, community facilities or affordable housing (see for example the findings of the NAO 1988). However, the Urban Programme was being used as a mechanism for funding voluntary organizations, and by 1987 they were receiving about 40 per cent of the total budget. This reflected the inability of local authorities to fund such projects from mainstream budgets more than their inclusion in any overall strategy. In addition, crucial aspects of inner-city life, such as health, social services, education and crime prevention, remained largely beyond the remit of departmental initiatives.

One of the few attempts to review the growing complexity of the government's inner-city policy in England emerged from the Audit Commission in 1989. The Commission's report, *Urban regeneration and economic development*, drew attention both to the extent to which government programmes were "seen as a patchwork quilt of complexity and idiosyncrasy" (Audit Commission 1989: 9) and to the important role local authorities could play in co-ordinating regeneration through "local regeneration strategies":

> Local authorities themselves must organize their urban regeneration efforts more effectively. They must integrate them into policy choices on their main programmes, acquire appropriate skills and acknowledge explicitly the limits of their role as enabler, leader and catalyst. They must develop only strategies that they have a realistic chance of achieving.
>
> The basis for these redefinitions should be a clear-sighted assessment of the needs of each deprived urban area: a local regeneration audit, developed in conjunction with the private sector and the local offices of central government departments. This should be the essential background against which the well intentioned efforts of all sides can be better co-ordinated. Local authorities themselves can play an important leading and co-ordinating role. (Audit Commission 1989: 2)

The Audit Commission unambiguously set out the way forward, so that the friction between different levels of government could be reduced by strongly favouring partnerships co-ordinated by local authorities:

Current initiatives provide opportunities for both partnership and conflict. There is a strong case for saying that the totality of effort devoted to urban regeneration is less than the sum of its parts. The Commission makes no apology, therefore, for focusing on how existing plans and programmes can be made to work better, rather than proposing yet more novel initiatives with catchy acronyms. (Audit Commission 1989: 7)

By 1990 the differing perceptions of the meaning of partnership were becoming more pronounced: different levels of government, development agencies, the private and community sectors – all perceived and defined it differently. Moreover, a further divergence was occurring in the application of partnership in urban regeneration in both England and Scotland. In England, partnership was perceived by ministers as the principal means of regenerating the inner city, but was seriously flawed in its application in that it was fragmented, exclusionary, biased towards one sectoral interest, and increasingly used as a smokescreen for the centralization of power and the reduction of local accountability.

In Scotland, a review of urban policy similar to Action for Cities was carried out by the Scottish Office. This time the tone was more measured and the evaluation of the interlocking programmes by the SDA, local authorities, local enterprise trusts and community businesses was more systematic. The use of the Urban Programme and SDA funds, such as LEGUP (Local Enterprise Grants for Urban Projects), had helped stimulate voluntary activity and private sector investment, together with Scottish Homes and community-based housing associations. Much had been achieved in GEAR and through local authority action, but much remained to be done, particularly in the peripheral housing estates constructed in the 1950s and 1960s. New Life for Urban Scotland (1988) therefore proposed to maintain the momentum of existing programmes, but also to launch a new partnership initiative in four peripheral housing estates in Castlemilk (Glasgow), Ferguslie Park (Paisley), Wester Hailes (Edinburgh) and Whitfield (Dundee). In addition, smaller partnerships had already been established on housing estates at Barlanark, Motherwell and Perth. The selected area of Wester Hailes contained a population of about 12 000 in about 6000 homes. The four partnerships were to be under the leadership of the Scottish Office, but also involving local authorities, the Training Agency, Scottish Homes, SDA, the health authority, business support groups and local residents organizations. The initiatives were expected to run for ten years and the objectives would be comprehensive: increasing economic activity in the wider area, improving residents' chances of finding jobs, improving the environment, upgrading and diversifying housing tenure, improving health, educational and recreational opportunities, and community facilities and structures, and reducing crime.

Two years later (Scottish Office 1990), the second report contained an upbeat assessment of progress to date in the four partnership areas, and hinted at a broader, more comprehensive strategy developing in the Scottish Office:

> A sound foundation has been built and achievements are beginning to flow. The Partnerships and other initiatives provide the right framework for pressing ahead and for continuing innovation, to complement the continued pursuit of the key policies already in place.
>
> There is scope for a similar strategic approach to be applied to other parts of our towns and cities. (Scottish Office 1990: 7)

By 1990, urban policy had evolved very differently in Scotland from to its equivalent in England. Ministers of the Scottish Office conceded that the harsher aspects of Thatcherism, such as UDCs, were not needed in Scotland because of the comprehensive reach of the SDA. For its part, the SDA had judiciously avoided being seen as the economic arm of the Conservative Government and had broadly won the support of Labour local authorities, and the business community, in selecting and running its area projects with considerable political sensitivity. The four New Life partnerships built on some of the lessons learned in GEAR and elsewhere on the need to include public, business and community interests, whereas the direct involvement of the Scottish Office reflected the continuing tensions between it and the SDA on who should claim credit for such initiatives. Gulliver (1984: 326) suggested that the SDA's area projects amounted not to a Scottish urban policy but to more of a convenient mechanism for delivering SDA products and services. By the early 1990s the Scottish Office was gradually moving towards the nearest thing to a strategic approach in Britain, based on what was beginning to look like a workable partnership between a broad range of local interests.

In Wales a similar strategic approach is being developed by the Welsh Development Agency (WDA) and the local authorities, leading to the integration of economic development and urban regeneration policies. The approach is to prepare urban investment programmes for towns and urban areas for implementation by both public and private sectors. Pavitt (1990) identifies three strands to the policy. Contractual joint ventures are drawn up between the WDA and local authorities on large sites where substantial investment is required. For small towns, a town development trust is more appropriate for carrying out small-scale improvements. The third model is a consortium of public and private sectors, often with local community representation, able to co-ordinate investment and improvement over an extended period. From 1991 this approach has been called Urban Development Wales (UDW), and has three advantages: it offers a flexible approach to identifying and meeting the needs of urban areas, it tackles problems holistically, and it is based on partnership through an integrated action plan. One of the added advantages of this approach is that investment plans can be used to lever additional moneys from the EU Regional Fund. In 1990–1 UDW had a budget of £4.8 million, but two years later this had increased to £21 million. The projected budget for 1994–5 is £35 million (*Planning Week* 1994). Although unemployment remains high in particular localities, the approach has brought significant environmental improvements and some inward investment to areas such as the Valleys and Cynon Valley. The UDW is building the foundations of a strategic approach that combines local initiative with a regional perspective within a European framework.

Post-Thatcherism: a return to local corporatism?

The reappointment of Michael Heseltine as Secretary of State for the Environment in 1990 and the re-election of the Conservative Government under John Major in April 1991resulted in a further phase in the evolution of the partnership approach in England, with several new initiatives. From the peak of the deregulatory boom of the late 1980s, property values slumped, and continuing recession forced a reappraisal of urban policy. The announcement in May 1992, that London Docklands' flagship development, Canary Wharf, was in the hands of administrators, symbolized in extreme form the effects on the balance sheets of many of the UDCs. Asset values had to be slashed and many UDCs sought more time and resources to complete their programmes.

The government's response was to commission a complete review of urban policy along the lines suggested by the Audit Commission report (1989), but in the meantime to add yet another layer of new initiatives over and above those previously heralded in Action for Cities. Thus, in 1991–2 the UDCs were still receiving 61 per cent of the total spend on inner cities and the Urban Programme absorbed 24 per cent, despite growing criticism of the effectiveness of both initiatives.

City Challenge

The first of the new initiatives, City Challenge, was announced by Michael Heseltine in May 1991. Drawing on several overseas visits while out of office, Heseltine reinterpreted the concept of partnership in what many claimed was a new and imaginative way. However, the level of expenditure was low and only ten "pacemaker" authorities were to be selected by competitive bidding in the first round (subsequently increased to 11) out of a total of 15 authorities invited to bid. Also , no new money was provided and the £83.5 million allocated for 1992–3 was found by recasting departmental housing and Urban Programme budgets. The innovative features of the initiative were that deprived neighbourhoods were to be targeted by independent regeneration agencies using public money and the leverage of private sources set up to prepare and implement action plans over five years. Action plans were required to identify a "vision" and to specify with clear targets both property-related and "people-orientated" strategies.

A further novel feature was that local authorities were accepted as having the task of "civic leadership – in forming partnerships, harnessing existing talent, energy and resource and developing imaginative and innovative solutions to the problems of urban decay" (DoE 1992b: 6). Although the City Challenge agencies would work closely with local agencies such as Task Forces, City Action Teams and Training and Enterprise Councils, central government would approve the action plans and authorize expenditure over agreed limits. Moreover, the "ownership" of the strategy would be assured by the direct involvement of all sectors:

> The City Challenge initiative is underpinned by the proposition that substantial and lasting urban regeneration requires efficient, entrepreneurial delivery mechanisms that promote effective collaborative relationships between all the key players. (DoE 1992b: 3).

The 11 pacemaker authorities were required to have their action plans approved early in 1992 and to be in operation by April. All have now set up regeneration agencies and most have been incorporated as companies limited by guarantee, with a management board made up of local authority representatives (in the minority), other public sector agencies, the private sector and community representatives. A second round of City Challenge was announced in April 1992 in which all 57 urban priority authorities were invited to bid. Twenty successful authorities were announced in July 1992 and each will receive £7.5 million per year over five years. Table 3.2 indicates the successful local authorities in rounds 1 and 2 and their deprivation ranking.

City Challenge raises some fundamental issues about the way urban regeneration is organized and managed, and both builds on previous initiatives and prescribes new directions. The ultimate test of its success will be the extent to which it can galvanize local stakeholders, central government departments and the private sector, all of which have very different priorities, to work towards a single set of objectives. Several commentators have emphasized the positive features of the initiative (De Groot 1992, Hambleton 1993, Parkinson 1993):

- the transfer of responsibility to local partners to apply imagination, flair and quality to the definition of local needs and to identifying ways of meeting them
- the flexibility to operate laterally across departmental and policy boundaries
- the emphasis on involving residents and building on the capacity of the community to play its full part
- the recognition that regeneration could best be achieved by combining physical and property-related strategies with those aimed at social and community needs, and
- the commitment to detailed action plans with clearly identified "milestones" and outputs. All of these qualities mirrored, in varying degrees, the weaknesses perceived in previous initiatives, such as the UDCs and Inner City Partnerships.

65

Table 3.2 City Challenge areas by deprivation ranking and rounds.

Authority	Deprivation ranking	Round
Hackney	1	2
Newham	2	2
Tower Hamlets	3	1
Lambeth	4	2
Brent	8	2
Manchester	11	1
Leicester	12	2
Wolverhampton	13	1
Lewisham	16	1
Birmingham	14	2
Liverpool	14	1
Kensington/Chelsea	17	2
Sandwell	19	2
Nottingham	20	1
Blackburn	21	2
Middlesborough	23	1
Bradford	26	1
Kirklees	31	2
Walsall	34	2
Hartlepool	35	2
Bolton	36	2
Newcastle	37	1
Sunderland	38	2
Derby	41	2
Stockton	46	2
Wirral	48	1
Sefton	50	2
Wigan	53	2
North Tyneside	54	2
Barnsley	55	2
Dearne Valley	*	1

* A joint bid by Rotherham (55), Barnsley (56) and Doncaster (51).
Source: DoE Press Notices 474 and 497, as reproduced in Atkinson & Moon (1994).

On the other hand, there are also serious flaws. Perhaps the most important is the continuing emphasis on identifying relatively small target areas for special treatment and in using a competitive process to identify "winners" and "losers". The selection of bids appeared to be far more related to ensuring an even geographical and political spread of local authority areas, rather than any real assessment of the quality of bids. Secondly, there was no new money available, but rather a rearrangement of existing budgets. In addition, those areas gaining from City Challenge are likely to lose far more from the capping of budgets for their main services and cuts in the Urban Programme. In the case of Newcastle, the £37.5 million for City Challenge over five years must be set against an estimated loss of £200 million for the city as a whole (Beecham 1993). Thirdly, the division of the £37.5 million into five annual payments of £7.5 million takes no account of the problems of achieving an even expenditure of resources, given other requirements to achieve leverage and a mixture of public and private funding. A real danger exists that action plans will become project-driven to meet budgetary targets, rather than needs-based. Finally, there is growing evidence that the lack of lead-in time has led to difficulties in fully involving local communities in the planning process. In many areas there is a danger that local residents are marginalized by better resourced players, well practised in promoting and mobilizing their own interests (Mabbott 1993). This also raises more fundamental questions about the extent to which collaborative organizational structures can be representative and democratically accountable.

A detailed review of the experiences of six of the pacemaker authorities concluded that it was essential to provide a lead-in time of four to six months to enable local authorities to consult the community and voluntary sectors. In addition, guidance on community involvement is needed, as is an audit of the capacity of the local population to play its full part in project and sector development. Funds should be allocated for use in community consultation and community sector project development during the bid preparation phase and to facilitate community involvement throughout the funding period (Macfarlane & Mabbott 1993).

The government's 1992 Autumn Statement was interpreted as both a serious loss of confidence in its urban policy and a surrender to Treasury economies. Although the third round of City Challenge was to be "suspended", it was also announced in the Urban Programme guidance for 1993–4 that UP funding would effectively be phased out, with a £60 million cut in 1993–4 and a further £158 million in 1994–5. Only existing commitments will be maintained, with many projects ending in each successive year. This, together with cuts in Section 11 funding to areas of high immigration, will inevitably cause redundancies in local authorities and the voluntary sector. In its place a Capital Partnership programme was set up, for which bids were invited. One element of this was an Urban Partnership Fund where £20 million of UP funds are to be used in conjunction with local authority capital receipts, estimated by the government as £1750 million, up until the end of December 1993. Priority is to be given to capital or revenue projects based on existing UP, City Challenge or UDC plans or commitments. This is seen as a temporary measure, while a review of the urban priority areas is carried out in the light of the 1991 census results. As part of the 1992 Autumn Statement, the Chancellor of the Exchequer also announced the Private Finance Initiative, whereby the private sector is encouraged to invest directly or in joint ventures in capital projects that previously would have been entirely publicly funded. The DOE's contribution was to publicize several sites for which private finance is sought in collaboration with local authorities or UDCs (DoE 1993e).

English Partnerships

A second manifesto commitment from the 1992 election, and a further proposal closely associated with Michael Heseltine, is the establishment of a urban regeneration agency for England, which was the subject of a departmental consultation paper in July 1992. It was proposed that the agency would have statutory powers to promote the reclamation of over 150 000 acres of development of derelict, vacant and underused land and buildings. It would take control of Derelict Land Grant and City Grant and would absorb the work of English Estates in providing industrial and commercial space in Assisted Areas. The consultative paper makes it clear that the agency would be flexible and entrepreneurial, but would work within the existing statutory planning framework. In addition, it would:

> . . . operate wherever possible as an enabling body. It would aim to pro-
> mote development with the private sector and would work closely with
> local authorities, the voluntary sector, and other bodies involved in urban
> renewal. (DoE 1992c: 4)

As the Leasehold Reform, Housing and Urban Development Bill passed through Parliament in 1993, debate focused on the nature of the agency and how it will work in practice. On the one hand, it is possible to see it as a "roving urban development corporation" in order to override local opposition and to impose a property-led solution. On the other hand, it could seek out existing or promote new partnerships to provide a local implementation mechanism. The selection of Lord Peter Walker as Chairman and the announcement in November 1993 that it is to be called English Partnerships (EP) perhaps indicates that the latter approach is more likely. However, when EP began work in April 1994, it had neither the broad range of economic development powers nor the level of resources, many of which are already committed, of Scottish Enterprise or the Welsh Development Agency. Because of these limitations, it is also unlikely to operate as an effective co-ordinator and catalyst across a broad range of policy areas. It will therefore be another small fish in a crowded pool.

In January 1994 EP announced that it had commissioned feasibility studies into the first four "flagship projects" at a $10 \, km^2$ area of Speke and Garston (Liverpool), a proposed new university site in Lincoln, an 80 ha site at Newburn Haugh (Newcastle), and the 31 ha Royal Arsenal site within the Greenwich Waterfront Development Partnership area and the Thames Gateway. The Liverpool and Greenwich sites had both been the subject of failed City Challenge bids in round two.

Government offices for the regions

In November 1993 the government announced moves to integrate 20 separate grant regimes into a single budget and the establishment of ten integrated regional offices in England for the Departments of Trade and Industry, Employment, Environment and Transport. Each office will prepare an annual regeneration statement, setting out the key priorities for regeneration and economic development in the region, and a Single Regeneration Budget from which bids will be invited. A Cabinet Committee on Regeneration will agree the resources and set guidelines for its allocation. In 1994–5 existing commitments will absorb the £1400 million budget, but bids are being invited from local authorities and partnerships for the £100 million available for the following financial year. English Partnerships, UDCs and Housing Action Trusts will continue to receive annual allocations from their integrated regional office. In the same announcement, London, Birmingham and Manchester were invited to prepare prospectuses of promotional activities for the next ten years under the banner of City Pride. As with the SRB, questions have been raised about how far City Pride is about promotional place marketing and how far the prospectuses will be integrated into existing planning and economic development mechanisms.

Bids for SRB will be encouraged primarily from partnerships incorporating significant local interests that have devised a city-wide strategy, intensive activity to regenerate a specific area, such as a town centre or housing estate, or for innovative projects. Objectives can include economic development, the leverage of private and European funds, housing improvement, as well as social priorities relating to health, facilities, the environment and crime prevention (DoE 1993b). Local authorities are encouraged to co-ordinate the relevant interests in submitting bids:

> The Government wants to stimulate proposals from a wide range of local players from the business, voluntary, education and other sectors working in partnership. The Government's view, based on recent regeneration experience, is that these partnerships are likely to be best formed by the local authorities and TECs working in unison to bring together the relevant parties and to submit bids on the budget. (DoE 1993b: 2)

Further guidance issued in 1994 suggests that the bidding process, the nature of the documentation required, the commitment to clearly defined and monitored strategies, and the preparation of exit strategies, relies heavily on the experience of the first two rounds of City Challenge (DoE 1994).

This announcement is significant, since it attempts to correct several criticisms of urban policy made in the past. First, it is an attempt to integrate the "patchwork quilt" of grant regimes into a single budget, as well as aiming to achieve a higher level of collaboration between at least four government departments; both go some way to make good the faults identified by the Audit Commission and by critics of the inner-city partnerships. Secondly, it is to be welcomed in principle in that it suggests central government is pulling back from direct intervention through a succession of model programmes designed to bypass local authorities. Thirdly, it suggests local authorities have an important role to play as co-ordinators and enablers of local bids. On the negative side of the equation, it is clear that each year the uncommitted proportion of the SRB will be very modest and that there will be far more losers than winners. It thus institutionalizes the growing practice of putting out government funding mechanisms to competitive tender, as in City Challenge, Estates Action and related programmes. It may, however, have the effect of mobilizing several new partnerships that can leverage private and European sources of funding.

It will not be until the bidding process for SRBs has operated for several years before conclusions can begin to be drawn about its impact and effectiveness. Much depends on the extent to which the regional offices effectively integrate their departmental spending plans and are able to achieve devolved decision-making powers from Whitehall. It also raises questions about how far other departments will be integrated, if health, education and crime, for example, are on the local agenda. Moreover, it is by no means clear that the political will exists to maintain and increase budgets orientated towards urban issues and to apply the principle of devolving decision-making and implementation to the lowest effective level of government. Stewart suggests that the introduction of Regional Directors and regional budgets signifies a realignment in central–local relations designed to pre-empt the growing trend towards devolution and regionalism evident in the other political parties that at the time of writing largely dominate local government (Stewart 1994: 142).

The evolution of the partnership approach in Scotland

In October 1993 the Scottish Office issued a consultation paper on the future of urban regeneration policy in Scotland (1993). This reviewed both progress and experience in the four "New Life" Partnership areas and it set out several options for using Scottish Office powers and Urban Programme resources in a strategic manner to target those areas in greatest need. The overall objective of the four Partnerships is:

> to pursue a comprehensive, co-ordinated, long-term, strategic approach to regeneration, harnessing the resources of the public and private sectors and local communities. (Scottish Office 1993: 1)

In reviewing progress in the existing Partnership areas, the report notes the importance of linkages between different aspects of regeneration, the need for an agreed strategy based on a co-ordinated approach, the importance of a local implementation team based in the area, the need to build monitoring and evaluation procedures into the strategy, and in having an agreed exit strategy. Progress is then charted in several key policy areas and the role of the private sector and local community reviewed.

The report then turns to the question of how Urban Programme (UP) funds might best be applied in future. Approved UP expenditure in 1992–3 stands at £83 million, supporting 1200 projects, and is channelled to local authority areas falling within the 10 per cent in greatest need as measured by deprivation indices. The two alternatives proposed are continuing the current system of allocation or targeting specific area-based regeneration initiatives beyond the four existing

Partnerships. In identifying and selecting areas for extending the partnership approach, the Scottish Office suggests that either local agencies should be responsible or the Scottish Office itself should designate several Priority Partnership Areas (PPAs). These would receive core funding to prepare a strategy and to provide basic running costs. In addition, the report proposes that PPAs could be selected by the Scottish Office, by competition or by prior negotiation, in which local agencies would be able to influence those that were accorded the highest priority.

Further observations are sought on whether partnerships should be managed by a board of sectoral representatives or whether a particular agency should take the lead: the Scottish Office, local authorities, Scottish Homes, local enterprise companies, local communities, and the private sector are all considered possible candidates. Finally, the consultation paper seeks advice on the future direction of the Urban Programme:

> – The Programme could be left in its present form with approvals given centrally on a project by project basis.
> – UP resources could allocated as a block to local authorities to be spent solely on qualifying activities in eligible disadvantaged areas.
> – To move towards more dedicated budgets for initiative areas with a regeneration strategy and a resource team in place.
> – To devise a strategy-based approach that represented a further extension of the third option, that is to part-fund the setting up of an area initiative, which would include an analysis of the area and the preparation of a comprehensive regeneration strategy; to fund the running costs of locally based implementation teams; and to fund projects contributing to regeneration in the initiative areas. (Scottish Office 1993: 36)

This consultation paper marks an important advance in the development of the partnership concept in that, although its starting point is the acceptance of integrated, comprehensive and multisectoral approaches to urban deprivation, it looks forward to how limited resources might be used strategically to achieve maximum impact in areas of greatest deprivation. The need for community involvement is also given equal if not greater weight than that of the private sector, which in any case is marginal in the most deprived peripheral estates. There is also the suggestion that delegation of decision-making and resource allocation to the lowest level of accountability is to be encouraged. As in England, no new resources are on offer and the possibility of a competitive basis to allocation is raised but not, at this stage, imposed. Although the underlying tensions between Labour-dominated local authorities and the minority party running the Scottish Office may have influenced the options proposed, there is no doubt that the experience of the four New Life Partnerships has genuinely informed policy. However, as commentators such as Hayton (1993) note, it is difficult to draw any firm conclusions about the New Life partnerships without detailed evaluation. The Scottish Office's proposals suggest that the increasing tendency toward the targeting of cash-limited resources on areas of deprivation will inevitably lead to smaller areas being deprived of resources, and the emphasis on supply-side training measures will simply displace labour from one area to another, if demand is also not also stimulated (Hayton 1993: 55).

The European Union Structural Funds

A further impetus to the formation of partnerships has come from the growing availability of European Structural Funds from Brussels. Regional groupings of local authorities, together with other public and private sector agencies, have developed innovative approaches to accessing and applying these funds. Three main funds are available: the European Regional Development Fund (ERDF), the European Social Fund (ESF), and the European Guarantee and Guidance Fund (EAGGF). Following the ratification of the Maastricht Treaty in 1993, there is also a new Cohesion Fund. The Structural Funds are allocated on a regional basis or to meet the needs of particular target groups, such as the long-term unemployed. They can also be used to fund voluntary organizations or bodies such as chambers of commerce. There are six objectives under which regions are selected:

Objective 1: to promote the development and structural adjustment of lagging regions (where per capita GDP is less than 75 per cent of the EU average). Currently Northern Ireland, Merseyside and the Highlands and Islands are designated under this objective. Objective 2: to convert regions seriously affected by declining industries (where there is a decline in industrial employment and the average unemployment and industrial employment rates are above the EU average). Examples include the West Midlands, central Scotland and the Lee Valley, London.

- Objective 3: to combat long-term unemployment (individuals over the age of 25 who have been unemployed more than a year).
- Objective 4: to facilitate the occupational integration of young people (job-seekers below the age of 25).
- Objective 5a: to adapt agricultural production, processing and marketing structures.
- Objective 5b: to promote the development of rural areas (based on the number of persons engaged in agriculture engaged in agriculture, their level of economic and agricultural development, the extent to which they are peripheral and their sensitivity to changes in the agricultural sector).

EU Structural funds are normally allocated through Integrated Operational Programmes involving consortia of local authorities and other (mainly public) agencies such as the TECs and UDCs. In the past, the only requirement was that the funds should be additional to other central or local government expenditure. However, the EU is increasingly looking for the leverage of other public and private sources and for the closer integration of funding partners. Quite large sums of money have been gained through successful applications to the EU. In the Black Country, four boroughs obtained £48 million in 1992–3 under Objective 2, and Merseyside has spent £35 million from the ESF and £50 million from the ERDF, with an additional £30 million from Objectives 3 and 4. Funding is used for major projects to improve transport and infrastructure, environmental improvements, the development of science parks, town centre upgrading and business advice and support.

In the bid for Objective 2 funding, submitted by twelve London Boroughs covering the Lee Valley and part of the Thames Gateway, it was proposed to establish an Integrated Development Organization made up of a development committee, operational programme committee and a permanent secretariat. It would be made up of representatives of the local authorities, TECs, LDDC and City Challenge companies, together with the four main government departments involved. In addition, consultation forums would be established to draw in other partners: employers, enterprise agencies, training and education providers and the community sector. In January 1994 it was announced that funding had been approved for only six London boroughs in the Lee Valley area. Although many local authorities have complained of the bureaucratic difficulties of applying for EU funds and the problems arising from Structural Funds being awarded on a calendar year basis, the benefits are potentially great. So far the British government has not taken any steps to integrate European funding sources with national procedures, for example the Single Regeneration Budget.

The 1994 review of urban policy

The 1994 review of urban policy represents one of the most comprehensive and exhaustive assessments of any area of public policy ever undertaken (Robson et al. 1994). It involved quantitative studies of the inputs and outcomes of urban expenditure on a sample of 123 local authority areas (including the 57 urban priority areas), surveys of residents and employers in target areas, and interviews with the "policy communities" of the conurbations of Greater Manchester, Merseyside and Tyne & Wear. The conclusions are detailed and wide-ranging, and not easily summarized. The overriding impression is of the limited impact of policy, and of the arbitrary and uneven distribution of policy inputs and the variable outcomes in both target and non-target authorities. Detailed criticisms are presented of the development and implementation of policy, the uneven response of both public sector agencies and the adverse financial constraints imposed on local authorities that severely limited their ability to play a full role. Evidence of "area loyalty" emerged from the residents' survey, suggesting "scope for a more focused social dimension to urban policy to capitalize on the place-loyalty of local communities" (ibid.: x). An overall assessment set out both the positive and negative elements of policy:

73

Our quantitative evaluation clearly suggests a complex mixture of pluses and minuses. There have been positive impacts associated with the expenditure of Action For Cities resources; there are, on the other hand, places where even large expenditures have had no demonstrable effect in reversing or slowing the urban decay reflected by increasing polarization. The cores of the large conurbations present deep and multifaceted problems that appear not to have been deflected by policy intervention; on the other hand some of the smaller and more peripheral Urban Priority Area (UPA) authorities have shown economic and residential improvements by comparison with non-UPA areas. Many of the criticisms levelled at the conception and implementation of urban policy – its lack of strategic coherence, the limited encouragement given to the full range of actors potentially involved in the creation of partnerships, its short-termism, its emphasis on property-led renewal at the expense of community development – seem likely to be addressed more effectively if many of the strategic principles that underlie City Challenge can be translated more consistently and broadly into the genesis and implementation of urban policy. (ibid.: 55)

The report takes the view that "the attempt to encourage the formation of partnerships has been a well adjudged priority" (ibid.: 50), but that this trend has been constrained by the limited incentives to encourage long-term private sector involvement and government moves in the 1980s to downgrade the role of local authorities as facilitators of partnership formation. Significant differences were detected between Tyne & Wear and parts of Manchester, where relatively strong coalitions emerged, and Merseyside, where the response was partial and weak. The first of five main recommendations from the report states:

There are clear indications of the importance of creating effective coalitions of "actors" within localities. Such coalitions are most likely to result from the development of structures and mechanisms which encourage or require long-term collaborative partnerships. (ibid.: 55)

Conclusions

This chapter has explored in some detail the development of the idea of partnership in the context of the evolution of urban policy. One of the first conclusions that needs to be drawn is that, as others have already noted, it is unrealistic to talk of a coherent urban policy: ". . . there have been some urban initiatives running simultaneously, sometimes in parallel, sometimes intersecting, but usually uncoordinated" (Atkinson & Moon 1994: 272). It is clear that the succession of initiatives that are described here are largely politically driven. They reflect the need for successive governments to present symbolic evidence of action in relation to politically sensitive issues such as poverty, unemployment, housing and immigration, as well as the imperative of successive Secretaries of State to devise new initiatives in line with their own political philosophy. Although individual programmes and policies have been evaluated independently, it was not until 1994 that any overall assessment of the cumulative impact of the totality of programmes was published. However, with the growing importance of EU funding on a regional basis, and the establishment of government offices for the regions and a Single Regeneration Budget in England, it may be that small area-based initiatives will gradually be phased out in favour of a broader strategic approach. This may well suggest that a transition from an exclusive focus on the "needle points of deprivation" (Hambleton 1993: 315) to a more European concern for regional development is finally under way.

In conclusion we set out the main parameters along which urban initiatives have evolved over the past 25 years:

- *Objectives*   These have normally been defined in general terms in relation to the physical, economic and social regeneration of an area. In general, broad objectives are fixed by central government, but complex monitoring arrangements are then imposed to ensure the funding is spent according to the government's intentions. On the other hand, continuing independent evaluation of impact and performance is not normally carried out, except in the cases of the Community Development Projects and City Challenge.
- *Agency*   Rather than giving new powers and responsibilities to an existing organization, such as local government, it has been considered necessary to set up new agencies to be directly overseen by the funding body.
- *Structure*   The structure of the relevant agencies has either been exclusive, in the sense of the agency being solely responsible for implementing the strategy, or inclusive, in that the agency has to work closely with other local interests, which may be co-opted into a management role.
- *Policy*   The policy of the initiative may be sectoral and largely departmental or involve a comprehensive approach towards the co-ordination of service delivery.
- *Area*   This variable concerns both the definition of the target area of each initiative and the process by which suitable areas are selected, for example by deprivation indices, political factors or competitive bidding. Several small and clearly defined target areas are normally favoured.
- *Funding*   A specific budget is normally allocated by central government over a fixed period, but more recently the maximum use of the leverage of private finance has been expected.
- *Life*   The lifetime of each initiative is normally defined in advance, for example five or ten years, but may be subject to extensions as in the case of the UDCs.
- *Accountability*   Financial and political accountability has largely occurred indirectly through the sponsoring department. In some cases, informal mechanisms for consultation with other agencies and the public have been applied. Mechanisms for direct local accountability are normally absent.

75

- *Patronage* Special agencies have normally been managed by representatives of local interests appointed by central government. Where local authorities and local communities are represented, they are usually in the minority.

Table 3.3 sets out a chronology of urban policy measures in England, Wales and Scotland.

The concept of partnership has had an increasingly important role to play over the past 25 years. In the context of City Challenge, English Partnerships and the SRB it could be argued that it is the overriding principle of urban regeneration. Like other aspects of urban policy, it has received little research attention, but has achieved a broad base of support from the main political parties. In the next six chapters, the ways in which the concept has been mobilized and applied is explored in case studies.

Table 3.3 Chronology of urban policy measures in England, Wales and Scotland.

Date	Dept of the Environment	Dept of Employment	Dept of Trade and Industry	Scottish Office	Other
1977	3 Inner Area Studies published. Policy for the Inner Cities White Paper.				Home Office transfers inner cities functions to DoE
1978	Inner Urban Areas Act. 7 Partnership, 15 Programme & 19 Designated authorities.				
1979					
1980	LDDC & MDC. 13 EZs. Comprehensive Community Programmes wound up.			Clydebank EZ	
1981	Land registers. Merseyside Task Force, Financial Institutions Group.		Loan guarantee scheme for small businesses		
1982	Urban Development Grant. 1 more EZ.				
1983		YTS & TVEI			
1984	14 more EZs. Liverpool Garden Festival.		New Assisted Areas. Revised Regional Development Grant		
1985	CATs set up in .... 5 .... Estate Action	... Partnership...	... areas wider remit for English Estates		

Table 3.3 Chronology of urban policy measures in England, Wales and Scotland.

Date	Dept of the Environment	Dept of Employment	Dept of Trade and Industry	Scottish Office	Other
1986	Trafford Park UDC. Stoke Garden Festival. URGs paid direct to applicant. Phoenix Initiative launched.		First 8 Task Forces		
1987	UPMI introduced. 4 more UDCs		8 more Task Forces		
1988	*Action for Cities* 2 more CATs 4 more UDCs City Grant More EZs British Urban Development launched Housing Action Trusts			4 New Life Partnerships. Glasgow Garden Festival	Welsh Valleys Initiative (Welsh Office) Home Office announces Safer Cities Programme –20 projects over 5 years.
1989	*Progress on Cities* Bristol UDC	10 more Compacts	3 more Task Forces		
1990	*People in Cities* Gateshead Garden Festival	12 TECs launched		Glasgow European City of Culture	
1991	Round 1 of City Challenge. Phoenix Initiative wound up.	70 TECs launched		Scottish Enterprise set up with 13 LECs	

Table 3.3 Chronology of urban policy measures in England, Wales and Scotland.

Date	Dept of the Environment	Dept of Employment	Dept of Trade and Industry	Scottish Office	Other
1992	Round 2 of City Challenge Private Finance Initiative Birmingham & Plymouth UDCs UP reduced. Urban Partnership Fund introduced. Urban Regeneration Agency announced. Integrated Regional Offices				Ebbw Vale Garden Festival (Wales)
1993	Single regeneration budgets. City Pride initiative for London, Birmingham, Manchester.			Lanarkshire EZ. Progress in Partnership review of up etc.	second 5 year Welsh Valleys initiative.
1994	English Partnerships becomes operational. Bidding Guidance for SRB published. Bids for round 1 of SRB to be submitted by September. Assessing the Impact of Urban Policy published.				

CHAPTER 4
Birmingham Heartlands

Origins of the Heartlands urban development area

Birmingham has always been seen as a city willing to embrace change, as well as traditionally taking a pragmatic approach towards the creative use of public and private money to achieve civic objectives. As one of the major centres of small and medium-size metal and engineering industries, it has always reflected locally the same periods of growth and decline as the national economy. In the 1950s and 1960s, economic prosperity was more or less taken for granted, when the city centre was redeveloped and links to the national motorway network were being constructed. By the 1970s the West Midlands economy was beginning to falter. In the 1980s, economic recession led to massive restructuring and growing levels of unemployment. The decline of employment opportunities, particularly among the city's growing ethnic minority population, was a contributory factor towards the street riots in Handsworth in September 1985. As England's second city, Birmingham provided an obvious location for a series of urban initiatives promoted by successive governments. In the early 1970s Peter Walker had selected Small Heath as the base for one of the three inner area studies, and the city was also one of the first Inner City Partnership authorities. At about the same time, Saltley was the location for a Community Development Project. Under the Conservative Government, Birmingham was also assigned one of the first City Action Teams in 1985, Handsworth was selected for the first round of Task Forces in 1986, and a further one was established in East Birmingham in 1988. By 1987 the Birmingham Partnership had an overall budget of £29 million, with £9.5 million going towards economic development and almost £4 million allocated to voluntary bodies (Deakin & Edwards 1993: 131). The city council was also noted for its innovative policies towards the legacy of nineteenth-century bylaw housing and for its willingness to enter into complex joint ventures with the private sector, such as the National Exhibition Centre, the International Convention Centre and the Aston Science Park. The West Midlands County Council, together with its satellite the West Midlands Enterprise Board, had until the Council's abolition in 1986 played an important strategic role in promoting investment in the city and in attracting additional funds from the European Union.

By the mid-1980s there was growing evidence that Birmingham's engineering sector had suffered from the recession and that the jobs created through prestigious city-centre developments were insufficient to absorb the growing numbers of the unemployed, who lived in the inner suburbs. Large areas of the inner city remained derelict through either factory closure or the clearance of substandard housing. The incoming Labour administration in 1984, led by Dick Knowles, was committed to economic regeneration through Birmingham's own brand of the Civic Gospel, and the new Chair of the influential Economic Development Committee, Albert Bore, instituted regular meetings with leading figures of the local private sector. There were also strong links with the Birmingham Chamber of Commerce and Industry. Clearly, the moderate Labour administration, unlike several other large cities at the time, found no difficulties in doing business with the corporate sector. This growing accommodation between the city council and the private sector gave rise to at least two collaborative approaches to urban regeneration. In the city centre the council adopted what has been called the prestige model of urban regeneration (Loftman & Nevin 1992, 1994) towards several cultural and commercial developments in the Broad Street Redevelopment area. These included the International Convention Centre, the National Indoor Arena, a four-star Hyatt Hotel and the Brindleyplace festival marketplace scheme, drawing heavily on examples in such US cities as Boston, Atlanta and Baltimore. In contrast, on the eastern fringe of the city centre, a coalition of public and private interests was constructed, designed, at least in part, to show that Birmingham could promote its own intersectoral model of regeneration and thus head off government attempts to impose a UDC.

The origins of Birmingham Heartlands

Immediately following the 1987 election, the city council, aware that the new Secretary of State for the Environment, Nicholas Ridley, was looking for suitable areas for a new generation of UDCs, raised the possibility of establishing an urban development agency that would be locally controlled but centrally funded. At the same time, John Douglas, managing director of a local firm of developers (R. M. Douglas), had gathered together several other interested parties and approached the City Action Team with a proposal to set up a private sector-led regeneration initiative. The response was positive enough to put the plan to the liaison meeting with the city council. The Birmingham Chamber of Commerce was very supportive and it deployed its large membership in support of the proposal. Moreover, a suitable area of about 1000 ha had been identified about 3 km to the east of the city centre: it had about 300 ha of derelict land and the Nechells ward scored among the 10 per cent most deprived wards in the country (Fig. 4.1).

In November 1987 the proposal for the urban development agency, which would be controlled by the city but with minority private sector involvement and

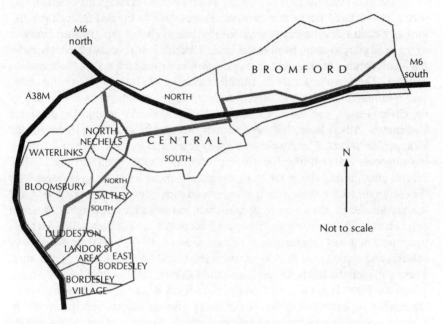

Figure 4.1 Plan of Birmingham Heartlands area.

would receive core funding from the DoE, was put forward for ministerial approval. Ridley was willing to accept the agency but exacted a high price. His terms were that no core funding would be provided, the agency must have a majority of private sector board members, and he wished to see the area designated as a Simplified Planning Zone. The outcome was that Birmingham Heartlands Ltd (BHL) was established in March 1988 as a private company, with 65 per cent of the shares held by five companies (R. M. Douglas, Galliford, Tarmac, Wimpey and Bryant) and 35 per cent held by the city council, with one share retained by the Chamber of Commerce and Industry. The original intention was that the company would play an active role in reclaiming derelict land and providing infrastructure. This hands-on approach proved impractical and it was soon modified, so that BHL was to be neither a landowner nor a source of development finance but an enabling agency that would prepare a development framework within which the activities of the partners and others would be co-ordinated. A sum of about £500 000 was made available by the partners for staff and running costs. BHL would be entitled to receive ten per cent of gross profits from developments in the area carried out by consortia owned by BHL shareholders, and a management fee would be deducted from grants negotiated by the company. Sir Reginald Eyre, a former MP and Conservative minister, was nominated as Chair of the board, and Councillor Dick Knowles his deputy. The Chief Executive was to be nominated by the developers, and the Finance Director by the city. In order to launch the new company, a development strategy was commissioned from Roger Tym & Partners, and this was made the subject of consultation in the early part of 1988.

The Tym Development Strategy for East Birmingham

In preparing a development strategy for the area, the consultants identified both opportunities and constraints, but indicated graphically the extent of the task ahead (Roger Tym & Partners 1988). The Heartlands area contained about 18 000 jobs, and the largest employment sectors were in vehicle manufacturing (DAF/Freight Rover, Metro Cammell, Jaguar, SP Tyres and Dunlop were some of the largest companies), food industries (HP Sauce) and wholesale distribution. In the period 1971–81 the area had lost 4500 jobs and a further 5900 between 1981 and 1985 and, whereas most of the larger surviving companies had gone through a period of retrenchment, there had been little new or inward investment. The area had, however, attracted several activities, such as vehicle repairers, scrap metal processors and container storage, which employed few people and had a detrimental effect on the environment.

The residential population lived in four areas lying to the west of the designated area in North Nechells, Bloomsbury, Duddeston Manor and Bordesley. According to the 1981 census the resident population had all the hallmarks of urban deprivation. Of the 12 632 residents at the time, 27 per cent were 15 years old or under, and 15 per cent were of pensionable age. The unemployment rate was recorded as 29 per cent, and 80 per cent lived in local authority accommodation, whereas only 10 per cent were owner-occupiers; 78 per cent of households did not own a car (Table 4.1). Of the jobs that were available in the area, less than 5 per cent were taken by local residents and over a third of these were in processing and making (Roger Tym & Partners Technical Appendix 1988: 7).

Environmentally, the area was visually bleak and dominated by derelict land, old buildings and redundant engineering structures. It lacked cohesion and was subdivided by railways, major utilities and canals. Environmental degradation, industrial contamination, rising groundwater levels and the spread of bad neighbour industries all provided further disincentives to investment. Access into the area by road was constrained by the obsolete road network and there were few railway stations convenient for local residents. The Inner City Partnership and Derelict Land Grant had resulted in some environmental improvements, such as to the canal towpaths, but these were scattered too widely to have much cumulative impact. The city council had carried out some improvements to its housing through the Priority Estates Project.

Overall, the consultants concluded that, although the area faced real difficulties in common with other inner-city areas, it also had several assets. It was accessible to the national motorway network; it was close to the city centre and

83

Table 4.1 Comparison of census data for the Heartlands UDC area for 1981 and 1991.

	1981		1991		1981–91 change
	No.	%	No.	%	%
Residents in private households	12632	99.7	9927	99.7	−21.4
Children aged 0–15	3431	26.9	2699	27.1	−36.4
All residents aged 60+	1942	15.2	1520	15.3	−21.7
In White ethnic group	n/a		7032	70.6	n/a
In Black ethnic group	n/a		1550	15.6	n/a
In Asian ethnic group	n/a		1048	10.5	n/a
Total private households	4774		4320		−9.5
Average household size	2.65		2.30		−13.2
Households moving within the city	n/a		317	7.3	n/a
Households moving from outside city	n/a		41	0.9	n/a
Households without car	3721	77.9	3246	75.1	−12.8
Total dwellings	n/a		4788		n/a
Owner-occupied	496	10.4	718	16.6	44.8
Rented with job	64	1.3	124	2.9	93.8
Rented privately	152	3.2	132	3.1	−13.2
Rented from a housing association	234	4.9	441	10.2	88.5
Rented from LA	3820	80.2	2899	67.2	−24.1
Houses overcrowded & lacking amenities	231	4.9	69	1.6	−68.2
Unemployed residents	1587	28.9	1261	31.9	−20.5

Source: 1991 Census of Population: Area Profiles. City of Birmingham.

Aston Science Park; some of the public housing was attractive and sought after; it had access to a large employment catchment area; it was associated with the city's "track record for municipal enterprise, collaboration with the private sector and the successful achievement of national projects" (Roger Tym & Partners 1988: 8); and it could exploit opportunities provided by two navigable canals.

On the other hand, the Heartlands area had "a disintegrated pattern of land ownership" that would make land assembly difficult for the private sector; it had a poor image and a social stigma attached to it; developers would be deterred by the low quality of existing development and insecurity about the future; access within the area, and to and from the motorway network, was confusing and obsolete.

The strategy proposed the joint aims of attracting new economic activity and jobs, and improving living conditions for the existing communities. These were to be achieved through a physical development strategy, a marketing strategy, an investment strategy, and measures to ensure that existing residents benefit from the changes. Opportunities for investment and development were identified in six areas:

- the creation of a new urban village at Bordesley
- major improvements to areas of public housing at Nechells, Bloomsbury and Duddeston
- a flagship commercial area near the Birmingham and Fazeley canal, to be known as Waterlinks

- the 32 ha Star Site near Spaghetti Junction to be developed as a national or international commercial area
- improvements and development of existing industrial sites at Bromford and Saltley
- improvements to the road and rail infrastructure through the construction of a new spine road and the Midland Metro.

In all, the consultants estimated that about 200 ha could be developed in a ten-year period, of which 87 ha would be residential, 31 ha flexible business use and 85 ha for industrial uses.

In response to extensive public consultation, the draft strategy was amended to extend the urban development area to include the Bromford industrial area, to investigate the possibility of forming a community trust to reflect local interests, to reduce the amount of housing proposed for Bordesley and Waterlinks, and to include safeguards on the Star site to protect existing retail centres. The City of Birmingham concluded that 7400 industrial jobs and 5300 commercial jobs could realistically be created.

Implementation

The original intention was that BHL operate as the primary developer and the city council would use its statutory powers of land acquisition. Major financial and legal difficulties emerged that required a change in approach to a less interventionist role. Instead, the board would approve a series of development frameworks for different sites, and implementation would be monitored through working parties. Commercial development would be undertaken by development companies, each chaired by a board member, whereas the City Council would remain responsible for its own housing and for planning matters. Table 4.2 sets out the membership of the BHL board.

Table 4.2   Composition of the BHL Board.

Sector	Name	Role or employer
Chair	Sir Reginald Eyre	Retired MP
Chief Executive	A. Osborne	Tarmac
Finance Director & Secretary	J. Weardon	City Council
City	Sir Richard Knowles	Council leader
City	Cllr A Bore	Chair, Econ. Development Cttee
City	Cllr R. Brew	City Council
Private	C. Bryant	Bryants
Private	J. Douglas	R. M. Douglas
Private	P. Galliford	Galliford
Private	M. Jennings	Tarmac
Private	M. Dowdy	Wimpey
Chamber of Commerce	J. Bettinson	Chamber of Commerce

Working parties were constituted for both geographical areas and topics:
- roads/infrastructure
- waterlinks
- Bordesley
- Star Site
- Heartlands Industrial
- Bromford Square
- housing (local authority)
- greening, screening, culture
- relocation
- training
- Community Trust
- education compact

Within the partnership the different sectors have different roles to play. The City Council remained responsible for planning, housing and highways for the Heartlands area. As the planning authority, the City Council was responsible for development control in Heartlands, and could sell land (it was able to do so on a best-price basis to developers involved in the partnership) and it can utilize its compulsory purchase powers to assist regeneration further, in accordance with the development framework. As the highway authority, the City Council was responsible for road improvement schemes, although BHL assisted by approaching central government for finance. As the housing authority and the major landlord in the area, the City Council was also seeking to refurbish its stock and to increase the proportion of owner-occupation through private housebuilding. In addition, the city continued to allocate a proportion of its Inner City Partnership funding to the area and designated part of Saltley as a Simplified Planning Zone in accordance with the earlier undertaking to central government.

The private sector's role in the Heartlands initiative was to act as a commercial developer, forming joint venture companies to develop specified areas of land in accordance with the agreed development framework. Naturally, the private sector was motivated by profit, although it was accepted that grants would be needed to make some schemes viable. A consortium of developers bought land and raised the finance from the private sector.

Central government did not have a direct role in Birmingham Heartlands Ltd, as was indeed the intention. However, through grant regimes, such as City Grant and Estate Action, central government provided indirect financial assistance to Heartlands. Also, the regional activities of the various central government departments were co-ordinated by the Birmingham City Action Team, and some of Heartlands social programmes benefited from the presence of the East Birmingham Task Force, which from 1988 was the informal evidence of the government's support for the strategy.

Projects

Roads and infrastructure

Initial projections suggested that about £150 million would be needed for roads and infrastructure coming from the Department of Transport, the Transport Supplementary Grant, developers' contributions and European sources. The roads and infrastructure programme was focused on the construction of a spine road running through the middle of the area and opening up several important sites for development and to improve access from the M6 motorway to the centre of Birmingham. The route was approved by the City Council in 1989. Central government promised £85 million in the following year, and by 1992 had approved a £100 million Transport Supplementary Grant towards the scheme. In addition to this, BHL needed to raise a further £13 million from the private sector, and by 1993 this had been secured. It was estimated that the road would be completed by 1997.

As well as the spine road, improvements were under way at Thimble Mill Lane at a cost of £8 million, Lichfield Road at £17 million, and by the end of 1994 had been completed at Saltley Gate, Richard Street, and Rupert Street. An important proposal by Centro, the West Midlands Passenger Transport Executive, is to create a rapid transit system linking Edgbaston, the city centre, Heartlands and the National Exhibition Centre. The necessary parliamentary powers have been obtained, but negotiations continue with the Department of Transport to raise the necessary finance. The first line of the Metro to Wolverhampton was agreed in early 1995.

Waterlinks

The Waterlinks area is 134 ha along part of the western edge of Heartlands, which lies adjacent to Aston University and Science Park, and includes the canal basins. It was originally identified for major office and business uses. Waterlinks was supervised by a BHL working party chaired by Jim Shedden (formerly a director of Tarmac) and the Waterlinks plc joint venture company was set up by Bryant, Douglas, Tarmac and Wimpey as the major development company for the scheme. In the first phase at Aston Cross a £6.2 million City Grant was contributed to a £26 million project providing 180 000 sq. ft (24 000 m²) of business space, a restaurant, wine bar and shops. In all, planning permission has been given for over 1 million sq. ft (130 000 m²) of commercial development linked to planning agreements to secure environmental improvements. A new two-star hotel is also proposed on an adjoining site. A City Grant of £1.1 million was also allocated to the refurbishment of Waterlinks House, originally built as a multi-storey factory, but now occupied by office users such as the Task Force and BHL (and subsequently BHDC) itself.

The Star Site

This 33 ha former power station site was identified by the Tym development strategy as suitable for the major flagship development in Heartlands, because of its location close to the motorway interchange. A major design competition was held in 1989, and the following year Star Site plc was formed to construct a major international business exchange providing office development with associated retail, leisure and cultural facilities. Because of the recession, the development has not progressed. Prospects improved when British Rail announced they were investigating the possibility of constructing a new InterCity station on the site, but this too has been dropped at least in part because of uncertainties associated with rail privatization. By early 1994 a consortium of Tarmac, Wimpey and Bryant were again examining the feasibility of a commercial and leisure development on the site.

Heartlands Industrial

The majority of the Heartlands area lying adjacent to the M6 motorway has been designated as Heartlands Industrial and it is to this area that the new spine road will bring the greatest benefit. There are several elements to the Heartlands Industrial project. One is the Bromford area, which includes the former Fort Dunlop building, for which the Tarmac Richardson Partnership was formed to promote a mixed use commercial development, including a hotel. The second is the Saltley area in which a Simplified Planning Zone had been designated, and the Heartlands Industrial Improvement Area was declared in 1990 to provide grants to firms already in operation in the area. By mid-1993 a new paper-recycling plant and four new business parks had been constructed in this area, but market conditions were not sufficiently favourable to enable the Fort Dunlop development to proceed.

Bordesley Urban Village

In Bordesley the BHL aim was to create a new urban village, with the focus mainly on the construction of new houses, but also the provision of associated community features such as a village green. The Bordesley area lies directly to the east of the city centre and covers 95 acres (38.5 ha). The area formerly consisted of mixed industrial uses and poor-quality residential areas, which housed approximately 1000 people. The Tym strategy proposed the construction of 900 new houses and flats, with facilities and public open space constituting a new residential area in the centre of the city. The 1987 development framework proposes an urban village, with 750 new houses and improvements to 350 existing houses and flats, together with a new park and improved educational and community facilities.

The development was undertaken by Bryant, Tarmac and Wimpey, with investment of £27 million initially predicted. The first phase of 118 houses was completed quite rapidly at a cost of £7 million development and was supported by a £1.4 million City Grant. A second scheme by Woolwich Homes and Bellway Urban Renewal was for 320 houses and flats of mixed tenure, valued at £17 million, for which a £3.7 million City Grant was provided, together with £3.2 million from the Housing Corporation. The local authority and housing associations have invested in the refurbishment of many of the existing dwellings in Bordesley, and also the Inner Area Partnership Programme was responsible for funding the new Kingston day nursery for the area. In all, by 1993 an estimated £60 million has been invested in Bordesley, with £35 million coming from the private sector. The private housing has sold well, despite the recession, and significant improvements have been made to the environment and to social facilities, such as the newly refurbished St Andrews school. More recently, the Bournville Village Trust has agreed to purchase a village centre for Bordesley, containing shops and community facilities, which is to be developed by Wimpey with the help of a City Grant.

Nechells

Nechells is the main residential area in Heartlands, containing over 2500 mainly local-authority dwellings in Duddeston, Bloomsbury and North Nechells. The 1981 census showed that nearly 7000 people lived in the area and that there were above-average proportions of lone-parent households, and high levels of unemployment, deprivation, housing density, ethnic minorities, and low levels of car ownership. In partnership with the City Council, BHL set up the Nechells Working Party to produce a development framework for the area. This was subsequently published in draft form in 1989 and approved after public consultation in the following year. In Bloomsbury an estate management board has been set up to give local people a say in the running of their estate and what happens to it in the future. The board was originally set up in 1984 as part of a Priority Estate Project and consists of twelve elected tenants, four council nominees and four co-opted members. It has housing management powers and it controls its own revenue budget. In 1990 it drew up a plan to redevelop the estate, carried out extensive consultation with tenants, and has the support of a consortium of housing associations in implementing the plan. Birmingham Friendship Housing Association, Estate Action (£15.5 million in total), the Inner City Partnership, the city's Housing Investment Programme, as well as other housing associations, have invested a total of £44 million in Nechells, which has included the refurbishment of five tower blocks, conversion of maisonettes into two-storey houses, some new building, and environmental projects.

Environmental improvements

By the early part of 1993 almost £4 million had been committed to environmental improvements, including £1.7 million on general landscaping, £0.6 million on Kingston Hill Park and £0.1 million on North Nechells Park, with a further £0.5 million on other environmental projects.

Training and education

BHL had established an education compact between Duddeston Manor school and various local firms. In November 1992, Joblink 2000 was launched with funding from the Task Force and City Council in order to provide customized training packages for local firms. Several companies moving into the area, for example in the Waterlinks development, have sought its help in providing staff with appropriate skills.

Table 4.3 summarizes the extent of completed or committed public and private investment in the area at May 1993.

By the end of 1991, BHL had been in operation for almost four years and a considerable amount had been achieved. Perhaps most importantly, it had been demonstrated that a major City Council could work closely with the private sector and the local community in implementing a development strategy, without the direct involvement of central government. Streamlined working relationships had been established between the City Council and the urban development agency, and additional investment had been brought to the area through the effective use of City Grant, an Industrial Improvement Area, Derelict Land Grant, Estate Action and the Inner City Partnership programme. The confidence of the private sector had been demonstrated through developments such as Waterlinks and a significant amount of private housebuilding. Although delays had occurred, for example with the spine road and light rail system, there was every prospect that these would ultimately bring substantial benefits to the area. Although local residents had not been represented on the board, BHL and the City Council had used "planning for real" and other consultation methods to ensure that there was general public support for the implementation of detailed policies. The improvement of estates in Nechells and Duddeston, and the development of the Bordesley urban village, including the provision of a new park and day nursery, carried widespread public support. Moreover, house sales remained buoyant, even in the recession, and a high proportion of the purchasers had strong family or work connections with the area.

However, the Heartlands development strategy had always been predicated on an improving national and regional economy, and by early 1992 there was evidence that progress could not be sustained. A declining property market, and retrenchment by local and national developers, gave rise to fears that the whole strategy might be at risk if public funding, over and above existing grant

Table 4.3 Committed or completed public and private investment in the Birmingham Heartlands area (May 1993).

Development	Estimated cost £m
Roads and infrastructure	
Spine road	100.0
Nechells Parkway–Aston Expressway	3.0
Lichfield Road	17.0
Completed schemes	3.0
TOTAL	123.0
Environment	
Land reclamation, new parks, landscaping,	
canals and Green Line.	4.0
TOTAL	8.0
Bordesley Village	
118 dwellings (£1.4m City Grant)	7.0
320 dwellings (£3.7m CG/£3.2m HAG)	17.0
300 refurbished la houses (£5m HAG)	6.5
New day nursery & refurbished school	2.5
Major acquisitions well advanced	200 houses
100 dwellings (incl. £3.5m HAG)	3.5
TOTAL	36.5
Waterlinks	
1m sq. ft. business space with pl. perm.	–
Aston Cross business scheme	26.0
Phoenix Business Park	6.0
Maple Leaf Business Park	3.0
Thyssen Haniel/Galley Pearl	1.0
Evans Halshaw	3.5
Mann Egerton	4.0
Waterlinks House (£1.1m City Grant)	7.5
TOTAL	52.0
Nechells Housing	
North Nechells: 40 dwellings	2.0
Bloomsbury	24.0
Duddeston Manor	18.0
TOTAL	44.0
Heartlands Industrial	
Saltley industrial area	
SPZ established	
Mainstream 47 business park	10.0
Paper recycling plant	3.0
Saltley business park	3.0
Bromfield:	
City Link business park with planning permission subject to s.106 on spine road	
Fort Dunlop proposals	
Holly Park business development	5.0
Remaining area	13.0
City Council Industrial Improvement Area	
5 year programme of investment	3.5
TOTAL	37.5
Training and education:	
Joblink 2000	1.0
School compact	2.0
TOTAL	3.0
Total invested or committed	297.0

Source: BHDC Report. 19 May 1993. (unpublished).

regimes, was not available. The initial response had been to submit a bid for the first round of City Challenge, but this had been turned down in the summer of 1991. The BHL board therefore agreed reluctantly that there was no alternative but to seek central government support, even if this meant a transition to UDC status – the one thing all the local interests had been concerned to avoid when BHL was first conceived. With a proven record behind them and this time Michael Heseltine as Secretary of State for the Environment, the board felt itself to be in a strong position to negotiate terms.

The transition to an urban development corporation

Negotiations over the transition from BHL to the Birmingham Heartlands Development Corporation (BHDC) continued through the latter part of 1991 and into 1992. The outcome involved compromise on both sides. Central government agreed to inject what was originally suggested as £10 million per year over five years, in return for appointing the new UDC board. BHL, on the other hand, ensured that the development strategy was maintained and that half the board should be nominated by the City Council. Thus, although the original strategy was retained and the close links with officers and members of the City Council enhanced, the main losers appeared to be the original five development companies and the Chamber of Commerce and Industry, which could no longer remain on the board because of potential conflicts of interest. However, the exact amount of financial support from central government still remained to be finally agreed.

The Birmingham Heartlands Development Corporation was formally set up on 10 March 1992, the day after parliamentary approval had been obtained. The Secretary of State's nominations to the board were made up of six members selected by the City Council, including the Leader, the former chair of the Economic Development Committee, the Leader of the minority party, the Chair of the Planning Committee and one local ward member. Sir Reginald Eyre agreed to remain as chair of the board and Sir Richard Knowles as his deputy. The private sector members were appointed by the Secretary of State. After some delay, Jim Beeston was appointed Chief Executive in July, having previously held the post of Deputy Chief Executive of BHL. Most of the other staff transferred to new posts in the development corporation. The composition of the BHDC is set out in Table 4.4 and the organizational structure in Figure 4.2.

Although continuity was maintained from the BHL board through the presence of the Chair, Deputy Chair and Albert Bore on the new board, the representatives of the five development companies formed Birmingham Regeneration Ltd to complete several developments in the Saltley/Small Heath area to the east of Heartlands.

The UDC's board also operates as four groups responsible for particular aspects

92

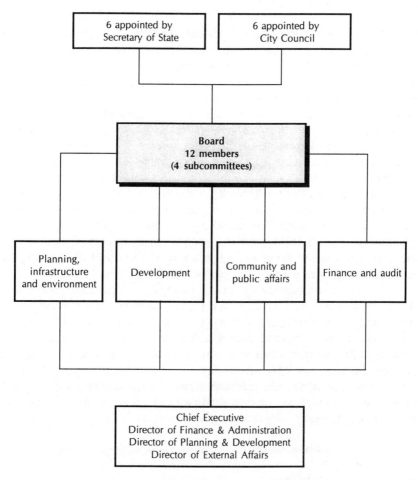

Figure 4.2   Organizational structure of BHDC.

Table 4.4   Composition of the BHDC board.

Private sector appointments

Sir Reginald Eyre	Chairman
Paul Sabapathy	IMI Titanium
Michael Wilcox	Grimley J. R. Eve
Jim Shedden	Formerly of Tarmac
Hazel Duffy	Journalist, Financial Times
David Brooks	Formerly of Cadbury Ltd

Public sector representatives

Sir Richard Knowles*	Leader of City Council and Deputy Chair
Cllr Albert Gore*	Chair of the Econ. Devt Committee
Cllr Randall Brew*	Leader of the Conservative Group
Cllr Fred Chapman	Chair of the Planning Committee
Cllr Kathy Finnegan	Nechells ward member
Cllr Reg Hales	Birmingham City Council

* Formerly of the BHL board.

of the development corporation's activities. The planning, infrastructure and environment group meets about every two weeks to deal with development control and all planning applications. The development board group deals with all grants for housing, industrial and business schemes. The community and public affairs group is responsible for community projects and public relations. The fourth group covers finance and audit. A small team of local authority planners make recommendations to the board on development control and planning matters.

The detailed implementation of the strategy is carried through by several area co-ordination teams chaired by board members, BHDC staff or representatives of the City Council and the private sector, originally established by BHL. These are both area-based, such as for Bordesley Village or Waterlinks, and topic-orientated, such as infrastructure, relocations, compulsory purchase orders and housing. These teams include representatives of relevant council departments, government agencies and departments, and private sector companies. All board meetings, and those of the co-ordination teams, are private, with the exception of the planning, infrastructure and environment board.

Liaison and co-ordination with the City Council is maintained through several mechanisms. The City Council's Director of Economic Development attends board meetings as an observer and officers from the Departments of Economic Development, Planning and Architecture, and the City Treasurer attends monthly management meetings with BHDC executives. The planning department provides planning and legal advice on planning matters in the area through a service-level agreement, and additional services, such as compulsory purchase orders, personnel services, quantity surveying and a baseline study are provided by other departments.

Progress in the first two years

When BHDC began work in the latter part of 1992, the level of funding from central government was still to be resolved, although all the indications were that it would be less than the £10 million per year originally suggested. It was finally agreed that the Corporation would receive only £5.4 million in 1992–3, £5 million in 1993–4, £7 million in 1994–5 and £9 million in 1995–6. An assumption is made that £11.1 million will be available in 1996–7. Throughout, the corporate plan (BHDC 1993b) sets targets for spending up to £50 million over the five-year period, although in reality only £37.5 million has been approved by the DoE. This suggests that, should further funding become available, it can be integrated relatively easily into the annual spending programmes. The corporate plan suggests that the shortfall in funding can be accommodated by purchasing land by agreement, rather than using compulsory purchase powers, and by seeking DoE approval to submit bids for City Grant directly to Marsham Street, rather than coming out of BHDC resources (BHDC 1993b: 18).

In the first year of operation, the main priorities for BHDC remained economic development, housing improvement and environmental upgrading, although greater emphasis was placed on the local economy. Increasing attention is also being paid to acquiring European funding through Birmingham's Integrated Development Programme. Social aspects continued to receive attention through support for Joblink 2000, the Community Trust and a proposal to establish a Groundwork Trust in the area. Initially £3 millon was spent on land acquisitions for housing and to secure access to the canal in the Waterlinks area, £750 000 on buying out BHL's assets and extending the office accommodation for BHDC in Waterlinks House. An additional £1.8 million was spent on environmental improvements, a new all-weather pitch at Duddeston Manor school and in upgrading canals in the area. In coming years between £4 million and £9 millon are likely to be obtained from the European Regional Development Fund for land reclamation, landscaping and vocational training schemes.

The BHDC Corporate Plan for 1993–4

In the first full year of operation, BHDC produced a detailed corporate plan setting out its objectives and estimated expenditure for the financial year and the five-year plan period. The approach was to build on the achievements and development strategy of Birmingham Heartlands Ltd, but to use its limited resources to maximum effect by "acting on the margin – intervening in the market place only where it is necessary and cost-effective; co-ordinating available resources from public and private sectors; and empowering local people to participate in the mainstream economy rather than developing an alternative one" (BHDC 1993b: 1). In tackling a wide range of economic and social objectives in collaboration with other local agencies, it claimed to be more akin to City Challenge initiatives than other UDCs (BHDC 1993b: 7).

Because of the shortfall in expected funding, the overall objectives are based on the assumption that the Corporation will continue in operation beyond the initial five years agreed with the DoE. BHDC thus aims to lever £950 million of private sector investment, and £300 millon of other public expenditure compared with the Corporation's (assumed) £50 million, create over 21 000 jobs in 8.3 million sq. ft (770 000 m^2) of floorspace, preserve 6000 jobs in the area with 1000 homes built or refurbished (BHDC 1993b: 4). The detailed objectives are set out in Table 4.5.

BHDC continues to promote several industrial developments originally conceived under BHL. As part of the restructuring of Leyland DAF and in order to secure a management buy-out, a site of 42 acres (17 ha) was sold to BHDC, with additional funding of £4 million from the DoE. This will provide an important opportunity to attract new industry to Heartlands, since no land was vested in the corporation. In February 1994 the board approved plans for an industrial and

Table 4.5   Key outputs during the plan period and assumed lifetime of BH UDC.

Output	Unit	Total lifetime	Plan period 1992–7	% to be achieved 1992–7
Floorspace created/refurbished (net)	sq. ft	8295129	2767129	33
New housing (net)	no.	570	493	86
Refurbished homes	no.	400	400	100
New jobs (net)	no.	21163	5083	24
Jobs preserved	no.	5990	5890	98
Land acquired	acres	51.7	50.1	97
Land disposed	acres	49.2	45.5	92
Land reclaimed or developed	acres	366.9	223.8	61
Public sector investment	£m	305.5	258.4	85
Private sector investment	£m	957.5	234.6	25

Source: BHDC Corporate Plan 1993–4.

warehousing complex for the site to be known as Heartlands Central, which is also being promoted nationally as part of the DOE's Private Finance Initiative. At the same time, interest in the Star Site was reviving and a review of the current state of the market was commissioned by Tarmac, Wimpey and Bryants.

Improving transport links and infrastructure is seen as crucial to the development of the area. The Department of Transport confirmed the necessary compulsory purchase-orders for the spine road in November 1993 and funding of approximately £100 million was agreed through a City Council Transport Supplementary Grant with an additional £13 million coming from private sources. Construction began in February 1994 and is likely to have been completed by 1997. Discussions are continuing with the passenger transport executive over the location of new stations on the proposed Metro Line 2 running from the city centre to the National Exhibition Centre.

The construction of new housing and the refurbishment of existing stock continues at Bordesley and Bloomsbury. The UDC has considered grant-aiding a new village centre at Bloomsbury, and Wimpey was awarded a City Grant of £300000 to develop the Bordesley village centre. A project manager is working with existing shopkeepers and local residents on the range of facilities to be provided. The area health authority and the City of Birmingham Social Services Department are considering providing a local surgery in the centre. BHDC will continue to promote the development of Bordesley village through the acquisition of industrial land to be used for housing, environmental and road improvements.

Training, skills development and enterprise development remain important initiatives in East Birmingham. An Enterprise Centre in Aston has been funded by BHDC, the Task Force and the City Council, to provide business support and advice. It opened in March 1994 and is run by an independent organization called Just for Starters. As a second stage, a listed school is being renovated in Bordesley to provide managed workspace for new companies employing about 40 people, to be run by the same organization. Joblink 2000 was set up in 1991 by BHL, the Task Force and the City Council, with the objective of increasing the recruitment of local people through the promotion of customized skills training for specific jobs where vacancies exist. By the end of 1992, 346 trainees had benefited from the programme and 58 per cent have obtained permanent full-time employment (DoE 1993d 12).

BHDC plans to spend over £1 million on community support in the five-year plan period. The Community Trust was launched under BHL and receives about £60 000 from BHDC. It has launched several environmental and community projects in the area and is hoping to produce a regular newsletter for local residents. It owns a company called Heartlanders, which is contracting to employ local people to carry out repairs to vacant property on council estates before it is re-let. The Trust employs sixteen people, of which ten work on building maintenance, two on the maintenance of canal towpaths, two on recycling and one as a community safety officer. It also owns a narrow boat, which is mainly used for school trips, and it has a seed-corn fund to support local groups. Although the Trust is the primary community organization in the Heartlands area, it has not sought representation on the BHDC board and is generally content with the level of consultation available. It takes the view that members of the board, including the Chair, are approachable, and representation is effectively carried out by the presence of senior members and ward councillors on the board. This opinion of the effectiveness of local consultation methods is broadly endorsed by staff in the Kingston day nursery in Bordesley, which was funded through the Inner City Partnership Programme.

Conclusions

The experience in Birmingham Heartlands provides an interesting test case of how regeneration can be promoted by harnessing the skills and resources of the private sector, while maximizing the use of public resources through the agency of a facilitating organization working with, but at arm's length from, the local authority. Although the development strategy has provided a vision of what might be achieved over a ten-year period and forms the basis for the statutory Unitary Development Plan, it has proved sufficiently flexible to enable adjustments to be made to respond to changing economic circumstances and broadly to reflect local needs and opinion. From 1988 onwards, BHL quickly developed an enabling and facilitating role to take advantage of development opportunities as they arose, while using its relationship with the City Council to gain access to funding mechanisms, such as Estate Action, Inner City Partnership and transport grants. In the longer term the development of the spine road and the Midland Metro hold out the possibility of significant benefits for the future. An important issue for consideration is whether, in retrospect, the Heartlands area might have been better served if a UDC had been established in the first place. On the one hand, additional resources would have been available from the beginning, but on the other, relationships with the City Council might have been more difficult and the board would not have had the high level of councillor representation it was able to achieve in 1992. As it is, the transition appears to have been reasonably smooth, although officers claim "their eyes were off the ball" for several months in 1992 while staff appointments and the budget were being negotiated.

The development strategy had the advantage of simplicity. There was little coherence to the area when first designated, apart from the prevalence of derelict and underused industrial land and four areas of predominantly council housing. The strategy successfully identified the long-term economic role for the area as providing well serviced and accessible industrial and commercial sites for new and existing companies, as well as defining subareas where more flexible policies could be applied, subject to prevailing market conditions. The four housing areas lying on the western fringes could be treated as relatively self-contained "urban villages", by co-ordinating the inputs of the city's housing department, housing associations and private developers. Thus, the nature of the area leant itself to applying different approaches: in some cases high-profile marketing strategies were needed to promote development, in others a co-ordinated and community-orientated approach was used to meet particular needs.

Overall, the development achievements of BHL were significant. By May 1993 approximately £170 million of public and private money had been invested in Heartlands and a further £57 million had been spent on roads, infrastructure and the environment (BHDC 1993a). Approximately £90 millon (including City Grant) had been spent on Waterlinks and other industrial sites. Moreover, plans were well under way for the £113 million spine road and the Metro. The Star Site and Fort Dunlop were the main casualties of the recession, but these and other industrial sites, such as Heartlands Central, were always going to be largely dependent on the approval of the spine road. It is significant that BHDC estimates that a large proportion of the new floorspace and jobs created will occur after the initial five-year plan period, when the spine road and possibly the Metro will have been completed.

There is little hard evidence on how far residents have benefited from the presence of BHL and BHDC. The census figures indicate that housing conditions have improved significantly and that unemployment had fallen 20 per cent between 1981 and 1991. However, it should be remembered that BHL was established only in 1988 and that the fall in unemployment may well reflect a comparatively high level of population turnover, not least as a result of slum-clearance and redevelopment.

The presence of the Task Force, and initiatives such as Joblink 2000, Just for Starters and the school Compact, suggest that attempts are being made to match local skill levels with the needs of local employers. The Community Trust and the Groundwork Trust also indicate a commitment to achieving wider community objectives such as environmental improvement, public safety and stronger community organizations.

Organizationally both BHL and BHDC indicate the importance of the City

98

Council's role in providing civic leadership. By having senior members of the council leadership on the board, the political importance of the agencies was immediately apparent. Other significant benefits arise from the close working relationship established with the City Council and the integration of the different local agencies and funding mechanisms through the area co-ordination teams. In addition, Sir Reginald Eyre as Chair, brought added political weight and extensive personal contacts that, together with the composition of both boards, helped establish a broad political and intersectoral consensus in relation to the needs of the area. BHL also brought into the partnership the five major development companies with extensive experience of working in Birmingham. Both agencies also managed to establish a flexible and unbureaucratic management style that soon dissolved the initial scepticism of local residents. It might be argued that this also could be seen as a relatively paternalistic approach in that the voluntary and community sectors were not represented on the board, yet this needs to be balanced by the commitment to public consultation, particularly in the implementation of the strategy in the four housing areas. BHDC has been considering establishing a community forum to advise the board, but there is little apparent pressure from residents for this to be set up.

In retrospect, it may well be that Birmingham has been fully justified in its approach to urban regeneration. From the strictures of Nicholas Ridley's refusal to fund BHL, to Heseltine's greater flexibility towards the formation of BHDC, it is perhaps central government that has learned most about urban regeneration over the past six years.

CHAPTER 5
Brownlow Community Trust

The history of Brownlow

The origins of Brownlow lie in the partial implementation of a regional strategy for Northern Ireland in the late 1960s and early 1970s. Brownlow was to be a small part of the New Town of Craigavon proposed in the 1960s to provide good quality housing and employment as part of an overspill policy to reduce over-crowding in Belfast. The proposal for a new town resulted from a two-year study by Sir Robert Matthew, completed in 1963. The study looked at the future and the development of Belfast in the context of the whole of Northern Ireland, and concluded that a new town should be located in County Antrim to house a grow-ing population displaced through slum clearance in the city.

Craigavon is situated 40 km to the southwest of Belfast (Fig. 5.1), and was to form a new linear city, joining the two existing towns of Lurgan and Portadown. Despite resistance from these two towns, the aim was to relieve housing pressure in Belfast by encouraging people to move, with the opportunity of jobs and good-quality housing with all the amenities and high-quality environment of a new town. At the time, optimistic assumptions were made about levels of employ-ment and the ability of residents to take advantage of a higher quality of life than they had been used to in Belfast. Construction of the new town began in 1968, and it was envisaged that it would become the regional centre of the much larger Craigavon Borough Council established in 1973. Initial projections assumed a population of 120 000 by 1981 and 200 000 by 2000, although these figures were subsequently revised downwards.

In fact Craigavon New Town never developed as was originally envisaged. By 1973, when the development commission was wound up, economic recession in the UK meant the inward investment targets for new industries were not achieved and in addition, as in the rest of the UK, the policy of population dis-persal from the major cities was reversed. Moreover, "the Troubles" cast a long shadow over all aspects of life in the province. Most notably they depressed busi-ness expansion and deterred inward investment. The most significant new com-pany in Craigavon was the Goodyear tyre factory, which at its peak in the mid-1970s employed 1800 people, but which closed in 1983, and with its closure vir-tually sealed the fate of the new town. In 1982 the DOE had reduced by two thirds

100

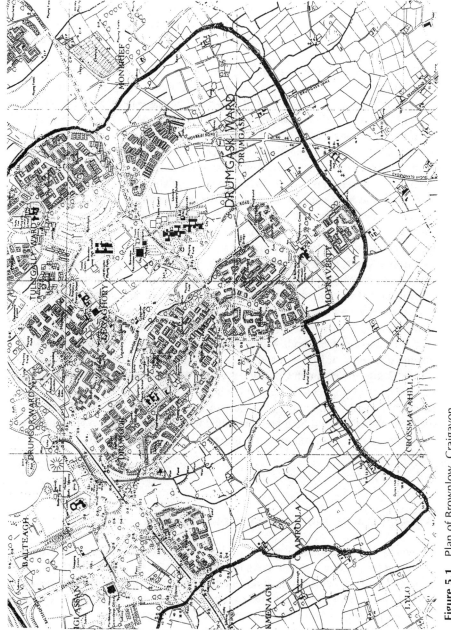

Figure 5.1 Plan of Brownlow, Craigavon.

the area of land available for industrial development in Craigavon. At the time of the closure of Goodyear, one third of the houses already built in the area were vacant and it became increasingly difficult to attract new residents. The planned development of new housing for Craigavon was curtailed at about the same time, after only one of the new housing areas had been built; this area was Brownlow. Approximately 75 per cent of the housing is now owned by the Northern Ireland Housing Executive.

Thus, through worsening economic conditions and changes in planning policy, the need for the new town had largely disappeared by the early 1980s. Brownlow was then left as a series of 23 urban housing estates, built on assumptions of high levels of car ownership, in the middle of what would otherwise be a rural area. Originally designed as purely a residential area, it has only one industrial estate and a regional shopping centre some distance from the housing. Many of the leisure, social and health facilities normally associated with new towns were never constructed. Brownlow's population has been declining for some time and now stands at about 8500, having originally been 12 000. There are four small and limited shopping facilities in the neighbourhood centres of Tullygally, Drumgor, Moyravety and Legahory, where the health centre, housing office and police station are also located. There has been some demolition of the housing stock, particularly in the less popular neighbourhoods, and a few private houses have been constructed. Nevertheless, much of the remaining housing in Brownlow is of good quality, relatively large and built at a low density. A legacy of new town planning is that Brownlow has a good road transport infrastructure and is well connected by road with the rest of the country. The area is poorly served by bus services, both within Brownlow and to the neighbouring towns, leading to a sense of isolation and social exclusion among those without cars.

The Craigavon Borough Council has a total population of 75 000 and contains three centres of population: Lurgan (23 000), Portadown (25 000), and Brownlow (8500) lying between the two. Lurgan and Portadown are towns with very different characters and both are committed to maintaining their own individual identities. Lurgan lies 3 km to the northeast of Brownlow, Portadown 5 km to the southwest.

A social and economic profile of Brownlow

Brownlow has a population structure biased towards the younger age groups, reflecting the relatively recent move for many from Belfast, but scores highly on most indicators of deprivation. It differs markedly from the rest of Northern Ireland: 37 per cent of the population is aged 15 or younger, 18 per cent is aged 16 to 25, 40 per cent is 26 to 60, and only 5 per cent is 60 or more.

The relative deprivation of the population is reflected in higher than average levels of unemployment and lone-parent families, low levels of educational attainment and skills, and an above-average score on several health indicators. These difficulties, coupled with a low level of car ownership, leads to social exclusion from opportunities to participate fully in the community.

The official rate of unemployment in Brownlow is currently running at an average of 28 per cent; twice the Northern Ireland average of 14 per cent, with unemployment in the UK at about 10 per cent. However, it has been estimated that if all those not working but not officially registered as unemployed (that is, those on training schemes and the economically inactive) are counted, then the unemployment rate in Brownlow is nearer 46 per cent. In some estates this rate of unemployment rises to around 75 per cent. Also, 74 per cent of those unemployed have no formal educational qualifications at all; only 5 per cent have GCSE O-levels and 2.4 per cent GCSE A-levels. Only 1.1 per cent have a university degree.

More than 44 per cent of the households in Brownlow receive an income less than half the average income in Northern Ireland. Half of Brownlow's residents live below the poverty line, which compares with 34 per cent in Northern Ireland as a whole and 28 per cent in the UK. At least 61 per cent of households in Brownlow are in receipt of welfare payments other than child benefit, and 85 per cent of the Housing Executive's tenants in Brownlow are eligible for housing benefit.

Brownlow also figures poorly in terms of health issues. Birth weights are low, and asthma, heart disease and cancer all have a greater incidence in Brownlow than is the norm. For a town with a population of 8500, Brownlow has 14 social workers, which is a higher proportion than average. At 20 per cent, the proportion of lone-parent families is one of the highest in Northern Ireland.

In all, the residents of Brownlow face real personal difficulties in competing in the wider labour market, as a result of educational disadvantage, ill health, geographical isolation, and the lack of job opportunities in the immediate area. Yet housing conditions are relatively good and those amenities that do exist have been provided to a high standard. However, by its nature, poverty and deprivation tends to lead to marginalization from all aspects of social and community life.

Community activity in Brownlow

The history of community activity in Brownlow goes back almost as far as the development of the town itself. The first community council was set up in 1969 by Brownlow residents themselves, and by 1972 the Craigavon Development Commission had recognized the residents' concerns when it set up the Brownlow Community Council to meet the social needs of incoming residents. The Brownlow Community Council consisted of representatives from the community who had been democratically elected by the residents themselves, together with representatives from the Craigavon Development Commission, and was therefore seen as a partnership between the two sectors. However, the Council functioned only until 1973, when the Development Commission was disbanded.

Community activity continued in Brownlow throughout the 1970s and 1980s, as it became clear that the town was not going to achieve its original target and the social and economic needs of residents were becoming more apparent. In June 1988, after several months of work by community groups and the statutory agencies, the Greater Brownlow Review was published. The review recognized that the problems in Brownlow were the same as those experienced throughout the whole of Northern Ireland, but also made the case that residents of Brownlow felt an increasing sense of isolation and alienation because of a lack of jobs and social facilities. It also emphasized the fact that, for a town with a population at that time of around 12 000, Brownlow had few of the facilities that would be expected in similar towns of this size, and that this was a significant contributory factor to the town's problems. The review recommended that the community and the statutory agencies in Brownlow work more closely together, and that through consultation and co-operation they should develop a common strategy for the future.

There were two outcomes from the Greater Brownlow Review. First, it led to the setting up of the Brownlow Community Development Association (BCDA) in December of 1988. Secondly, it persuaded the DOE to appoint consultants to investigate the economic regeneration opportunities for Brownlow. The BCDA held its inaugural meeting on 12 December 1988, attracting 23 representatives from the statutory, community and voluntary sectors involved in the Greater Brownlow area. The BCDA was formed as a non-sectarian, non-political organization for the whole of Greater Brownlow, with membership open to all community groups in the area. The statutory agencies could attend BCDA meetings, but were not allowed to vote. One of its first tasks was to produce a strategy called Brownlow 2000, which explored the opportunities for economic development in Brownlow to coincide with the Association's first annual general meeting in March 1989. The BCDA was acknowledged at ministerial level as a positive step forward, and Brownlow 2000 was later to prove very important in Brownlow's application to the European Union's (EU) Poverty 3 programme.

The second outcome of the Greater Brownlow Review was the preparation of what became the Brownlow Initiative, by the consultants David Mackey and Associates. Mackey held that the opportunities lay in the "motivation, encouragement and support of local people to bring forward and implement projects that would improve economic and social performance" (Gillespie 1992). The key to this process of motivation and encouragement, it was suggested, was in encouraging all sectors to work together. Mackey went about this by first of all networking with relevant officials within the public sector, local professionals and community leaders and other local residents, and then by organizing a series of workshops in early 1989 with local people in order to find out what their views were. Local residents were initially suspicious of the consultants and the involvement of the public sector. A community leaders' group and a joint officers' group (made up of the statutory agencies) were established to examine the implications of consultant's study and to develop a strategy for the future. Three main recommendations emerged:

- a community company would be the best body to take the initiative forward
- Brownlow needed the development of a village centre to improve the provision of shops and other services
- the improvement of the physical structure in Brownlow would lead to an improved image for the town.

The recommendation that a community company would be the best vehicle for taking the initiative forward resulted in the formation of Brownlow Limited, a company limited by guarantee open to membership on the part of any Brownlow resident for a fee of £1. Brownlow Limited has a board of directors drawn from local companies, the statutory agencies and the borough council, as well as elected community representatives. The company was set up to:

emphasize the community base of the initiative; embody the regeneration partnership between community, business and public sectors interest and; ensure that there is a "trusteeship" of the objectives. (Gillespie 1992)

The remit of this new community company was the economic regeneration of Brownlow, and to this end it has been involved in several employment and training programmes and in small business development, and has co-ordinated the planning of the Brownlow village square development. It has also been working on a longer-term development for tourism and housing near the existing regional centre. In terms of employment and training, Brownlow Limited is responsible for the running of the job placement agency (discussed later), a training links programme, and the Euro-youth and Wider Horizons projects. Brownlow Limited has also refurbished the Tullygally Centre to provide five shop units and a community hall, and has developed several small business units in derelict housing on the Rosmoyle Estate creating the Bluestone Business Centre in late 1993. The "Heart for Brownlow" was identified by Mackey as a priority for the economic regeneration of the town, and Brownlow Limited commissioned a feasibility study for the project. By 1993, plans had been drawn up and finance was being sought from the DOE and other private sector sources. The new village square development at Legahory is considered essential in order to provide a central focus for the town, to increase the range of shops and other facilities, and to "upgrade Brownlow to become a town in its own right" (Brownlow Ltd 1993).

A potentially far larger project, subsequently taken on by Brownlow Limited, is the Craigavon Central Area Development Study, commissioned by the DOE in 1990 and paid for by BCT. The study looked at the development potential of approximately 60 ha around the balancing lakes and the existing administrative and shopping centre. A mixed-use commercial and leisure development was proposed, with the potential for 1000 new jobs to be promoted by a development consortium composed of the DOE, the borough council, Brownlow Limited and the private sector, at a total cost of £54 million. Although a new spine road to the M1 has been constructed, no development has yet taken place, although (at the time of writing) Brownlow Limited was confident that this will happen soon. The BCT is concerned that the proposed development offers few benefits for local residents and that BCT has not been able to achieve representation on the consortium.

The third European Poverty Programme

The European Poverty Programmes arose out of the recognition by the European Union that it suffered from significant regional imbalances. In research using various economic indicators, the EU attempted to measure the scale and intensity of these imbalances; 36 regions were identified as having economic circumstances significantly below those of the EU average. Only two of these regions were in the northern sector of the EU, one in the Republic of Ireland, the other in Northern Ireland.

The first Combat Poverty programme ran from 1975 to 1980. Although originally planned to last two years, in 1977 it was extended for a further three years, at which time projects in Naples, London, Bavaria and Belfast were added. The second Combat Poverty Programme ("Poverty 2") from 1985 was much larger and more extensive than its predecessor, and involved 91 action research projects throughout Europe. Between the first and second programmes it was acknowledged that the incidence of poverty was changing, with economic restructuring and the overall decline in employment in manufacturing industries becoming more prominent, as well as growing social exclusion. The second Combat Poverty Programme ran for four years until 1989, when the third Poverty Programme ("Poverty 3") was launched. In the UK, Brownlow was selected, along with Toxteth in Merseyside and Pilton in Edinburgh. All three projects are being extensively evaluated, both in the UK and at the European level. Poverty 3 was designed to build on the ideas and experiences that emerged from Poverty 2, and is based on six basic principles:

- *Partnership*   This implies more than the setting up of an inter-agency steering committee to submit an application for EU funding, or simply distributing funds, but playing a direct role in drawing up and implementing an inter-agency strategy.
- *Inter-agency strategy*   This suggests not only identifying innovative projects, but also analyzing the causes and dynamics of poverty in the target area, reviewing the existing policy and actions of significant agencies and developing a coherent strategy that achieves synergy between the partners and tackles aspects of poverty and need previously unmet.
- *Multidimensional poverty*   This involves researching the interconnections between different types of poverty and exploring the extent to which dep-

rivation in one aspect of life (e.g. ill health or unemployment), has repercussions on other elements (e.g. debt, the breakdown of relationships, and housing problems). Likewise, projects need to be integrated and targeted in order to reduce poverty.

- *Economic and social integration* This is based on the recognition that strategies to combat poverty have to link economic and social objectives and to target resources on both supply- and demand-side measures. For example, training projects can help the unemployed to find jobs, but action also needs to be taken to increase the range of jobs available. The provision of childcare facilities may also be an important factor in improving access to jobs and in raising household incomes.
- *Additionality* It is an essential component of the third Programme that EU resources are seen as being additional to the expenditure of other agencies involved, not as a replacement. These resources should also be used for projects that would not otherwise have taken place.
- *Participation* It is essential that representatives of the target groups in the project area are directly involved in the planning, development, management and implementation of the strategy, in order to avoid some of the consequences of "top-down management" experienced in the early US anti-poverty programme.

The challenge in the Poverty 3 programme was therefore to develop strategies that linked:

- economic and social measures
- supply-side and demand-side measures
- top-down and bottom-up processes and organizations
- economic development and community development
- grassroots power and public, private and voluntary agencies (Gillespie 1992: 17).

Poverty 3 was to last from 1989 to 1994, and consisted of 39 local projects, of which 27 were model actions and 12 were to be innovative initiatives. Three of the projects are in Ireland: two in the Republic, and one – Brownlow – in Northern Ireland. The way in which Brownlow came to be chosen for the Poverty 3 programme is outlined in the next section.

Brownlow Community Trust

As part of the recognition of the less fortunate areas within Europe, the application form for inclusion in the Poverty 3 programme was received by the Southern Health and Social Services Board (SH & SSB) of Northern Ireland. The application was completed within a few weeks, with the original DOE consultants, Mackey and Associates, being commissioned to assist in its preparation. In accordance with the stated principle of partnership, the initial work on the application was prepared by the SH & SSB, the BCDA and the Northern Ireland Voluntary Trust (NIVT). The work was co-ordinated by a new body, Brownlow Community Trust (BCT), which was established initially as a steering group of representatives from the above organizations, with assistance from the Southern Education and Library Board (SELB) and Brownlow Limited.

The application for Poverty 3 drew heavily on the previous work in Brownlow by various groups: the Greater Brownlow Review, Brownlow 2000, and The Brownlow Initiative, all discussed earlier. In particular, Brownlow 2000 was acknowledged as embodying many of the same principles as were fundamental to Poverty 3. The formation of a social partnership was seen as the way forward for Brownlow. The application to Poverty 3 included an assessment of the causes of poverty in Brownlow, the identification of specific target groups within the community, suggested projects, the objectives of the partnership, the outputs envisaged, and the team required to implement the projects. These are listed below.

Causes of poverty in Brownlow
- the restructuring of the industrial and employment base
- the high proportion of the population reliant on State benefits, unemployed households with large numbers of children, and single parent families
- the poor housing conditions on some estates
- the lack of local shopping facilities exacerbating the problems of living on a low income
- high population turnover
- social and cultural exclusion from Lurgan and Portadown

Target groups identified
- the long-term unemployed
- the young unemployed
- single-parent families
- children.

Objectives
- to build community cohesion
- to decrease the sense of dependency of local people
- to encourage enterprise and initiative in the social, economic, and cultural aspects of Brownlow
- to enhance the quality of life and to improve the environment in Brownlow.
- to improve services and promote co-ordination and integration in their delivery.

Outputs envisaged
- to improve the economy of Brownlow
- to removing the social deprivation, poverty and isolation affecting local people
- providing a sense of place and a focus to Brownlow
- developing a new status for Brownlow that would be recognized by every one both inside and outside the area

- enabling the public authorities to learn that by working in a practical way with each other and collectively with local people great progress would be made towards solving problems that appear insoluble.

Projects
- women's project
- unemployed project
- health project
- children and families project
- community arts project
- job placement agency incorporating open learning centre
- Brownlow High Street development.

Team required
- project leader
- women's project worker
- unemployed project worker
- health project worker
- children and families project worker
- community arts project worker
- job placement agency incorporating and open learning centre
- Brownlow High Street development worker

Source: Gillespie (1992)

The Brownlow application to the EU's Poverty 3 programme was successful, and the resulting organization and activities of Brownlow Community Trust are discussed below.

Organization and funding

Brownlow Community Trust (BCT) is a company limited by guarantee with charitable status. It has a board of management that consists of 23 representatives from the statutory agencies and the community. There is no private sector involvement on the board of management, because of the limited presence of the private sector in the area. BCT is one of the EU's model action projects, which means that EU funding is designed to elicit "transferable methods and models of good practice in combating exclusion . . . to inform social policy at local and European level" (BCT 1992). The membership of the BCT board of management is made up of nine representatives of statutory agencies, two councillors from the borough council, four from Brownlow Community Development Association, four from local agencies operating in the area, and four community representatives elected annually (Table 5.1 and Fig. 5.2).

Table 5.1 Membership of the Brownlow Community Trust Board of Management.

Denis Preston (Chair)	Unit General Manager, Southern Health & Social Services Board
Martin O'Neill	Senior Community Worker, SH & SSB
Joe Wright	Voluntary Activity Unit, DHSS
Gregory Butler	Youth Advisor, Southern Education and Library Board
Eileen Keville	Senior Education Officer, SELB
Clifford McIlwaine	Senior Planner, Department of Environment
Bert Wilson	Regional Housing & Planning Mgr, N. Ireland Housing Executive
David Capper	District Manager, NIHE
Paul Sweeney	Director, Northern Ireland Voluntary Trust
Cllr Fred Crowe	Craigavon Borough Council
Cllr Patricia Mallon	Craigavon Borough Council
Tony Moore	Community Director, Brownlow Ltd
Eamon O'Reilly	Brownlow Community Development Association (BCDA)
May Gray	BCDA
Sam McMullan	BCDA
Mary Sheen	BCDA
Jim McWilliams	Brownlow Unemployed Group
Alice McCabe	Brownlow Childcare Action Group
Clare McCann	Brownlow Women's Forum
Gerry McIlroy	Community representative
Cllr Peter Smyth	Community representative
Philomena Gallagher	Community representative
Francis O'Neill	Community representative

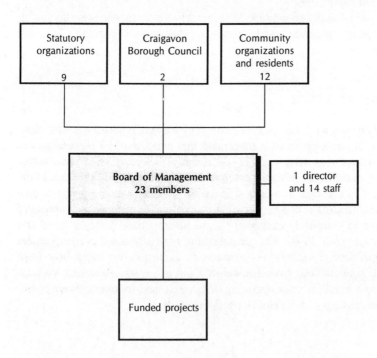

Figure 5.2 Organizational structure of Brownlow Community Trust.

Staffing the project team

- The project team is made up of 13 employees under the direction of Roisin McDonough, who was appointed in May 1990. Staff perform the following roles:
- 2 secretaries
- 1 office manager
- 1 information/publicity manager
- 1 women's project officer
- 1 unemployed project worker
- 1 community health worker
- 3 lay health workers
- 1 play policy-worker
- 1 project historian/researcher
- 1 non-traditional skills worker

The Poverty 3 programme requires funding from the statutory bodies involved to match that from the EU. In the case of Brownlow this means that, over the project's five-year lifespan, BCT will have a budget of almost £2.2 million, with just under £1 million of European Union funding. The requirement of the EU is that this matching funding should be additional to that which would have been allocated to Brownlow, although in practice several of the agencies offered staff-time and benefits in kind. It is also a stipulation of the EU that the funding derived from the Poverty 3 project cannot be used to finance capital expenditure; instead, it must be used to provide grant aid to community groups and others whose objectives coincide with those of the programme itself.

Because Brownlow was selected by the EU as a model action project from which lessons will be learned and applied in other circumstances throughout the EU, the monitoring and evaluation of the project is crucial, and a strict requirement of the annually received EU funding. BCT is the subject of several evaluation programmes, both internally and externally. The Trust has its own internal evaluator and project historian, and there are two evaluators from the University of Ulster appointed by BCT. Regular meetings are also held between all the evaluators of the UK Poverty 3 programmes, co-ordinated by the project Research and Development Unit at the University of Warwick.

Target groups and projects

- The Trust identified four target groups in its original application to the Poverty 3 programme:
- the long-term unemployed
- the young unemployed
- single-parent families
- children.

These target groups have subsequently been revised and are listed in *Progress through partnership* (BCT 1992) as:

- women
- children
- long-term unemployed
- young unemployed.

There is also a "strong health focus which cuts across all these areas" (BCT 1992) and a "non-traditional skills project" developed out of work on the women's project, with young women on training and employment opportunities in non-traditional areas of work.

Defining the project's objectives

After carrying out extensive research and public consultation, BCT identified three overriding principles underlying all its activities, which are also in accord with the EU's Poverty 3 programme. These are participation, partnership and an integrated approach (BCT 1992: 11):

participation – that local people must be involved in the decisions taken about how government bodies and others formulate and carry through their policies in Brownlow;
partnership – that statutory bodies and local people need to work together on an equal basis to jointly develop a plan that will set the foundations for the long term social and economic regeneration of Brownlow;
an integrated approach – that tackling poverty needs an approach that brings together a wide variety of measures in different areas such as in training, housing, education, health, the environment, employment, leisure, culture, as well as income.

In preparing an economic strategy for Brownlow, BCT set out the following mission statement:

Brownlow Community Trust will promote the social, economic and cultural integration of those marginalized by poverty by (Smith 1993: 15):
(a) promoting their participation in the wider decision making and policy process.
(b) securing their active involvement in interrelated strategic aims.

Priority groups: women

The decision to target women within BCT's Combat Poverty Programme was taken because of several factors. First, women tend to carry many of the burdens of poverty and deprivation, and themselves often experience difficulties in gaining access to the jobs market. Secondly, because of the role women tend to play within a family unit, they are more likely to have to deal with the consequences of poverty, for example in managing the family budget and in looking after children. Brownlow offers little choice in shopping, further compounding the problem of a tight budget, and public transport to alternative shopping is poor. Also, because Brownlow was built as a new town, there is little family support for women to draw on. A lack of childcare facilities often means women are unable to participate fully in the community, and many women in Brownlow express a fear of going out after dark.

Chrysalis Women's Centre
The Chrysalis Women's Centre was opened on 8 March 1993 and is located on the ground floor of an old Southern Health and Social Services Board (SH & SSB) family centre on the Burnside Estate. The centre was developed by the Burnside Centre Planning Group, which consisted of local women, representatives from the SH & SSB, the Northern Ireland Play Association, and Craigavon Unemployed Workers Centre Mobile Creche Group (see below). Chrysalis is managed by local women and it exists to facilitate meetings and various training courses, as well as to provide a creche. The women's project officer, appointed in January 1991, helped in negotiations with the SH & SSB, with the raising of finance for the centre and in developing a programme of courses.

Young mothers
The idea for a young mothers project in Brownlow originally came from a similar project in Bristol. An inter-agency planning group was formed under the direction of the women's project officer, which included representatives from SH & SSB, the Education and Library Board Youth Service, Craigavon Borough Council and members of the lay health scheme, as well as local mothers. Since April 1992, the young mothers group has been holding regular meetings, and has instigated a programme of classes in personal development.

Asian women's group
This group of local women is supported by the BCT women's project. In particular, BCT was involved in the successful application by the group to the Northern Ireland Voluntary Trust for the employment of an Asian lay health worker.

Training
A successful application for European funding under New Opportunities for Women (NOW) has meant that a fast-track 36-week training course could be offered, which includes computing, word processing, business languages, accounting, supervision and management. The BTEC course in computer technology was initially completed by six women, and funding was obtained to enable the Trust to run further courses.

113

Non-traditional skills project

In October of 1992, BCT appointed an officer to work on the development of the non-traditional skills project. The project is aimed at young women and hopes to promote opportunities and awareness, and provision of training, for young women in areas of work not normally thought of as traditional occupations for women. BCT has worked with the two secondary schools in Brownlow, trying to increase awareness, and has run two conferences on "Opportunities for All in Industry". The Trust has also worked with the providers of training, raising awareness as to the problems faced by young women who are wanting to avail themselves of training. In particular BCT has been working with the Craigavon Government Training Centre.

Priority groups: children and young people

Just over half of the children in Brownlow live in low-income families; there-fore, the targeting of children and young people, from both the children's point of view and for the benefit of their parents, was identified as a priority for the Trust. In particular, childcare facilities, which might allow parents to become more involved in other community activities, are still lacking in some areas of Brownlow.

Play

In 1992, BCT appointed a play policy-worker to establish an inter-agency work-ing party to help devise a "plan for play" in Brownlow. This followed a study by Playboard Northern Ireland, which highlighted the importance of play in the educational and social development of children, and suggested ways of increas-ing the opportunities for play. The Education and Library Board Youth Service funded a playboard foundation course to help increase awareness of the impor-tance of play.

Children's Policy Forum

The Children's Policy Forum is an inter-agency forum that was set up in early 1992. Its objectives are: to prepare a workable plan for play and childcare facil-ities within Brownlow; liaison with statutory agencies, voluntary organizations, and community groups; sharing information and ideas; promotion and support of innovative childcare and play ideas; help with the raising of finance; improve awareness of childcare and play policies of the statutory agencies; encourage childcare and play opportunities for minority groups, particularly travellers; and to promote better healthcare for children.

Funding and support for local groups

Funding and support for local groups are aimed at improving the provision of childcare and play facilities by providing, for example, local playgroups, sum-mer schemes, after school play schemes, and healthy eating.

Cultural provision

The Trust has organized workshops, competitions, story telling, and bursaries in an attempt to increase the exposure of local children to cultural activities.

Daycare

BCT produced a report on childcare needs in Brownlow in 1991, in which it suggested ways to optimize the use of existing facilities as well as calling for the provision of facilities, particularly in areas where none currently exist.

Schools

Teachers in the local schools have been encouraged to work with BCT officers, and currently many local children now save with a credit union. Also, BCT has been involved in the Brownlow Campus Project, which is hoping to obtain money from the European Regional Development Fund to extend the provision of outdoor leisure facilities for use by schools, as well as by the wider community.

Priority groups: the long-term and young unemployed

The Unemployed Project

The overall aim of the Unemployed Project is to empower local people to enable them to compete on an equal basis with others from outside Brownlow. A project worker was appointed in January 1991, managing many of the activities that take place under the umbrella of the Unemployed Project. The following are some of the individual projects:

- *Craigavon Unemployed Workers Centre*   This opened in 1987 in response to a change in Unemployment Benefit entitlement and is now fully supported by BCT. It is located in a house on one of the Brownlow estates and it exists to help achieve social justice for the unemployed of Brownlow. For example, it runs a benefits take-up scheme to ensure that claimants are receiving their full entitlements. It is estimated that this scheme has brought in over £1 million to Brownlow in extra benefit payments. The centre concentrates on counselling, education and training, and campaigning.
- *Craigavon volunteer bureau*   This opened in 1992 to provide facilities, resources and training for the volunteer workers in Brownlow. The Bureau is funded by the EU INTERREG initiative, Craigavon Borough Council, Lurgan Further Education College, Social Services, and the Community Volunteering Scheme. In particular, the Bureau can provide money to cover the costs of transport, meals, and childcare for volunteers.
- *Job placement agency*   BCT provides £35 000 out of £50 000 running costs in 1992–3 for the Job Placement Agency run by Brownlow Limited.
- *Brownlow Community Trust's economic strategy*   This was produced by the unemployed project worker in 1993. The strategy examined the economic and social needs of Brownlow, the agencies concerned with training

and employment, and the priorities to be adopted. The main points to emerge from the strategy were that Brownlow needed an integrated social and economic development plan that would ensure that those who live within Brownlow have equal opportunities for employment. Access to training and the development of appropriate skills were highlighted as key elements of the strategy, which aims to improve the overall quality of life of the residents of Brownlow.

- *Community business programme*   This was extended to Brownlow, following negotiations with the Local Enterprise Development Unit (LEDU), and the Newry and Mourne Enterprise Agency. The Programme, funded by the International Fund for Ireland and LEDU, offers training in business skills.

- *Business in the Community*   In furthering the objective of partnership, BCT facilitated several visits to Brownlow by BItC. BItC is now represented on the management committee of the Craigavon Volunteer Bureau, for which it provides financial and management expertise. The relationship is reciprocal, since BCT's Unemployed Project Worker was asked to be involved with BItC's Directions for the 1990s initiative.

- *Challenging debt*   BCT, with the Lurgan Credit Union, launched a successful pilot scheme offering loans through the Credit Union to those in need. The scheme emerged from an inter-agency group that was formed following findings by the SH & SSB that concerns about income and debt were the greatest causes of stress in Brownlow.

- *Tullygally 18+ Group*   This is a partnership between BCT, SELB, the Youth Service, and the Aldervale Project (a community care project for which BCT assumed management responsibility), which facilitates this group on the Tullygally Estate in running a programme of personal skills development and self-help.

- *Drumgor unemployed group*   The BCT Health Project Worker (see below for details of the Health Project) has been involved with the unemployed group on the Drumgor estate.

- *Edenbeg Unemployed Group*   Set up in November of 1991 by BCT with the SELB and Craigavon Borough Council, this group on the Edenbeg Estate aims to develop the skills of unemployed residents. Its projects include access to childcare, community education and driving lessons.

- *Craigavon leisure centre pilot scheme*   With the BCT Health Project, the Unemployed Project has been jointly running a scheme for low-cost access to the Craigavon Leisure Centre. A report by Craigavon Borough Council recommended that it should continue providing childcare and structured leisure programmes for local children.

- *Cultural activities*   It has been acknowledged that poverty contributes to a low level of access to cultural activities, and it was with this in mind that the BCDA set up a Brownlow Community Arts Group, following a successful community arts day in early 1991. Now Craigavon Borough Council,

SELB, and BCT are involved with the group, the main aim of which is to help finance and develop the arts in Brownlow. In November 1992 a community artist was appointed under the Artists in the Community Scheme funded by the Northern Ireland Arts Council. Ken Parker worked one day a week in Brownlow and has been involved with local schools in preparing murals for the health centre, the Aldervale Project and at the Chrysalis Women's Centre. Brownlow Community Arts Group has also organized a local festival, the most recent of which took place in May in 1993.

- *Historical and environmental projects* The unemployed project has been involved in the restoration of the Lynastown graveyard, which is thought to be one of the oldest Quaker burial grounds in Ireland. Volunteers, including local people, have been helping with this restoration.
- *The Brownlow stream* BCT was first involved in the production of a video to highlight to the statutory agencies the health and safety problems posed by the Brownlow stream, which is used by some as a dumping ground for rubbish. Consultations took place with Northern Ireland 2000, Friends of the Earth, and Conservation Volunteers Northern Ireland, and BCT have been negotiating with the statutory agencies to carry out environmental improvements.
- *Brownlow Community Trust census* The Unemployed Workers' Forum was involved in preparing and carrying out a census questionnaire that collected data on the social and economic characteristics of Brownlow's population.

Health

BCT's health project is designed to underpin all its other activities, and many of the schemes run under the umbrella of the Health Project are operated in conjunction with other BCT projects. The underlying philosophy behind the project is that a holistic approach is required to improve health, which affects all aspects of life in the community.

- *Health Project Steering Group* This group oversees the Trust's Health Project, and is made up of representatives from the statutory agencies, voluntary organizations and community groups. The group was set up after a Community Health Day in March 1992 and has been meeting regularly ever since.
- *Lay health workers* Since February 1992 BCT has employed six lay health workers who act as neighbourhood health information officers for their allotted part of Brownlow. The lay health workers have also been involved in setting up a health information centre located in the community house in Burnside, in order to lend videos and books on health issues to the community, although this centre is now run by volunteers.
- *Leisure centre initiative* This is being run in conjunction with the unem-

ployed project and is designed to increase access to the leisure centre for those on low incomes.

- *User groups* The Brownlow health centre users group is made up of both individuals and community groups, who have been meeting since May 1991, helping with the production of a health centre users' guide, running a creche and in organizing an open day at the centre.
- *Older people's planning group* An inter-agency group set up in late 1992 to explore the particular problems that affect older people in Brownlow.
- *Community development and networking* BCT has been networking with other health projects across Northern Ireland and the rest of the UK, as well as with other groups within Brownlow itself.
- *Grant-aid for community organizations* In addition to support for the projects listed above, BCT has a grant-aid scheme whereby existing community organizations in the area can make an application to the BCT board for funding. In 1991–2 £226 000 and in 1992–3 £204 000 was distributed to organizations such as the Unemployed and Residents Groups, play schemes, youth clubs, summer festivals, and others subscribing to the objectives of BCT and meeting the funding criteria.

Conclusions

In statistical terms, Brownlow represents one of the highest concentrations of multiple deprivation in Northern Ireland, yet the past four years have indicated that, with sufficient motivation and resources, much can be achieved by developing community participation and by co-ordinating the efforts of public sector agencies. BCT has thus achieved a great deal by working as a catalyst in running demonstration projects and by making the public agencies less remote to the people they serve. However, the expenditure of £2.2 million will not reverse the indicators of deprivation that have been in evidence for almost 25 years.

On the positive side, BCT has achieved significant improvements in relation to the three principles underlying the Poverty 3 programme. The participation of Brownlow residents has increased substantially, both in contributing 11 out of the 23 places on the board of management and in working as employees, volunteers and recipients of the wide variety of projects funded by the Trust. Although inevitably there was some mistrust of the approach among residents, and fears that the experts from the statutory agencies would dominate the project in the early stages, these have largely been dissipated. Indeed, some interviewees remarked on the increasing assertiveness of the community representatives on the board, to the extent that new projects are unlikely to be approved without their support. Others reported that there was an element of cynicism and frustration in the early days that, for example, posts should have been offered to local residents first before being advertised nationally.

With regard to partnership, there is also positive evidence that the statutory bodies (which are largely run by unelected agencies) have learned to consult local people and to co-ordinate their activities more closely. Four of the main service providers, together with Craigavon Borough Council, are represented on the BCT board, although it is significant that the Industry Development Board (IDB) and the Local Economic Development Unit are not directly involved. These organizations could have a greater impact on the economic wellbeing of the town if they worked more closely with BCT. The IDB, for example, contributed £16.9 million to companies in Craigavon in 1990-1, which is the largest amount allocated to any district council in Northern Ireland.

The Northern Ireland Housing Executive, which owns 85 per cent of the houses in Brownlow, has a local office in the Legahory centre and claims that the work of BCT has caused it to become more sensitive to local needs. It has recently prepared an improvement strategy for the Edenbeg Estate, where arson and theft have caused some residents to move out, and is considering ways of encouraging greater tenant involvement in the management of the estate. Ironically, reorganization in the Executive may lead to the closure of the local office. Likewise, the DOE (also with a local office in Craigavon) is carrying out public consultation for a new district plan for Brownlow.

There is also increasing evidence of the third principle – an integrated approach –emerging from the involvement of the public and voluntary sectors on the BCT board. All the agencies are aware of the interrelated nature of the problems of the area, and, as far as their budgets allow, are all working towards giving Brownlow high priority in resource allocation. On occasion, the BCT has also taken the lead, for example in preparing an economic strategy for Brownlow (Smith 1993) and targeting the training needs of the population in particular.

Over and above these three principles, BCT has adopted a fourth, which is promotion – of both the achievements of the project and the principles underpinning it. This has been done partly to publicize more widely the benefits of working in partnership, but also in order to secure funding for a second phase of the project. The concept of partnership is less developed in Northern Ireland, where the transfer of services from local to central government, and the profusion of government agencies, are more apparent than in the rest of the UK. To this end, BCT was instrumental in organizing a conference called "Towards 2000" for the public and voluntary sectors in the province in order to "develop a strategic framework in which a holistic approach to broad social and economic policy and planning issues in Northern Ireland can be discussed with a view to their long term implementation".

The additional EU funds from Poverty 3 have clearly had an impact in terms of mobilizing community support structures and in stimulating closer integration between residents and the statutory agencies. However, major problems remain for the future. Perhaps the greatest need in the area is a massive increase in employment opportunities in order to absorb the high level of unemployment and to increase household incomes. This was particularly difficult to achieve between

1989 and 1994, because of the diffusion of responsibilities between several different agencies. Although the DoE owns most of the land, the NIHE owns 85 per cent of the housing. As a result of the various studies carried out in the late 1980s, Brownlow Limited emerged with a separate employment and training remit, whereas BCT developed a primarily community development role and was not permitted to acquire land or buildings. The Craigavon Borough Council has very few powers and only a modest budget for tourism and economic development. The Central Area Development Study indicates some of the difficulties that could emerge from a regionally significant development that could bring great benefits, but from which Brownlow residents currently feel excluded.

While the future of BCT remains uncertain and the EU has still to confirm whether it will fund a Poverty 4 programme, it may be that a new form of partnership is needed along the lines of the New Life partnerships in Scotland, or the City Challenge agencies in England. This would be funded directly by central government and would involve the DoE, IDB, NIHE, and SS & HB and would build on the community development role of BCT. Its primary task would be the regeneration and expansion of Brownlow and it would have the powers to operate holistically across all government policy areas, while continuing to build the capacity of residents to play a full part in the process.

CHAPTER 6

Greenwich Waterfront Development Partnership (GWDP)

The Greenwich Waterfront

The Greenwich Waterfront Partnership area is made up of approximately 1012 ha of the London Borough of Greenwich and includes about 11 km of the south bank of the River Thames, with almost half the area lying in Thamesmead town. The London Docklands Development Corporation operates in part of Southwark to the west and on the north bank of the Thames. The area has a resident population of about 70 000 living in several identifiable communities, such as Deptford Creek, Greenwich town centre, East Greenwich, Woolwich and Thamesmead.

The land uses in the area are predominantly industrial (161 ha), vacant (150 ha), residential (98 ha), other uses (including roads; 95 ha), and commercial (46 ha). There are approximately 31 000 jobs in the area, 370 industrial operations and an unemployment rate of about 20 per cent in 1992.

The housing is predominantly rented: 57 per cent from the local authority, 16 per cent from private landlords and 8 per cent from housing associations. Only 19 per cent is owner-occupied housing. The Partnership has identified at least 324 ha of land as having development potential, including the 121 ha Greenwich Peninsula site owned by British Gas, and the 31 ha Royal Arsenal.

Origins of the partnership

At the height of the property boom in 1988, pressures were growing to develop several sites in the area in a piecemeal fashion. The London Borough of Greenwich began to realize that a strategic approach was needed to both co-ordinate development and fend off the possibility that the DoE might incorporate part of the area into the remit of the London Docklands Development Corporation. Brit-

121

ish Urban Development, the newly formed private sector organization, had already been investigating the possibility of co-ordinating the development of the British Gas Port Greenwich site on the Greenwich Peninsula.

Greenwich's approach was to begin to carry out public consultation for the whole area, with a view to preparing a strategic plan. This began as a planning brief that would eventually be incorporated into the unitary development plan, but, as time passed, a corporate strategy was seen as being more relevant. The Civic Trust Regeneration Unit was retained to advise on carrying out consultation and preparing the strategy. Since Greenwich was already a member of the Docklands Consultative Committee, this was commissioned to do an independent consultation exercise with community groups. In addition, other consultants were employed to prepare reports on specialist topics. PA Cambridge Economic Consultants produced a report on *The southeast London economy and the Single European Market* (1989), Transport Planning Associates submitted *Greenwich Riverside – transportation strategy review* (1989), and Comedia produced *Greenwich 2001 – a concept study* (1989). At the same time, workshops were organized internally between the departments of Greenwich Council to feed into the strategy.

The organization of the partnership

From the beginning, the Council was convinced that, to co-ordinate the development of the Waterfront fully, all interests in the area should be involved in the process and that a detailed strategy was needed with appropriate agencies to implement it. There were two distinct stages in the process. The first involved detailed community consultation, discussions within the council, reports by consultants, and open meetings for all participants, leading up to the publication of the Greenwich Waterfront Strategy in January 1991. The second stage has involved setting up and operationalizing the Development Partnership, including representative forums for the community and local businesses, and implementation agencies for specific areas such as the Greenwich and Woolwich town centres.

Phase one: the Waterfront strategy

For about two years there was a period of extensive debate inside and outside the Council, public consultation (including exhibitions and publicity) and consultants' reports, leading up to the publication of the Waterfront Strategy in January 1991. This was prepared jointly by the Greenwich Planning Department and the Civic Trust Regeneration Unit, and was described as "an urban regeneration strategy for seven miles of the Greenwich Waterfront. It contains development guidelines, an urban design framework, targets for community provision and a partnership framework for implementation" (London Borough of Greenwich 1991).

The document was presented in the form of a "vision" of how the area might be developed. There are three main sections covering guidelines and urban design principles for the main land use sectors, a discussion of the unique characteristics and opportunities in the five main subareas, and an outline of the mechanisms and procedures needed to implement the plan. The strategy is couched in terms of providing principles that all partners can subscribe to and it aims to balance the interests of the council, the community and the private sector, while exploiting the historic, cultural and environmental potential of the area. The strategy set out the guiding principles thus:

The place

- complements and enhances the character and identity of Greenwich and does not dominate it
- integrates new with old and provides continuity of buildings, spaces, communities and activities
- builds upon the variety and activity that is so fundamental to metropolitan rivers throughout the world
- demonstrates quality and high standards in terms of design and architecture
- is based on green principles – is sustainable, energy-efficient, people-friendly and takes account of the need to achieve environmentally sustainable economic and social progress.

The people

- is based on the direct involvement of the local community
- benefits local communities and does not ignore them
- is based on equality of access and makes special provision for people with disabilities to enjoy the benefits of changes to the Waterfront
- creates opportunities to encourage and enable local people to get involved in a partnership for the future of their area
- secures affordable housing for existing and future generations
- provides new access to the Waterfront and new opportunities to enjoy it
- provides a balanced and accessible range of facilities for community use
- improves cultural provision and community participation in the arts
- improves public transport.

The economy

- secures new, quality jobs and protects existing industry and employment
- stabilizes and strengthens the local retail economy including local shops
- secures a lasting contribution to the local economy from the tourist trade.
  (London Borough of Greenwich 1991).

In the final section, "The way forward", proposals for how the strategy might be taken forward over the following ten years are set out. Partnership is the key theme because "the resources and roles required are beyond the scope of any single agency acting alone" (London Borough of Greenwich 1991: 68). The three

123

primary functions that partnerships will have are: marketing and promotion, "do it" functions, and community involvement and empowerment. Thus, a three-tier structure is proposed, involving a Waterfront board and management team to develop a marketing and promotional strategy, mobilize funding, identify, investigate, package and market development opportunities, to encourage and facilitate community involvement, and to help establish and support local agencies. Secondly, local agencies would be set up to oversee implementation in identified subareas, for example the town centres and the peninsula. Thirdly, a Waterfront forum would be set up on which all local groups would be represented. This would provide a means of co-ordinating the responses and actions of the community across the whole Waterfront. The forum would also elect representatives to sit on the Waterfront board.

The Waterfront strategy was officially launched at a conference attended by about 100 people from local and national environmental organizations and about 35 officers and members from the London Borough of Greenwich. It included presentations by the Leader of the Council, the Borough Planning Officer and the Director of the Civic Trust. Discussion groups focused on how the strategy might be carried forward.

Phase two: setting up the Development Partnership

After the conference in January 1991 the Council began work on setting up appropriate agencies to push forward the strategy and identify priorities for action. To begin with, the lead was taken by officers in the planning department. A total of 234 policy proposals were reviewed and discussed in a further period of consultation.

During the first phase, several issues had come to light that would need resolution before further progress could be made:

- It was recognized that time was essential in order to establish confidence with all parties and to integrate their disparate interests. Yet action was needed early on in order to establish the reputation of the partnership.
- Certain deficiencies were perceived by both the community and local businesses in the way the council operated. Gaps were evident in the way services were co-ordinated and delivered, and there was a degree of mistrust, particularly between the local authority and the private sector. Some found the council's attitude uncaring and sometimes hostile, and some landowners had little or no contact with the council. In essence, the council's credibility in being able to deliver was being put to the test.
- The local community was fragmented and apprehensive about whether they would be bypassed as the strategy unfolded.

In order to progress the strategy and to establish appropriate agencies, the team of officers began by translating into action many of the proposals discussed in the first phase. Initially, attention was given to setting up an independent staff team, to formalizing the constitution of the Development Partnership, and to setting up representative forums for local business and the community.

The Greenwich Waterfront Development Partnership

This was launched in June 1992 as the strategic body to oversee the regeneration of the Waterfront and is intended to be a company limited by guarantee and, when formally constituted, would have 16 members representing the following interests:
- 5 from the London Borough of Greenwich
- 5 business representatives elected by the Waterfront Business Forum
- 5 community representatives elected by the Waterfront Community Forum
- 1 representative from Thamesmead Town Ltd.

In March 1993 it was agreed to increase the number of community representatives from four to five, in order to allow for representation by the Black and ethnic minority community. The community forum was also invited to set up a steering group of members from ethnic minorities to advise the partnership board member.

The remit of the board would be: to co-ordinate action across the whole Waterfront; to progress projects that have strategic implications; to bring together government, landowners and communities to solve problems; to raise the profile of the area; to promote new ideas; to encourage consensus; and to provide a means for the sustained participation of residents and businesses.

Until the board is formally constituted, an interim advisory board was selected and is composed of: the Leader and Deputy Leader of the Council, the Chair of the Planning and Transport Committee, a councillor each representing Greenwich and Woolwich town centres, and a councillor from the minority party. In addition, there are five business representatives from the Woolwich Building Society, the National Maritime Museum, British Gas, Tunnel Refineries and Barclays Bank.

The five community representatives come from the Greenwich African Welfare Organization, Riverside Churches, Greenwich Action to Stop Pollution, the Greenwich Arts Forum and the East Greenwich Community Centre. A subgroup of the board is currently investigating the alternative constitutional mechanisms for setting up the Partnership as an independent company.

The board's implementation programme was announced in December 1992 and was circulated widely for consultation. The responses were discussed at the advisory board meeting in March 1993. This meeting also discussed the basis for a marketing strategy, using £10 000 pledged by the South London Training and Enterprise Council, and considered instigating a Millennium project leading to a major festival in the year 2000, based around the concept of the meridian line.

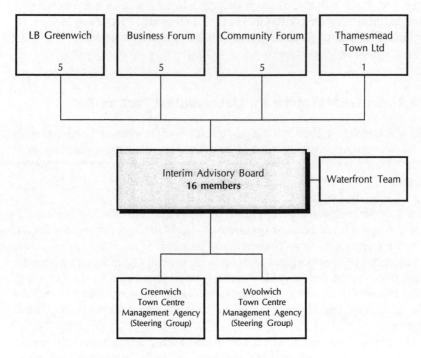

Figure 6.1   Organizational structure of GWDP.

This is the largest project contemplated so far and could be used to unify and promote the whole Waterfront area. In the summer of 1993 Greenwich was awarded Assisted Area status by the Department of Trade and Industry. This also provides access to the European Regional Development Fund.

Overall, the South London TEC has agreed to contribute £150 000 in 1993–4 towards the provision of an Adult Guidance and Assessment Centre in Woolwich and nine enterprise projects generated by the business forum task forces, for example a property database for the whole area and funding for site feasibility studies.

Staffing the Waterfront team

The team working on the Waterfront strategy has gradually expanded since its origins with a few officers in the planning department. By May 1993 the team comprised 17 people working from offices in Greenwich, Woolwich and Thamesmead. The team leader is David McCollum, who worked half time for the Partnership and half as Director of Leisure for Greenwich. The post of

126

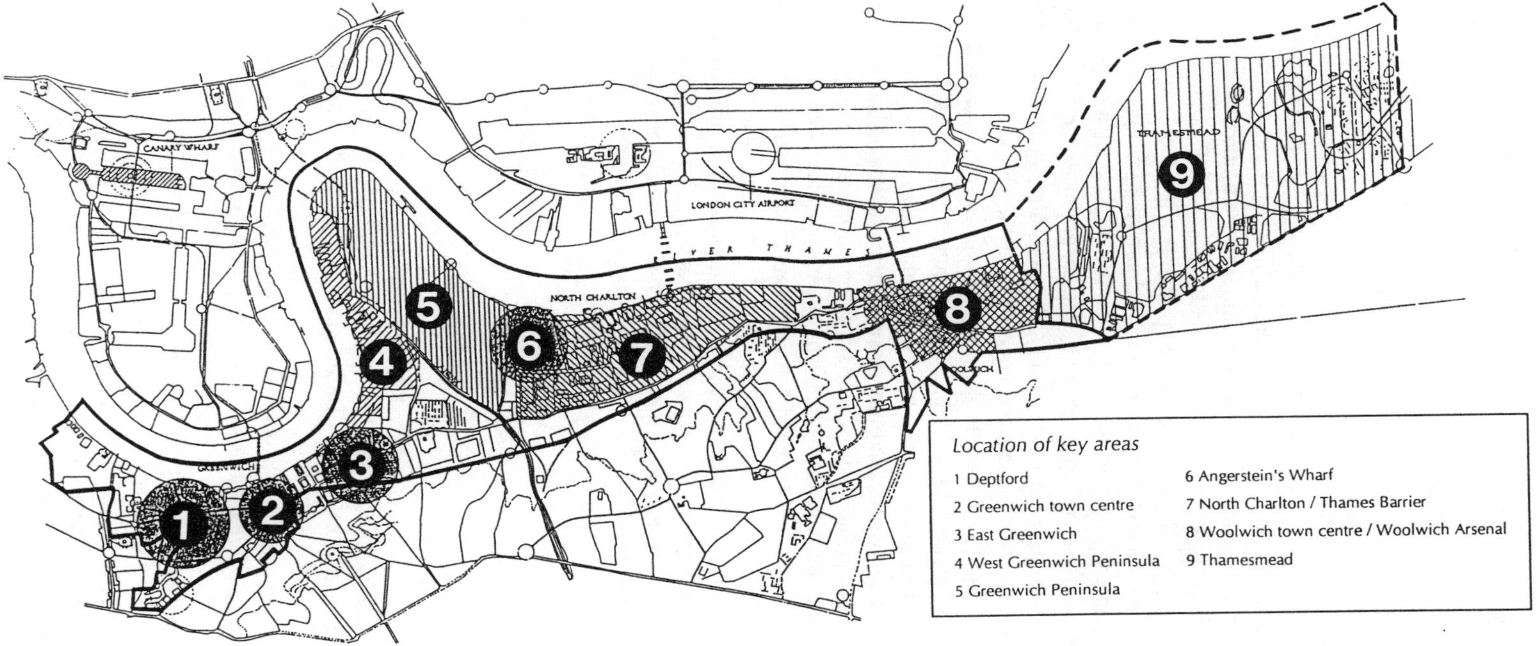
CANARY WHARF
GREENWICH
LONDON CITY AIRPORT
RIVER THAMES
NORTH CHARLTON
WOOLWICH
THAMESMEAD
1
2
3
4
5
6
7
8
9
Location of key areas
1 Deptford
2 Greenwich town centre
3 East Greenwich
4 West Greenwich Peninsula
5 Greenwich Peninsula
6 Angerstein's Wharf
7 North Charlton / Thames Barrier
8 Woolwich town centre / Woolwich Arsenal
9 Thamesmead

Figure 6.2 Plan of the GWDP area.

Waterfront Co-ordinator was funded by the Urban Programme until March 1994. The remainder of the staff include a Town Centre Manager each for Woolwich and Greenwich, a Business Forum Adviser and specialists on such topics as training and education, housing and crime prevention. The Community Forum Manager had been seconded from the Benefits Agency and the Property Adviser from the Woolwich Building Society. Other members of staff are based in Greenwich Council departments such as Planning and Press & Publicity, but work part time for GWDP. Three others provide secretarial, research and administrative services.

The team's approach is to work through the existing partners as far as possible in order to implement the GWDP strategy. There is no separate budget over and above those of the individual partners.

The business forum

Soon after the launch of the strategy, Coopers & Lybrand asked if they could assist by working with and advising the local business community. It was agreed that Janet Mackinnon should be seconded to the Partnership to liaise with local businesses in order to form a business forum and agree a clear set of objectives. From her initial discussion with local companies, she found that the business community was fragmented, rarely communicated with each other and were concerned about the complexities of getting planning permission and the number and variety of government agencies concerned with funding, training and transportation. Particular concerns about the area were the problems of local traffic management, especially in town centres, and poor environmental quality. She saw her role as getting the commitment of as many local businesses as possible to the objectives of the Partnership and devising a set of promotional activities and specific projects. The forum was launched in June 1992 and a series of meetings were held with local businesses to explain the strategy and to encourage them to participate. By October 1992, 120 businesses were affiliated and several projects were being drawn up under the guidance of the business forum steering group. This steering group was chaired by a representative of British Gas and it included senior executives of six companies with a local presence, four members of GWDP staff, and Greenwich's Deputy Director of Planning.

In addition, seven task forces were set up to cover River Thames development, local economic development agency co-ordination, marketing and inward investment, transport, cultural industries, ethnic minority businesses, and industrial property.

The community forum

From the early days of preparing the strategy, there had been many active tenants, residents and environmental groups in the Waterfront area, and some, such as the Greenwich Environment Forum, claimed some credit for bring the needs of the area to the council's attention.

The Docklands Consultative Committee was heavily involved in liaising with at least 95 local groups that have since affiliated with the community forum. It will elect five representatives to the Partnership board. From January 1993, a newsletter has been circulated to all groups to keep them in touch with the implementation of the strategy.

The forum hoped to gain access to £40 000 of Urban Programme funding for community projects for 1993–4, but this was not approved because of the DOE's decision to cut UP funds severely. A questionnaire was circulated to all groups to find out their main concerns and to identify possible environmental improvements needed in the area. Subgroups have been established to focus on issues such as housing, transport and the river, and a formal constitution has been adopted for the forum.

Local agencies

So far, two town-centre management groups have been set up for Greenwich and Woolwich. Each is affiliated to and has a representative on the Partnership board. Each area has a town centre manager.

Greenwich Town Centre Management Agency

Greenwich town centre has several important cultural assets and a wide range of shops and other commercial uses, such as a market, but also serious environmental problems. The Royal Naval College, the National Maritime Museum, the Observatory, the market, St Alfege's church and the Cutty Sark draw over 2 million visitors a year. The planned extension of the Docklands Light Railway from the Isle of Dogs to Greenwich and Lewisham, together with an upgraded service on the South London line, will greatly improve access. Greenwich also has substantial development opportunities such as the Dreadnought Seamen's Hospital, the Devonport Nurses' Home and a large site in Stockwell Street.

Yet the town centre also has substantial problems. It is choked by through-traffic, causing difficulties for residents and visitors. There is a need to broaden the appeal for tourists and spread the load away from the narrow area around the Cutty Sark. Historic buildings are in a state of neglect, public spaces need enhancement and the facilities for residents are poor.

The agency was formed in January 1992 in response to pressures to initiate action in the town centre along the lines of the strategy. The Town Centre Manager, Todd Strehlow was appointed after funds were obtained through contributions from 18 local organizations and businesses. The Civic Trust Regeneration Unit was also commissioned to prepare an action plan. This was published in February 1993 and it set out a detailed set of recommendations for the conservation and improvement of all aspects of the town centre.

The following organizations are represented on the steering group:

- Greenwich Society
- Greenwich Forum
- Haddo Tenants Group
- Ashburnham Tenants Group
- Meridan Tenants Group
- Greenwich Hospitals estates
- Spread Eagle Antiques/Restaurant/Greenwich Theatre
- Alexander Sedgeley
- National Maritime Museum
- Port of London Authority
- English Heritage
- L. B. Greenwich officers and members

The agency began by setting up the following projects:

- *Town centre action plan*   The Civic Trust has prepared an action plan that was officially launched in March 1992.
- *English Heritage Conservation Strategy*   English Heritage has prepared a detailed conservation strategy for the area (English Heritage 1993). This has subsequently become the first pilot for a Conservation Area Partnership scheme, on which English Heritage issued a consultative paper in May 1993. The proposal is that English Heritage, the local authority and other local interests would commit resources in a detailed action plan, setting out targets for the improvement of an agreed conservation area. In March 1994 it was announced that Greenwich town centre will receive £180 000 from English Heritage, to be matched by £100 000 from the council in 1994–5.
- *King William Walk*   Major environmental improvements are proposed in order to link the main pedestrian route from the Cutty Sark to Greenwich Park. An application has been made to English Heritage for additional resources to use traditional materials and specially designed street furniture. English Heritage agreed to contribute an additional £50 000, and the National Maritime Museum and Greenwich Hospital estates are also making contributions.
- *Urban Partnership Fund bid*   A bid for £500 000 has been made by Greenwich to the DOE for this funding, which replaces the Urban Programme. If successful, part of this sum would have gone towards new paving, street furniture and improvements to the market canopy. In February 1993 Greenwich was notified that it had been awarded only £125 000

towards improvements to the Woolwich Industrial estate and £170 000
towards setting up the Trinity Employment Centre. In the event, some
other parts of the bid, such as improvements to the Greenwich market, pro-
ceeded with private funding.

- *Signage* The Business Forum Signage subgroup has continued to meet
regarding signage throughout the town centre, focusing especially on
informational, interpretive and directional signs for visitors.
- *Deptford Town Trail* The Agency has worked closely with Deptford City
Challenge in creating a theme trail connecting Greenwich and Deptford.
The trail will include informational plaques on notable buildings and an
associated map and guidance leaflet.
- *Cutty Sark Gardens study* Consultants have been appointed by Greenwich and the English Tourist Board to undertake a study of Cutty Sark Gar-
dens. A bid has also been submitted for about £1 million to the EU LIFE
programme for funding for a sustainable tourism and transport project.
- *Christmas Festival* Discussions were held with the Greenwich Traders
Association about organizing a Christmas Festival in 1993.
- *Metropolitan Police liaison* Contact has been made with the police to discuss ways of meeting partnership objectives by carrying out a crime audit
and crime prevention programme.
- *Newsletter* A regular newsletter is to be distributed primarily to local
shops.
- *Devonport Nurses Home and Dreadnought Seamen's
Hospital* Discussions continue with Greenwich Hospital estates regarding marketing these vacant buildings. In November 1993, planning applications were submitted by the University of Greenwich to use the
Devonport to house the Faculty of Health, and Dreadnought as an administrative centre for the university.
- *Greenwich Reach Developments* Contact has been made with the developer to encourage them to revise plans to develop the site.
- *Heavy Goods Lorry Screen* Possibilities have been explored for funding
a feasibility study for an experimental screen to keep lorries out of the town
centre. Consultants have been briefed and the necessary approvals are
being sought.
- *Other priorities* These include launching a shopfront grant scheme and
an award for the best shopfront; to examine the feasibility of a new primary
healthcare facility to serve the Haddo and Meridan estates; to investigate
and agree designs for new signage and street furniture; to promote a sub-
scriptions and membership campaign; to determine other priorities from the
action plan; and to develop contacts with key interests in the town centre.

The Woolwich Town Centre Agency

Woolwich is a relatively old town centre that has seen little or no new retail investment since the days when the Royal Arsenal employed large numbers of people. The town centre is dominated by the headquarters of the Woolwich Building Society and, although the London Borough of Greenwich has closed the main shopping street to traffic and made improvements to the main square, there is considerable evidence of recession and decline. Shopkeepers and residents complain of poor signposting and of difficulties of access by bus and car. A market operates on a paved area close to the entrance to the Arsenal. In 1993 it was announced that the Royal Artillery Museum would occupy one of the vacant buildings in the Royal Arsenal. The remainder of the 31 ha Ministry of Defence site is the subject of a feasibility study commissioned by English Partnerships, because of its important location in the Thames Gateway.

The second local agency set up under the umbrella of the Partnership is the Woolwich Town Centre Agency. This was launched in February 1993 and was chaired by the District Manager of the Woolwich Building Society. The steering group was made up of representatives from national and local retailers, the University of Greenwich, the Asian Chamber of Commerce, Greenwich Borough Council and the Metropolitan Police.

In preparation for Greenwich's bid for the second round of City Challenge funding, the Town Centre Manager was seconded in April 1992 for two years from his previous post as manager of the Woolwich branch of W. H. Smith. He works from an office in council property in Woolwich, although he is part of the Partnership team. He sees his role as promoting a series of projects to improve the environment, develop vacant and underused sites, and to attract new retail and related investment by working with local landowners, retailers and the community.

Apart from assisting in setting up the Agency, the Town Centre Manager has worked on several projects to improve the appearance of the area, to improve signage and create a heritage trail, to encourage the police to carry out a crime audit and to discuss traffic management improvements and car parking with the Borough Engineer. Already at least five local companies have agreed to sponsor particular projects in the area.

The consultants URBED have been commissioned by the DOE to carry out a study of how management might improve three town centres, of which Woolwich is one. It is likely that some of the recommendations can be applied locally.

In 1993 a successful bid was submitted for EU funding under the KONVER programme, designed to encourage economic diversification in areas affected by the closure of defence industries. A sum of £552 000 was awarded to assist with environmental improvements, restoration of listed buildings, business advice and training in connection with the conversion of the Royal Arsenal site to alternative uses. An additional £810 000 was committed in matched funding (GWDP 1993).

Woolwich and Plumstead City Challenge bid

When the second round of City Challenge was announced by the DoE in April 1992, Greenwich realized the potential of achieving an additional source of funding for a deprived area of the borough already identified as part of the Waterfront strategy area. In particular, the imminent loss of the final 1300 jobs and the release of the 31 ha Royal Arsenal site provided a unique opportunity to reverse decades of decline in Woolwich. In 1991 male unemployment reached 34 per cent in the City Challenge area and 60 per cent in Arsenal ward.

By using the £37.5 million City Challenge funding to lever an additional £232 million, it was hoped to create 1450 jobs and construct 700 new homes for 2000 people. £5 million would be used to renovate the many listed buildings on the Royal Arsenal site for use as a mixed heritage and retail centre, and additional objectives would be the reversal of the decline of the town centres, an improved manufacturing and business economy, new housing to diversify tenure and new facilities for the University of Greenwich. A request was also made that the area should benefit from an Inner City Task Force to complement City Challenge funding by providing training programmes, funds for managed workspace, and by providing advice and support to small and medium-size enterprises.

The proposed implementation agency would have been a company limited by guarantee with the following representatives:
- 4 from the private sector
- 4 from the local community
- 3 from LB Greenwich
- 1 from the Training and Enterprise Council
- 1 from the University of Greenwich
- 1 from the metropolitan police
- 1 from the Greenwich Housing Association Group
- 1 from the public sector
- the Task Force director as an observer.

The staff of eleven was to include the town centre manager who, it had already been agreed, would be seconded for two years from W. H. Smith.

In July 1992 Greenwich was informed that its bid was not among the 20 successful submissions. However, work will continue to implement the strategy within the wider context of the Waterfront strategy, and in 1995 this area was the subject of a successful bid for SRB funding..

The Partnership: implementation programme for 1993–4

In March 1993 the Partnership board discussed its implementation programme for 1993–4. It was stated that in the two-year period from the publication of the Waterfront Strategy much had been done to promote the Waterfront as an area with unique identity and with co-ordinating plans for regeneration. In terms of development, there had been advances of both a strategic and a local nature that could provide a springboard for development in the future. Among the strategic developments claimed were:

- granting of planning permission for major developments at the Greenwich Peninsula
- government approval for the extension to the Jubilee line
- progression of developments at Deptford Creek
- progress of the extension of the Docklands Light Railway
- upgrading of rail services on the North Kent line and the rebuilding of Woolwich Arsenal station
- establishment of Town Centre Manager posts in Greenwich and Woolwich.
- development of programmes for improved training opportunities
- retention and planned development of the University of Greenwich.

However, some substantial problems remained: the attraction of inward investment at a time of recession, contaminated land, high levels of unemployment and crime, and the quality of local housing and primary healthcare are a source of dissatisfaction. In approaching these issues it was felt necessary to refocus the Partnership board's role:

- to oversee the programme of economic, environmental and social regeneration of the Greenwich Waterfront area
- to maintain and develop the Partnership of government and local authority agencies, business and community interests
- to secure resources for the programme
- to set objectives within which task force groups, local agencies and staff can operate.

It was proposed that the Partnership should pursue these objectives through ten programme areas: economic development, community development, education and training, culture and recreation, environment and design, transport infrastructure, housing, health, crime prevention, and anti-poverty measures.

In pursuing of these objectives the board also agreed a set of operational principles:

- balancing the needs of the whole Waterfront area and the needs of specific communities
- actively promoting the notion of partnership between government, local government, business and community groups
- empowering groups to determine their own priorities within the strategic framework
- involving government as fully as possible by working with its urban initiatives such as English Partnerships, Capital Partnership, Derelict Land Grant, and City Grant
- promoting the identity of the Waterfront area and marketing it to achieve increased inward investment
- developing principles of equality of opportunity for all residents.

Two relatively discrete sites in the Waterfront area are the Greenwich Peninsula owned by British Gas and the former Greater London Council development, now called Thamesmead Town.

The Port Greenwich development site

Port Greenwich Ltd is the company formed by British Gas to develop the 121 ha site on the Greenwich Peninsula. It was originally used by British Gas for the manufacture and distribution of town gas, but, with the change to natural gas, only part of the site is required for distribution. The site is in a commanding position in relation to the river and is directly opposite Canary Wharf in London Docklands. Part of the site is reserved for a third crossing to expand the capacity of the Blackwall Tunnel. An essential element of the redevelopment proposals is that an Underground station will be located in the centre of the site as part of the extension of the Jubilee line to Canary Wharf and Stratford.

In the period before publication of the Waterfront Strategy, a planning brief had been prepared and this gave rise to an outline planning application in October 1990, which was subject to extensive consultation. The outcome of this was that Greenwich requested more open space in return for an increase of 1 million sq. ft (93 000 m^2) of offices. The Jubilee line was also realigned to include a station on the peninsula and, as a result, it was decided to prepare a master plan in order to develop the site in phases. British Gas had originally proposed to set up a joint venture company with British Urban Development (BUD) in order to access government grants, but when BUD hit difficulties, British Gas decided to go ahead alone.

For the master plan the site was divided into two sections. The southern part was designed by Koetter, Kim and Associates International Ltd and the northern section by Foster Associates.

The outcome was a master plan that sets out proposals for the development on the east side of the existing A102(M) leading to the Blackwall Tunnel. The northern part of the site would be allocated to a riverside walk and a large high-density commercial development based on a new Jubilee line station and car parking with 500 spaces. Adjoining this would be a mainly residential and mixed-use area. In the southern part of the site there would be a central business district of residential, retail, educational, and sports and leisure facilities integrated with an area of open space of about 10 ha.

In December 1991 a revised outline planning application was submitted to Greenwich for the following uses:

- Residential development of up to 5400 units, ranging from one-bed units to family accommodation. The gross area of residential development extends to approximately 54 ha gross and includes accommodation sited within the mixed-use area and within the central activities zone and central business district.

135

- employment development comprising retail, office and industrial uses extend to approximately 21 ha gross, including such activities located within the mixed-use areas, central activities zone and CBD.
- a mixed-use development area comprising employment, residential, retail and leisure on 1.2 ha gross.
- a central activities zone comprising principally retail, business, residential and community facilities on 7 ha gross. This area will include a community centre, library, health centre, multi-screen cinema, hotel and retail super-market of up to 45 000 sq. ft (4200 m^2) gross.
- a transport interchange comprising a bus station, taxi ranks and private vehicle drop-off on 1 ha is located adjacent to Ordnance Crescent.
- a central business district to include high-density residential development (up to 60 habitable rooms per hectare), local shopping facilities and office floorspace of up to 700 000 sq. ft (65 000 m^2) and a 500 space car park associated with the Jubilee line station on 1 ha.
- a primary school and day nursery on a site of 1.2 ha gross, of which part will be in the form of a shared school/public open space extending to .4 ha.
- public open space will extend to 17 ha net, including the riverside walk but excluding the shared-use facility adjacent to the school site.
- miscellaneous uses, including a sailing club and utilities plant areas, will be sited as shown on the land-use master plan.
- a movement network comprising highways and footpath/cycle ways. (Port Greenwich Ltd 1992)

In October 1992 Greenwich Council resolved to grant outline permission sub-ject to 27 conditions, the signing of a Section 106 agreement and the company's making a contribution towards the construction of the Jubilee line extension. In addition, the Department of Transport imposed an Article 14 Direction, requir-ing land to be made available at the northern end of the site for increasing the capacity of the Blackwall Tunnel crossing. Discussions are continuing about whether a new access road to the A102(M) can be created from the northern end of the site. A series of options for the third bridge crossing were published by the Department of Transport for consultation in May 1993. However, little development is likely to take place until the Department of Transport finalizes the route and the funding of the Jubilee line extension. A decision was expected in the summer of 1993 and British Gas was optimistic about the outcome after the European Investment Bank agreed in April to find the first payment of £98 million. Government approval for the Jubilee line was finally given in November 1993, but it was not until July 1994 that agreement was reached between the Department of Transport and British Gas on the latter's contribution towards a new station on the site. The London Borough of Greenwich welcomed the announcement, not least because it makes the selection of the site for a millen-nium festival more likely.

In the meantime, the site is heavily polluted and Derelict Land Grant is being sought to enable the development to proceed. Initial site investigations are already under way, with a grant of £285 000 from the DOE in preparation for a DLG application. It is estimated that up to £60 million will need to be spent on infrastructure, excluding contributions to the Jubilee line.

The intention is that 25 per cent of the site will be allocated for social housing. Negotiations have been carried out with a consortium of eight local housing associations about how this target might be achieved. The Section 106 agreement specifies that 4 ha should be given free to one or more housing associations, with additional land being sold at market value. British Gas favours selling all the land for social housing at below market value in order to benefit their cashflow.

British Gas is already talking to housing developers, but takes the view that, in current circumstances, the site is not commercially viable. It may well postpone development until the property market improves or it can negotiate additional subsidy from public sources. The Department of Transport has stipulated that up to 200 houses can be built before additional infrastructural works are carried out to connect the site to the A102(M).

Major development is thus unlikely to begin until the route, funding and stations on the Jubilee line have finally been agreed. The trigger will be a first payment by British Gas of about £25 million towards the line, at which point the Section 106 can be signed subject to outline planning permission being given. The mix of uses and phasing will depend very much on market conditions over the next 10–15 years.

Thamesmead Town Ltd

Thamesmead lies at the eastern end of the Waterfront area and has a population of about 22 000. The land, which was then attached to the Royal Arsenal, was acquired by the Greater London Council (GLC) in 1964 and was developed from 1967 as a self-contained new town within Greater London. About two thirds of the town lies in the London Borough of Bexley; one third is in Greenwich. In 1986 a ballot was held among residents as to whether the town's assets should transfer to the London Borough of Greenwich or whether it should become a self-managing company. The outcome was a vote in favour of transfer to a new company in July 1987, when it became solely responsible for its management and development. The board of directors is made up of nine locally elected residents, who also appoint three executive directors, together with an independently appointed chair. In March 1992, the company employed 253 staff.

Thamesmead has continued with the GLC's development programme, but has also diversified the tenure by involving housing associations and private developers. A £100 million expansion of the town centre was refused outline permission by Greenwich in 1990 and was rejected at appeal in November 1991 on the grounds that it would adversely impact on Woolwich town centre, which had been identified by the GLC as a strategic centre. Approximately 242 ha remain to be developed, including 105 ha for housing and community uses, 40 ha for industry and 76 ha for open space and recreation.

In the early years, relationships with Greenwich were difficult, particularly after the rejection at appeal of the new town centre. A reappraisal took place with the appointment of a new Head of Development and it was decided to work more closely with the local authority. This coincided with the launch of the Waterfront Strategy and it provided an opportunity to integrate Thamesmead in the development of the wider area. Key officers now play a leading role on the interim advisory board and as members of the business forum taskforces.

Thamesmead is particularly keen to contribute to the development of the Royal Arsenal site, just to the west of its border, and is in detailed discussions with Hillier Parker, agents for the Ministry of Defence and the Crown Commissioners. Thamesmead has a large site ready for development adjoining the Royal Arsenal, which could help spread some of the commercial benefit into Thamesmead and reduce its relative isolation. Officers have also contributed to the submission of a bid for a Millennium project, which could involve some of the vacant land in the town.

Thamesmead has also made a submission to English Partnerships, arguing that it is in a position to contribute towards the development strategy for the Thames Gateway.

Conclusions

The Greenwich Waterfront Development Partnership is an example of a local authority mobilizing and collaborating with a wide variety of partners in order to initiate the regeneration of an area. This is a different approach from that of Birmingham Heartlands Ltd, in that the partnership was conceived as a means of giving residents' organizations and the private sector, together with the London Borough, equal representation and influence in decision-making. By carrying out extensive public consultation, and in commissioning research into local needs, the borough has always been aware of the need to carry local opinion with it. Although criticisms have been expressed by, for example, the private sector and the DOE, about the complexity of the organizational framework, and the close relationship with Greenwich Council, local residents' organizations feel involved and they consider that they can influence the way the partnership develops.

Like Birmingham Heartlands, the GWDP has divided the area into separate subareas. Special agencies have been set up to promote the regeneration of the two town centres, and a bid for City Challenge was unsuccessfully submitted for the Woolwich area, including the Royal Arsenal site. The Greenwich Peninsula, owned by British Gas, has been approached as a relatively self-contained area on which development may proceed once the complicated infrastructure arrangements are resolved. Likewise, Thamesmead is part of the wider Waterfront area, but is largely the responsibility of Thamesmead Town Ltd. In early 1995 the future of the largely vacant Deptford Creek area and the Royal Arsenal was still unresolved, but the intention was to incorporate them into the wider pattern of development, from which jobs, housing, leisure opportunities and community facilities should arise.

Given that GWDP has no additional resources to fund its regeneration programme, it is forced to rely on the borough, its partners and local agencies such as the TEC. It has therefore adopted a promotional strategy by which opportunities are sought from central government. The Partnership has lobbied for infrastructural improvements such as the extensions to the Dockland Light Railway and the Jubilee line, both of which would open up important development opportunities. Unsuccessful bids have been made for City Challenge and EU Objective 2 status, but additional funding has been obtained from the Urban Programme, Assisted Area status and the EU KONVER initiative. English Heritage was persuaded to carry out a detailed conservation study of Greenwich town centre (English Heritage 1993) and then to adopt it as one of the first Conservation Partnership Area Schemes. The South London TEC has been supportive in funding an Adult Guidance and Assessment Centre in Woolwich and in assisting with marketing. Bids for Derelict Land Grant for the British Gas site and funding for a major project from the Millennium Fund had still to be determined in January 1995.

At this stage it is impossible to assess the net additional benefits arising from the work of the Partnership. Because it lacks resources, its strategy has necessarily been a promotional one, as well as about improving the delivery of the council's own services. This has tended to lead to an emphasis on encouraging and co-ordinating development in the hope that some of the benefits can be redistributed to the most deprived sections of the community. It is difficult to identify any purely redistributive strategies within the overall programme, beyond those sponsored by supporting agencies such as the TEC. As the area is strategically located as a gateway to the Thames Gateway, significant benefits may arise in the future from the involvement of English Partnerships and through the SRB.

The GWDP might best be described as a coalition of local interests where the Partnership aims to promote and attract development, to co-ordinate and integrate it into the existing physical and social structure in order to maximize local benefits, by capturing public capital and revenue funds from central government and thereby also attracting inward investors. The speed at which this can be done is necessarily dependent on the limited capacity of the local authority to assist with land assembly, capital finance, improved service delivery and promotional support. However, this capacity has been significantly increased through the ability to attract secondees to the agency. The extent to which those involved in the community and business forums remain committed and perceive real benefits arising, will perhaps be the ultimate test of the Partnership.

The location of the Waterfront is of growing strategic importance, in that it offers much vacant land close to several strategic initiatives: Docklands, the Thames Gateway, and some major public sector transportation routes, not least the fast rail link to the Channel Tunnel. If the Partnership can ensure that a series of interconnecting and integrated developments take place where real benefits arise for local residents, much will have been achieved. At this stage, until some of the major decisions are made about infrastructural development in the area by government departments largely beyond the influence of the Partnership, little substantial progress is likely to be made.

CHAPTER 7

The Newcastle Initiative

Introduction

The Newcastle Initiative (TNI) in Newcastle upon Tyne was the first Business Leadership Team set up by the Confederation of British Industry's (CBI) Task Force on Business and Urban Regeneration (CBI 1988). The Task Force was set up at the CBI's 1987 Conference; it consisted of 15 prominent business leaders and was chaired by Tom Frost, Group Chief Executive of the National Westminster Bank, working with consultants from McKinsey and Associates and Charles Barker plc. The objective of the Task Force was to:

identify what further steps business should be taking to assist in the process of urban regeneration. (CBI 1988: 7)

The rationale behind the formation of this Task Force was that:

Business has a massive stake in the nation's cities. Employees and customers live in them; many companies operate from city locations, and their balance sheets reflect the cost and value of the assets involved; the retail, banking, insurance, tourist, leisure, manufacturing and construction industries will all be affected by the economic vitality and social health of the communities concerned. (CBI 1988: 7)

The outcome of the Task Force's work was the report Initiatives Beyond Charity published in September 1988, which came to four main conclusions about the role of business in urban regeneration. First, the Task Force felt that it was the local business community that should provide leadership for regeneration, with high-quality leadership being the key to building confidence in an area. Confidence, according to the Task Force, determines prosperity.

The second conclusion of the Task Force was that urban decay is too large a problem to be tackled by business on a charitable basis alone. Action is needed that is beyond the scope of charitable donations and the public sector by itself. "The resources needed to turn decline into growth in our major cities will therefore have to spring from sound economic development, driven by private investment decisions taken on the basis of the commercial returns available, not from a sense of charity" (CBI 1988: 10). Thirdly, the CBI report maintains that urban regeneration, regardless of the particular situation, can follow a common process. This process should aim to create prominent "flagship projects" in order to generate "conspicuous success", which should then be exploited to the full to create a self-sustaining momentum for regeneration. While following this process, the key issues of physical development, creation of employment opportunities, community involvement, and working in partnership should form the themes of the regeneration programme. Finally, the CBI's Task Force felt that business should commit itself to leading the way forward for regeneration in certain major cities, and therefore act as a catalyst for change at a national level. Accordingly, Newcastle was chosen as the pilot project for the Task Force. TNI was the first business leadership team designed to be a partnership between local business leaders, the local authority, central government and other public sector and voluntary organizations. Business Leadership Teams were concerned from the outset with the process of regeneration, focusing heavily on the idea of creating a vision, adopting flagship projects through which to inspire confidence, and by exploiting early successes to maintain momentum. In December of 1988 the Business in Cities forum was created by the CBI, Business in the Community and the Phoenix Initiative as "the central support for stimulating local leadership of business initiatives" (Business in the Community 1990), and it was this new forum that influenced the development of TNI. The CBI has subsequently launched business leadership teams around the country, based on the TNI pilot project, although all have subsequently evolved in different ways. The CBI now takes the view that the principle of private sector involvement in urban regeneration through partnership organizations has been fully accepted and that other organizations, such as Business in the Community, are now better placed to act as lead agency in the field.

The formation of TNI

It is uncertain why Newcastle was chosen as the location of the first business leadership team. It may have been because the city is relatively compact, with a well defined business community, so that the key players within the city already knew each other. It may also have been that Professor John Goddard of the University of Newcastle, and John Hall of Cameron Hall Developments Ltd, were both from Newcastle and were members of the CBI Task Force. However, Newcastle also displayed the characteristics associated with many of the UK's older industrial towns and cities. It suffers from high levels of unemployment, much vacant and derelict land, underused local resources, but had several urban regeneration initiatives under way. Newcastle also had a corporate elite, drawn from both the public and private sectors, who were committed to promoting the city as a manufacturing and commercial centre for the North East. In fact, many of the city's business leaders were already involved in other initiatives in the city.

As Shaw (1993: 252) notes:

> There are certainly important changes in the contemporary approach to urban regeneration in the North East, such as the expansion in the formal role of business interests within inter-organizational coalitions, and the shift towards an acceptance of post-industrial forms of economic development. However, such changes also need to be considered alongside the fact that, in areas such as the North East, economic decline has long generated alliances between local politicians, capital and labour, in defence of the local economy . . . such alliances have traditionally been based on tripartite representation, operating within non-elected agencies, and have long advocated some of the strategies now associated with local growth strategies or with what Harvey has referred to as "urban entrepreneurialism" (Harvey 1989).

Shaw goes on to discuss the close interweaving of membership on the various boards of partnership organizations, although, as he points out in relation to TNI, the role of the local authority remains central. Table 7.1 identifies the main economic development organizations in Tyne & Wear (based on Shaw 1993: 253).

Table 7.1   Unelected economic development organizations in Tyne & Wear.

Type	Examples
Urban development	Tyne & Wear Development Corporation
City Challenge	West End Partnership
	North Newcastle
Training & Enterprise Councils	Wearside tec
	Tyneside tec
Business leadership teams	The Newcastle Initiative
	The Wearside Opportunity
Regional development agency	The Northern Development Company
Local enterprise agency	Entrust
Local economic development company	Tyne & Wear Economic Development Company
Port authority	Port of Tyne Authority

The Task Force's core team began work in January 1988, bringing together senior business leaders in Newcastle, along the lines of the CBI's recommendations. The core team began by conducting background research on Newcastle and the initiatives that were already in operation, and from there went on to identify the key leaders in the city, from both the public and private sectors. Through consultation with both sectors and by holding presentations and producing supporting literature, the core team helped identify and establish a local leadership team that could provide direction and establish priorities for the initiative.

Once the leadership team began to take shape, the process of identifying potential flagship projects began. During this time new members were recruited and in the latter stages a Chair was selected. The core team went about the process of "securing leadership commitment" through a series of dinners and private discussions, "establishing change agents" involved identifying the ten most important private sector players, together with those in the public sector from the City Council and local development agencies, and "building momentum rapidly", which meant setting up project task forces to pursue the major projects identified earlier in the process.

The board was initially composed of ten private sector representatives and four officers from the public sector. Serving the board was an executive office staffed by a Chief Executive seconded from British Telecom, and an assistant executive seconded from Newcastle City Council. Five flagship projects were selected: the Theatre Village and Chinatown, Grey Street Renaissance, Japanese Links, business action in the community, and publicity.

After the core team had been working on the initiative for five months, the Newcastle Initiative was launched on 14 June 1988. The cost of setting up the initiative was estimated by the CBI as being approximately £110 000. This includes actual expenditure and contributions in kind made by companies.

Organization

Early on it was decided that the TNI board would be composed of a majority of private sector representatives. Apart from the ten private sector members, the chief executives of Newcastle City Council, the Tyne & Wear UDC and the Northern Development Company were invited to attend board meetings, but would not have voting rights. The Chair would be selected from the business community. It was also decided that the board would not have an executive capacity, but "will seek to initiate concerted action through the various organizations and companies represented, and other companies and agencies within the Newcastle area" (CBI 1988). The executive office was to be staffed by a Chief Executive and an Assistant Executive, who should hold the posts for no more than two years. The first Chief Executive, Bill Hay, was seconded from British Telecom and was replaced by Danny Sharpe in April 1991, who in turn was seconded from the DTI Regional Office. John Collier, a chartered accountant from Price Waterhouse, took the post at the end of 1992 and worked three days a week for TNI. There were two full-time Assistant Chief Executives; one is a secondee from Barclays Bank, the other came from the Benefits Agency.

Operating below the TNI board are several task forces for the flagship projects. These task forces were each formed by the member of the TNI board who had been appointed its "champion", and was given the responsibility of putting the team together. The task forces are seen as the primary agent for implementing the TNI strategy. Finance is raised from the private sector on a commercial basis, linked with public sector pump-priming where appropriate. It is the role of the board to determine overall strategy, motivate and encourage the task forces and to maintain an effective network between senior managers in the leading companies and local public sector agencies. Board members are drawn from some of the major industrial and property companies in the North East, financial institutions, universities, development agencies, government departments and the local newspaper (Table 7.2).

Table 7.2   TNI board members at March 1994.

Mr A. Pender (Chair)	Chief Executive, English Estates
Mr A Balls	Chief Executive, Tyne & Wear Development Corporation
Prof. L. Barden	Vice-Chancellor, University of Northumbria at Newcastle
Mr G. Black	Director, Chestertons
Dr J. Bridge	Chief Executive, Northern Development Company
Ms A. Chant	Chief Executive, Contributions Agency
Mr M. Clasper	Managing Director, Proctor & Gamble Ltd
Mr G. Cook	Chief Executive, Newcastle City Council
Ms P. Denham	Senior Regional Director, DTI
Prof. J. Goddard	CURDS, Newcastle University
Mrs O. Grant	Chief Executive, Tyneside tec
Sir J. Hall	Cameron Hall Developments Ltd
Mr A. Hill	Managing Director, Newcastle Chronicle and Journal
Mr A. Hogg	Regional Director, Barclays Bank
Mr R. Maudslay	Managing Director, Rolls–Royce Industrial Power Group
Mr D. Midgley	Group Managing Director, Newcastle Building Society
Mr D. Morris	Chairman, Northern Electric
Mr J. Ward	Northumbrian Water
Mr J. Wright	Vice-Chancellor, Newcastle University

Funding

The budget of TNI is approximately £200 000 per year, with about £120 000 of this being received in kind from the private sector. In 1992 the £120 000 received in kind included the salary for the Chief Executive seconded from DTI, office accommodation within the Tyne Brewery building, all telecommunications from British Telecom, a car for the use of the Chief Executive from Northern Rock Building Society, twelve return flights to London per year for the Chief Executive, salaries for the Assistant Chief Executives, and a Secretary. Newcastle City Council is not expected to contribute any funding towards the day-to-day running of TNI.

In addition, TNI raises money for specific projects. For example, TNI was involved in the production of a promotional video to attract inward investment to Newcastle upon Tyne, for which it raised £20 000 by offering those who contributed marketing opportunities within the video. Another example is the £20 000 raised for TNI's environmental initiative.

Figure 7.1 illustrates TNI's organizational structure.

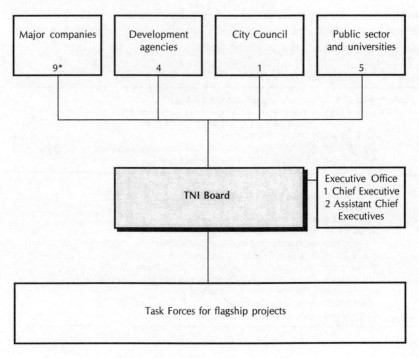

Figure 7.1 Organizational structure of TNI (* seats on the board).

Projects

The five flagship projects adopted initially by TNI were: the Grey Street Renaissance, Theatre Village and Chinatown, Business Action in the Community, Japanese Links, and publicity. However, as the initiative progressed, some of the projects were modified or dropped altogether, and some new projects have been introduced. In particular, TNI reassessed its activities on the appointment of John Collier as Chief Executive in December 1992, who felt that the Initiative had lost some of its original focus. A lengthy consultation process in early 1993 (carried out through a series of business dinners) produced ideas for taking the Initiative forward with a revised list of five projects: the Grainger Town Initiative, continuing involvement in Cruddas Park and support for Newcastle's two City Challenge initiatives, the arts and urban regeneration, the environment, and higher education.

The Grey Street Renaissance

The Grey Street Renaissance project is centred around Grey Street in the town centre, but also includes the adjacent streets and extends from the city centre down to the Quayside (Fig. 7.2). The whole area of the project lies within the Central Conservation Area of the city and contains many listed buildings. Grey Street itself has been described as one of the finest early nineteenth-century architectural set-pieces in England. It suffered from the 1960s speculative office construction boom in Newcastle, which attracted companies away from the centre and left many properties on Grey Street underused and neglected. The Quayside area was the first commercial centre of the city until the mid-nineteenth century, when a fire destroyed many of the buildings that were subsequently replaced by Victorian office blocks.

Despite the decay suffered by the Grey Street area from the 1960s onwards, it was still a prestigious address for Newcastle's business sector, and restoration and cleaning work began with the City Council using Urban Programme funding. However, progress was slow and, with the creation of TNI, a special taskforce based on partnership between sectors took over the project. The Grey Street Renaissance task force consists of representatives from the council, the Tyne & Wear Development Corporation, English Heritage, and the DoE, with all of these partners having allocated financial resources for the project. The task force acted as a catalyst, and derived its strength from the ability of the private sector to persuade others to contribute. Although the council and the UDC can resort to compulsory purchase powers, much of the improvement work was carried out through partnership and persuasion. The task force was primarily concerned with the promotion and marketing of the development opportunities within Grey Street and is not directly involved in the implementation of individual restoration or redevelopment schemes. This is the role of property owners, using discretionary grants such as City Grant, the Urban Programme, Conservation Grants and English Tourist Board grants.

In the past the fact that nearly all the buildings fronting onto Grey Street and Dean Street are listed was seen as a constraint to development. More recently, with the revival of the office market in the late 1980s and the rise in demand for high-quality office space in particular, this is seen as a positive opportunity. By the end of 1992 there was only one building in Grey Street that was still in need of restoration and cleaning, and it was therefore decided to enlarge the target area to include a larger part of the historic urban core. This was to become the Grainger Town Initiative (Fig. 7.2).

The Grainger Town Initiative

The physical appearance of Newcastle city centre has long been a concern of TNI, particularly the state of the buildings on the approach into the centre from the

147

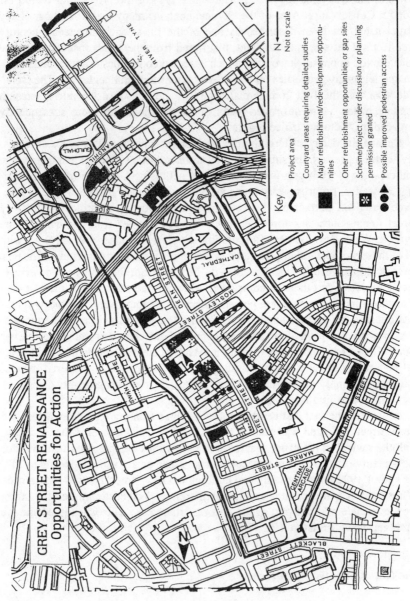

Figure 7.2 The Grey Street Renaissance area in the centre of Newcastle upon Tyne.

railway station. One of the main problems perceived as contributing to the run-down nature of some of the central buildings is the high proportion of vacant floorspace above shops, together with the fact that many of these buildings are listed and therefore could add substantially to the character of the city if brought back into use. It is this issue that the Grainger Town Initiative, launched in early 1993, is designed to tackle. In doing so, TNI works closely with an officer in the planning department, who is responsible for co-ordinating the regeneration strategy. The aim is to bring historic buildings back into beneficial use, to promote better use of upper floors, to improve the appearance of the streets around the central shopping area, and thus to attract more investment into the city centre. TNI is also investigating the possibility of using vacant upper floors for student accommodation. In March 1994, English Heritage announced that £325 000 was to be made available to Grainger Town under its Conservation Area Partnership Initiative, to be matched by a similar sum from the city council.

Business action in the community

TNI has adopted the Cruddas Park Community Trust as its Business Action in the Community project. The Trust "aims to improve the Cruddas Park and Loadman Street areas of Newcastle upon Tyne, both socially and economically, in order to make it a place in which people want to live through forging a partnership between tenants, public agencies and private industry" (Cruddas Park Community Trust 1992).

Cruddas Park and Loadman Street are two inner-city housing estates in the West End of the city constructed in the 1970s. They comprise 11 multi-storey blocks of flats and three blocks of low-rise high-density housing, containing around 1000 households in total. On a wide range of measures of deprivation, including housing conditions, unemployment, environmental quality, educational achievement and access to facilities, the wider area was identified as a major concentration of urban deprivation and was thus the subject of a bid for City Challenge funding in the first round (University of Newcastle 1992). Since large-scale clearance and redevelopment took place in the late 1960s, the West End has been the focus for several experiments in urban regeneration. Benwell had been identified in the early 1970s for one of the Community Development Projects and later in the decade formed part of the Newcastle–Gateshead Inner City Partnership. Although population turnover has always been relatively high, there has been a considerable history of community activity in the area.

TNI became involved in the area after consulting the city council about where it could best assist in the process of urban regeneration. The Cruddas Park and Loadman Street area was suggested because of its high score on indicators of deprivation. A team was assembled, made up of a secondee from the Department of Employment, and a part-time secondee each from the City Council and a Youth Enterprise Agency, under the direction of James Wood. This team began

149

working in the area in December 1988 and completed their work in February 1989. It initially met with a certain amount of hostility from the local community, as before its arrival no community consultation had taken place. Therefore, community involvement in the feasibility study became a priority and, accordingly, the two existing tenants' associations, albeit with a limited number of active members, were asked to help with a 30 per cent survey of the area. This investigated local perceptions of needs in the area and produced an economic profile. The needs of the private sector were also examined in terms of recruitment and training, particularly with regard to the availability of local labour and the potential role of community businesses. The delivery of local authority services was also examined through discussions with the directors of all major departments and the central government Departments of Employment, Environment and Trade and Industry were also consulted for the study (Wood 1992).

The results showed that the Cruddas Park and Loadman Street area suffered from the following problems (Wood 1992: 172):

- concerns over vandalism and the fear of crime
- few facilities for children and young people
- the high degree of social isolation
- high levels of long-term unemployment, low levels of skills and self-confidence
- a perceived lack of access to jobs and training.

The major recommendation was that a community employment and enterprise centre, with community work and employment staff, should be established in the area. The centre opened in October 1989 with three staff seconded from the Employment Service and with two additional posts funded by the Urban Programme and the local authority. After the feasibility study was completed, a steering group of six local tenants was formed to oversee developments following the study's adoption by the supporting agencies. This was later enlarged into a community council that now meets on a regular (initially weekly) basis and forms the policy-making body for the area. Initial meetings of the community council were often turbulent, reflecting some unresolved conflicts between local factions in the area. From this community council, the board members of the Cruddas Park Community Trust are elected, which was set up as the executive body for the community council in order to undertake those activities that incur a financial or legal liability. In addition, the Trust has several non-executive representatives from the local authority, the Departments of Employment and Environment and the private sector on the board. John Ward was invited to be the independent Chair of the Trust. At the time he was Regional Director for Barclays Bank and the Chair of TNI, until his retirement in 1993. By this means the link between TNI and the Cruddas Park Community Trust was cemented.

The Community Trust operates the Community Enterprise and Employment Centre, a holiday caravan, and four community businesses. These are a workwear clothing manufacturing business, a launderette, a desktop publishing business, and The Rock public house, which was re-opened by the Community Trust after it had closed as a result of drug-related problems. Thus, through TNI the Trust forms a direct link between the local residents and the key interests in the city. The Community Trust also has a business support group made up of a group of young professionals who are available to provide free advice to the community on a regular basis. John Collier was involved in the business support group before becoming the third Chief Executive of TNI.

The Trust is involved in the following areas: housing and housing management, support for the tenants' associations, training needs, gay support, the running of a community flat, newsletters, adult education, food and health, crime strategies, childcare, and an after-school club. Up to mid-1992, 208 people in the area had been found jobs with local firms and in excess of 300 people had been through the Trust's training and education programmes. However, unemployment remains high, since once people became employed they often want to move out of Cruddas Park.

For the future, the Cruddas Park Community Trust is aiming to sustain and build on the range of employment initiatives, and to increase the involvement of local residents in improving local living conditions and work opportunities, and in reducing social exclusion. The Trust is an important community-based organization, which at the time embodied many of the principles of City Challenge and is therefore well placed to contribute towards the overall strategy for Newcastle's West End.

Theatre Village and Chinatown

The Theatre Village and Chinatown Project focuses on an area to the southwest of the city centre. Generally neglected, with many derelict and run down properties, the area was the subject of a study by consultants on behalf of TNI, and it was this that defined the Theatre Village and Chinatown as a marketing strategy. The Westgate Development Trust was formed by TNI and Newcastle City Council as the agency through which to promote regeneration. The project emphasizes the entertainment, leisure, and tourism potential of the area, as well as providing commercial office development and housing. The project has since declined in importance to TNI, partly because it is now located within the area of the West End Partnership (funded by City Challenge), but also because a major road proposal created blight in the area. TNI claims credit for having created a vision for the area, and is now prepared to leave it to others to implement the strategy.

Publicity

The original TNI list of flagship projects included one concerned with publicity and promotion. However, when Danny Sharpe became Chief Executive of TNI he took the view that publicity could best be achieved through the medium of the other projects and the other marketing and development agencies in the city.

East meets West: Japanese Links

The encouragement of increased linkages with Japanese business, and the promotion of Newcastle upon Tyne as a "welcoming and attractive" (TNI 1988) location for Japanese investment was one of the initial flagship projects of the business leadership team. However, the project was dropped by Danny Sharpe, when he held the post of Chief Executive, as he felt the links had already been established with the formation of the Anglo–Japanese Society, which he helped set up some years earlier when he was Deputy Regional Director of the DTI.

Environmental initiative

TNI's environmental initiative was not one of the original flagship projects, but was launched when Danny Sharpe was Chief Executive. The environmental initiative produced a good-practice guide for businesses, including information on the legal requirements arising from environmental legislation and a list of relevant professionals who were offering guidance in this field.

The aims of TNI's environmental initiative are threefold (TNI 1991):

- to inform businesses and others of legislation, both current and impending, both UK and EC, which must be complied with
- to encourage businesses to think about the advantages to be gained from taking the environmental message on board and acting upon it to retain or even gain market share
- to encourage the business community to do something to improve the environment of Newcastle; this might entail a "tidy up" around workshop premises, a "face lift" to shop fronts, or sponsoring attractive litter bins or hanging baskets in the city centre.

In a more recent development, a subsidiary company has been set up, called TNI Environmental Services Ltd. Funding has been obtained from the Advisory Committee for Business in the Environment, which itself is a partnership between the DOE, the DTI and the corporate sector. Additional sponsorship has been obtained from three Newcastle-based companies –Northern Electric, Rolls–Royce and Procter & Gamble. TNI Environmental Services Ltd will use the funding to encourage local small and medium-size enterprises to focus on, and to make savings on energy consumption, waste and products. Training will be provided for key company staff to carry out environmental audits of their company's activities, in order to reduce energy consumption, recycle waste and to meet packaging and labelling standards (TNI 1994b).

TNI also helped organize a group of local businesses to sponsor the floodlighting of the Tyne Bridge at a cost of £180000. The opening coincided with a visit by the Cutty Sark Tall Ships Race.

The arts and urban regeneration

Promoting investment in the arts in Newcastle is seen as an important vehicle for economic development and urban regeneration. The development of a £30 million international concert hall in the city has been planned for some time, although has been delayed by financial difficulties. There is also a proposal for a £15 million extension to the city's art gallery. TNI is giving its support to fund-raising and promotional campaigns for both these projects.

Further and higher education

The idea of a project to foster closer links between business and the city's two universities was proposed by the Chief Executive of Proctor and Gamble, one of the largest company members and contributors to TNI. The project aims to "find common ground amongst the academic institutions in the city, to ensure that business leaders are aware of their needs and to promote the concept of Newcastle as the best youth city in the UK" (TNI 1994a).

The West End Partnership

Newcastle was successful in the first two rounds of City Challenge. The area selected in the first round lies to the west of Newcastle City Centre and comprises five distinct areas: Cruddas Park, Arthurs Hill, Elswick, Scotswood and Benwell. All of these areas have similar problems of unemployment, poor housing, and poverty. The total population covered by the City Challenge area is around 35 000, made up of approximately 16 000 households. The area is therefore relatively large in comparison with other City Challenge areas. The main objectives of the West End Partnership are concerned with employment, training, housing improvement, environmental improvement, community and social infrastructure, and community participation.

The connection between TNI and the West End Partnership is that the City Challenge area includes Cruddas Park and a small section of the Theatre Village and Chinatown, so that initially there was some common interest in the same geographical area. A further connection was through John Ward, formerly TNI Chair, who also sat on the board of the West End Partnership. TNI decided to offer its help at the beginning of discussions about City Challenge when the first Newcastle bid was being prepared. This led to suggestions that the business support group, who provide an advice service in Cruddas Park, could extend this throughout the whole City Challenge area. However, this was rejected by the local people in the adjoining areas, as they did not see themselves as being like Cruddas Park and did not wish to use the Cruddas Park facilities. This highlights one of the main problems encountered with City Challenge: that the area is very large and is made up of several tightly knit communities. Danny Sharpe, when Chief Executive, referred to this as the problem of defining what is meant by "the community". He took the view that, although an initiative may work very well in a particular area, there can be problems in trying to replicate it elsewhere without carrying out a detailed examination of local needs and opportunities.

Reassessing the role of TNI

With the change in Chief Executive at the end of 1992, the future direction of TNI was reviewed. The initiative had been running for four years, and the incoming Chief Executive spent some time investigating whether the project needed to be refocused. In the event, the City Council was keen that TNI should continue, and from 1993 the Initiative has at least a further three years of operation agreed, with finance of about £250 000 secured for each of those years. With this reassessment of the role of TNI and the raising of additional finance, greater attention is being paid towards recruiting new members, particularly from the small business sector.

Conclusions

When TNI was formed in 1988, it represented the first of several business leadership teams set up in different towns and cities arising from the CBI report, *Initiatives beyond charity*. The original intention was that it should be managed by a board drawn entirely from the private sector, with representation (but no voting rights) from the public sector. Its purpose was to identify flagship projects where business leaders could use their marketing and management skills in order to create a vision to which all could subscribe. By 1994, 9 of the 19 board members were drawn from public sector organizations.

The CBI report drew heavily on examples of private-sector–led urban regeneration in American cities such as Baltimore, Boston and Philadelphia. These examples relate closely to the Logan & Molotch (1987) descriptions of urban growth coalitions. From this perspective, at the height of the trend towards privatism in the USA and the UK, the private sector was perceived as providing many of the solutions to urban problems in the two countries.

As this chapter has shown, TNI has adopted several flagship projects aimed at promoting different themes and geographical locations in the city of Newcastle upon Tyne. However, in the majority of cases, detailed implementation has been undertaken by public sector agencies: the local authority, the Tyne & Wear Urban Development Corporation, City Challenge agencies and the Northern Development Company. Perhaps in response to this, an increasing proportion of representatives of public sector agencies have been nominated to the board.

Several commentators have drawn attention to both the crowded arena on which agencies such as TNI operate and the continuity of such partnership arrangements in economically peripheral areas such as the North East (Wilkinson 1992, Shaw 1993). Promotional, growth-orientated organizations such as TNI need to invent new flagship projects continually and to launch effective campaigns in order to maintain their own momentum. Hence, the stipulation that the Chief Executive of TNI should be seconded to the post for only two years. One result of this has been the refocusing of TNI's activities after each new Chief Executive has been appointed and the continual search for promotional opportunities not otherwise adopted by other agencies.

TNI is perhaps most effective in that it created a network of senior managers from the public and private sectors who are involved with locally dependent private companies, the universities and the local newspaper, or local development agencies. A broad consensus about the need for growth in Newcastle, and several geographically specific flagship projects, has arisen from this elite. Detailed implementation of the latter has fallen to the public sector organizations such as the City Council, the UDC, City Challenge agencies and the TEC. However, TNI can claim to have helped attract additional private and public resources to Newcastle. For example, helped prepare two successful City Challenge bids, brought additional English Heritage funding to Grainger Town, and raised sponsorship for floodlighting the Tyne Bridge and for TNI's environmental initiative.

As an organizational model for urban regeneration, TNI has its limitations, in that the private sector can rarely achieve much by itself and development agencies in the public sector are increasingly using their own resources to launch place-marketing campaigns in order to attract inward investment. As Shaw notes (1993), the North East has a long history of corporatist approaches to urban regeneration, and has more than enough agencies involved in overlapping and often competitive promotional and place-marketing campaigns. In addition, TNI makes no claims to involve local people, or even small and medium-size companies, in its management or the selection of its projects. Its reliance on informal and non-bureaucratic procedures also reduces transparency and diffuses accountability, except very indirectly through member organizations, such as the local authority. Business leadership teams such as TNI are thus most reminiscent of the American growth coalition model and they reflect the high point of the government's commitment to business-led regeneration, which was promoted in the mid- to late 1980s.

The Newcastle Initiative is thus best seen as a network of contacts between the major locally dependent interests in the city, which see individual and collective advantage in creating a coalition around a group of objectives relating to growth, development, inward investment, and the promotion of the city as an attractive location in which to live and work. Critics argue that organizations such as TNI are primarily concerned with the social and cultural transformation of the city, to bring it into line with a consumption-led regeneration strategy. This is problematic in terms of both its sustainability and the growing competition between urban areas offering a very similar "product" (Amin & Tomaney 1991).

CHAPTER 8
The Wester Hailes Partnership

Partnership in Scotland

In 1988 the Scottish Office published *New life for urban Scotland*. This proposed the creation of four partnership initiatives led by the Scottish Office: Castlemilk in Glasgow, Ferguslie Park in Paisley, Whitfield in Dundee and Wester Hailes in Edinburgh. The principles upon which the four partnerships were to operate were summed up in the subsequent Scottish Office report *Progress in partnership*. The three key principles were (Scottish Office 1993):

- an integrated approach to economic, social and physical regeneration firmly grounded in an initial analysis and long-term strategic plan (10 years); this requires partnership and concerted action across a wide range of public sector bodies;
- the inclusion of the private sector in partnership, both to secure the benefit of advice, expertise and resources, and to help breakdown the economic isolation of the areas;
- the full involvement of the local community in the decision-making process, partly to ensure that decisions taken reflect the needs of the community, but also to allow local people to take responsibility for their areas, thus securing the commitment required to ensure that improvements will be sustained in the long term.

The Partnership area

The Wester Hailes estate lies some 8 km to the southwest of the centre of Edinburgh (Fig. 8.1). The Estate was planned in the 1950s, and the first residents moved in 1969. By 1975 most of the housing had been completed. However, at that time, although the indoor shopping centre had opened, as had an hotel, "there was no secondary school, no library, no social club nor any other meeting place for adults. There was no health centre, no local social work department, no police station. There were no playgrounds for the young children, no discos, billiards or pool rooms, cafés or other facilities for teenagers. There was no local

157

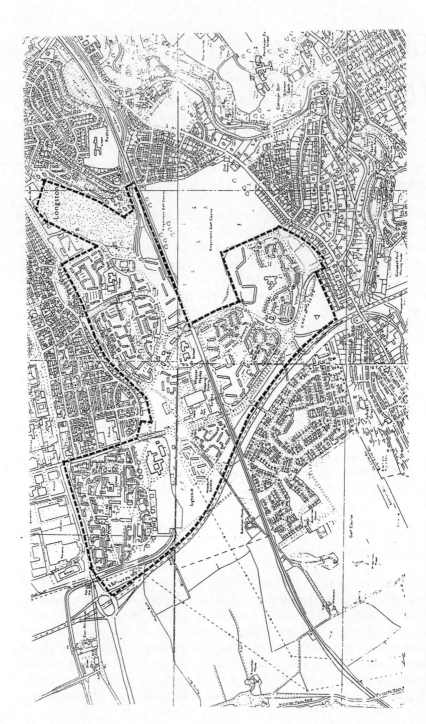

Figure 8.1 Location of Wester Hailes, Edinburgh.

industry . . ." (Gilloran 1983: 7). The lack of facilities was demonstrated clearly in a report in 1977 – *Wester Hailes speaks for itself* – in which residents compared their amenities with those in Musselburgh (a town of similar size to the east of Edinburgh). There were 9 food shops compared with Musselburgh's 51; no social facilities at all, as against the 16 social clubs and 27 restaurants, pubs or cafés in Musselburgh; and 1 doctor compared with 9.

The population of the area was 11 148 in 1991, having fallen from 15 503 in 1981 and from a peak of 18 000. It can be characterized as being a publicly rented commuter estate – although such a broad characterization masks both the fact that the majority of the residents do not travel to work and that there is a growing proportion (currently some 15 per cent) of owner occupiers on the Estate. It can also be characterized as being poor. In 1992 the unemployment rate was over 20 per cent, and in 1988 80 per cent of households had an income of less than £10 000 per year and 50 per cent had an income of less that £5000. Table 8.1 shows a few key statistics about the area, plus a comparison with Edinburgh; these figures are taken from an analysis of the 1991 census undertaken by the Partnership.

Table 8.1   Indicators of deprivation for Wester Hailes and Edinburgh (% of population).

Indicator	Wester Hailes	Edinburgh
Under 25 years old	46	31
Under 5 years old	10	6
Economically active as percentage of 16+	62	62
Looking for work	22	9
Owner-occupied households	14	66
Lone-parent households	18	4
No access to a car	69	39

Source: Wester Hailes Partnership 1993.

These figures give some indication of the depth of problems and nature of the issues facing the area. It must be stressed, however, that Wester Hailes is not unique. A look at either the other Partnership areas in Scotland, or at some of the other peripheral estates in Edinburgh, would provide comparable figures to those for Wester Hailes.

The choice of Wester Hailes

The apparent basis for the choice of Wester Hailes as one of the four Scottish Office Partnership areas was the analysis of the standard indices of urban deprivation, derived mainly from the 1981 Census of Population. However, other factors were taken into account, notably the possibility of achieving a measure of success in the ten-year period and the history of community involvement in the area. However, both of the local authorities – the City of Edinburgh District Council and Lothian Regional Council – resisted having Wester Hailes as the Partnership area. There was a widespread feeling that it was not the worst-off estate in Edinburgh and some would have preferred another Edinburgh estate – Craigmillar – to be chosen. Some people have made the link between the choice of Wester Hailes and the fact that it lies within the constituency of the then Secretary of State for Scotland, Malcolm Rifkin.

The doubts about the choice of area are still felt. A project has been set up in Craigmillar by Edinburgh District Council. The regional Council has never accepted that Wester Hailes was the most damaged estate, but has accepted its role in the partnership as long as this has not meant that resources will be swung away from other areas or that the Urban Programme will be biased towards Wester Hailes.

Previous initiatives in Wester Hailes

It is worth looking in some detail at the history of community involvement in the area, both because this was one of the major contributory factors in the choice of the area for Partnership status and because it raises the question of whether the existing forms of partnership on the Estate could have achieved a significant degree of change without a more formal Partnership being set up.

The involvement of the Wester Hailes residents in tackling some of the problems inherent in the Estate began before the last residents had moved in. In 1973 the Wester Hailes Association of Tenants (WHAT) was formed with the aim of fostering "a community spirit by promoting the health, education, social and recreational development of the inhabitants of Wester Hailes" (Gilloran 1983: 7). By 1975, there were six tenants associations covering different communities on the Estate. In the same year, Edinburgh Corporation's Social and Community Development Programme was established. This was funded by the EU, the Scottish Office and the two local authorities, in order to try to combine and concentrate the resources from several different policy programmes into geographical areas. Wester Hailes was one of the four areas in Edinburgh chosen for this experiment.

By 1978, the residents had built an adventure playground, a community workshop (which included a café, and offices for community workers and the community newspaper) and the Education Centre (which combined a secondary school with a community education centre). In that year an Urban Aid grant was approved, which allowed the staffing of a new co-ordinating committee of residents groups. Two years later, Wester Hailes Community Enterprises Ltd was established to try to provide work for local people, and one of its first jobs was to help to build community facilities in each of Wester Hailes' neighbourhoods. The community enterprise company later became a Community Programme manager. In 1981 the need was seen to have a more representative and widely based group than just the representatives of the tenants associations and of voluntary and interest groups in the area. In that year the Wester Hailes Representative Council was established. This was designed to give the residents of the area more of a voice, as opposed to the predominance of the voluntary sector on the former association. The Representative Council is discussed later in this case study.

Composition of the board

The board is made up of seventeen members representing the following bodies:
- the Scottish Office: one member plus the Chair
- Wester Hailes Representative Council: five members
- Lothian Regional Council: two members
- the City of Edinburgh District Council: two members
- the Employment Service
- Scottish Homes
- Health Board
- Business Support Group
- Capital Enterprise Trust
- Lothian and Edinburgh Enterprise Ltd

Figure 8.2 illustrates the structure of the Wester Hailes Partnership.

Funding and budget

The project has a budget of some £0.5 million per year for running costs. All the other financial resources come from within the budgets of the relevant local authorities and quangos. The Urban Programme has £2 million per year set aside for the Wester Hailes Partnership and Scottish Homes has been granted some extra funds, although the Wester Hailes Partnership is only one of the bodies with a call on these funds.

In a funding regime of this nature, it is difficult to separate those funds that are related to the Partnership and those that would have been spent in the area anyway. Table 8.2 is derived from the 1994 Partnership Progress Report and it gives a good picture of the levels of funding from different sources over time.

Table 8.2 Total expenditure in the Wester Hailes Partnership area by member organizations (£k).

Organization	1989/90	1990/91	1991/92	1992/93	1993/94
Lothians & Edinburgh Enterprise Ltd	–	51.1	2111.0	1247.0	1213.8
Scottish Office	444.0	414.3	2536.7	2921.7	939.2
Edinburgh District Council	2621.7	4613.1	5015.1	5767.7	6684.6
Lothian Regional Council	19.8	42.9	408.5	682.6	791.1
Scottish Homes	1170.0	2786.0	3062.0	5943.2	5833.0
Employment Service	6.0	87.4	97.4	76.7	54.3
Capital Enterprise Trust	5.0	6.0	2.0	2.5	6.5
Health Board	68.7	110.9	127.9	32.0	140.3
Business Support Group	–	2.2	0.2	10.5	2.1

Source: Wester Hailes Partnership 1994b.

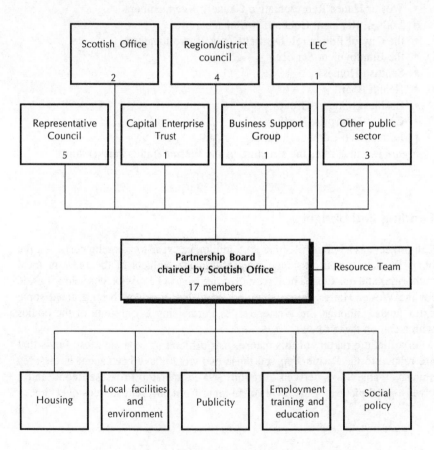

Figure 8.2 Organizational structure of the Wester Hailes Partnership.

The resource team

The Partnership is managed and run by a small resource team. The Leader from 1991 until 1994 was Sorrel Brookes. The team has 11 other staff (one of whom is part-time). Three staff are seconded, two from the Scottish Office and one from Lothian Regional Council, with the rest being directly employed. There are no secondees from the private sector, despite that fact that the 1989 Partnership Strategy recommended that there should be.

The suggested roles of the team were set out at the beginning of the project in *Realising the potential: the partnership strategy for Wester Hailes* (Scottish Office 1989). This set out five initial areas of work, including dealing with new and existing contracts, co-ordination of fund raising and of applications for grants and to carry out research and developmental work on new policies. The strategy stated that "the developmental role will be very important" but made it clear that "the resource team will take on jobs which lie between several organizations and which no one group has the time or the scope to take forward" (Scottish Office 1989: 62). It had been understood that the resource team would only service the Partnership Board and not take a more proactive role, but that it was the Scottish Office that required a fuller role in policy work.

The changes in role are reflected in a report prepared for the Partnership Board in December 1992 on *The role of the partnership resource team*. This identifies four roles for the team: ensuring implementation of the Board's decisions, contributing to policy development, monitoring and evaluation, and servicing the Board and its subgroups and panels. The report places its role in policy development in a different light by expressing some apparent annoyance that "other Partners have been too often content to leave policy development to the Resource Team . . . rather than committing their own specialist expertise to working things up . . . real commitment from the Partners is needed to make the process more efficient" (Wester Hailes Partnership 1992). Some suggest that the resource team be given even more responsibility to act in an advocacy role for the area.

The Wester Hailes Representative Council

The Representative Council has based its structure on 27 neighbourhood areas, each containing between 80 and 300 households. These elect their own neighbourhood councils, which in turn elect a member to serve on the Representative Council. This Council itself has an Executive Committee and two Subcommittees: the Spokespersons Co-ordinating Group and the Neighbourhood Subcommittee. The Council has its own staff, led by a co-ordinator, and in 1994 there were 22 people working for the Council or employed on a project. Their funding comes mainly from the Urban Aid programme. This totalled £567 511 in revenue grant and £126 134 in capital grant in 1993-4.

It is the spokespersons that are the key in the relationship between the Representative Council and the rest of the Partnership. There are twelve spokespersons: for training and employment, environment, low income, equal opportunities, education, economic development, youth, housing, publicity, childcare; community care and community facilities. In addition, there is a crime prevention group. Several of these responsibilities directly cover the remit of the Partnership's five working groups, which are described below. The spokespersons are members of those groups and they have small working groups that advise them. Attention has been given by the Council to the need to improve its members' skills in presentation and negotiation. Equally important, care is taken to ensure that spokespersons do not feel isolated when dealing with representatives of the other bodies in the Partnership, and board or subcommittee meetings are preceded by briefing meetings.

The Representative Council is involved in a wide variety of other activities and campaigns. During 1993, for example, the Council negotiated for a disused local-authority building to be used for childcare, and secured funding for a childcare organizer, organized some community events, and examined wider issues such as the community ownership of land and other resources.

The approach and goals of the Wester Hailes Partnership

The overall emphasis is, perhaps naturally, on partnership. The strategy states that:

> Our goals will only be achieved if all the public bodies who have a contribution to make to the regeneration of Wester Hailes work together in partnership with the local community and with private enterprise. None of us can bring about the transformation of Wester Hailes alone, but all of the partners have a vital contribution to make . . . This means sharing a common vision and goals and an agreed strategy for realizing them, with clear objectives, jointly discussed and well-defined arrangements for the coordination of policies and their implementation. (Scottish Office 1989: 10)

The 1994 Partnership Progress Report elaborates on this focus by setting out the benefits of the partnership approach. These are that (Wester Hailes Partnership 1994b: 1):

- agencies can work together towards common goals
- the ideas and resources of all partners are pooled
- attention is given to all aspects of the problems identified, with all the relevant agencies able to use their time and resources to find a complete solution.

The priorities of the partnership are shown by the remit of the five subgroups set up by the Partnership Board. These cover housing, local facilities and environment, publicity, employment, training and education, and social policy. The overall aims have been focused into seven aims covering the work of the sub-groups. These have been refined since the original strategy and the 1994 Progress Report (Wester Hailes Partnership 1994b: 2) cited them as:

- Housing: to create demand for housing in Wester Hailes across the full spectrum of types of house and types of tenure.
- Environment: to create a mix of high-quality facilities and environment of sufficiently high quality that at least 50 per cent of people questioned in any market survey state that they are "quite satisfied" or "very satisfied" with the facilities and the general environment in Wester Hailes.
- Publicity: to enhance the image of Wester Hailes in the eyes of residents, investors, employers and the wider community.
- Employment and Training: to halve the gap between the Wester Hailes unemployment rate and the substantially lower rate for Edinburgh over five years.
- Economic Development: to develop a community that has the appropriate level of economic activity and services for its size and which has also taken advantage of its location on the edge of a rapidly growing economic development area.
- Social Policy: to increase average household income in real terms.
- And, more generally, to give the community a stake in the new assets to be created locally and a share in the process of their creation.

Even further, some more specificity has been added since the original aims, these are still broadly based statements and they do not serve to identify the means by which such laudable ends may be achieved. Such an approach could serve to strengthen the role of the Resource Team by giving it the responsibility for turning agreed aims into an action programme. A clearer impression of the work of the Partnership to date can be gained only by looking at the work of each of the Partnership subgroups in turn. Even this overview must remain partial, as there is a very diverse range of activities and actions being carried out under the general heading of Partnership.

Housing

The 1989 Partnership Strategy for Wester Hailes sets out five aims for housing in the area (Scottish Office 1989: 29):

- to improve physical standards
- to reduce the current high level of turnover
- to provide a mix of housing that more suited to the current and likely future population, including additional low-rise housing and special-needs housing
- to create a sense of identity by fostering the growth of small neighbourhoods that increasingly share in the control and management of their housing, and
- to provide a wider range of choices – both in housing and in tenure – for present and future Wester Hailes residents.

165

The task is not an easy one. Of the 6000 homes completed by the mid-1970s, 33 per cent were in high-rise blocks of seven storeys or more and 66 per cent were in tenement blocks. In 1989, 95 per cent of the residents were tenants of Edinburgh District Council.

A housing strategy for the second half of the Partnership period was agreed on 17 May 1994. This restates the goal that was agreed in 1992: "to create demand for housing in Wester Hailes across the full spectrum of types of house and types of tenure". It is relevant to note that the subgoals had been refined, and references to reducing high turnover had been omitted, and new aims relating to equality of opportunity and to management quality had been added. This reflects a view that high turnover is not a problem in itself but reflects other problems that should be tackled. The strategy states that the area cannot provide enough houses to meet all the potential demand. It also points out the lack of available land. Therefore, the strategy places an emphasis on the demolition of high-rise and its replacement by low-rise housing. This is shown most clearly in the neighbourhoods of Hailesland and Westburn. In the former area the demolition of three high-rise blocks would reduce the number of such homes from 518 to 261, and would increase the number of low-rise homes from 320 to 418. In Westburn the changes were even more dramatic, with all 442 high-rise flats being demolished and 150 new houses with gardens replacing them. In other neighbourhoods the emphasis was placed more on housing rehabilitation and environmental improvements.

The difficulties inherent in widening the tenure base are apparent from the strategy and were the subject of lengthy debate within the Partnership. A particular focus for this discussion was the balance between housing for rent and housing for sale. The finally agreed split for this was 55:45. This agreement represented a degree of success for the Representative Council in reducing the target for housing for sale. Progress to date has not been dramatic. As far as new-build private sector housing is concerned, only 20 new homes have been built, raising the proportion of such owners from 0.4 per cent to 0.8 per cent between 1989 and 1994. The Right-to-Buy legislation has had more effect, with the proportion of households owning by this means rising from 4.6 to 13.4 per cent in the same period. Despite this slow start, the housing strategy sets a target of 32.6 per cent for owner-occupation by 1999.

One of the important partners in the implementation of the housing policies is Scottish Homes. Scottish Homes was established in 1989 by merging the work of the Scottish Special Housing Association and the Housing Corporation for Scotland. It works with local authorities, housing associations, the private sector and its own tenants, in order to deliver a national housing strategy for Scotland. It is closely involved in all four of the Scottish Office's Urban Partnership areas, with a total funding for these of £29 million in1992–3.

In Wester Hailes, Scottish Homes has worked through the Partnership to draw up a housing action plan. This is based on three interrelated aims: to remove some of the high-rise and run-down housing that characterized the area, to widen the tenure base of the area, and to contribute to its environmental improvement. These aims in turn contribute to the other main aims of the partnership. For example, a local employment clause has been included in the contract for the environmental works on the main pedestrian spine through the Estate.

Much of the implementation of the strategy relies on the Wester Hailes Community Housing Association (WHCHA). In 1990 three high-rise blocks were demolished at Hailesland by the Association, and the site has been used for the construction of 97 low-rise family homes. A further 250 homes are being built at Westburn. These will be used to rehouse tenants from the Westburn Gardens high-rise blocks, prior to their demolition. The WHCHA has also bought 180 houses at Wester Hailes Drive from the District Council in order to improve them.

Private sector involvement in the provision of housing in the area has been slow. WHCHA has agreed to sell on 40 of the Wester Hailes Drive houses to the private sector for a low-cost home-ownership scheme. Scottish Homes can provide financial support for private housing developers through its GRO grants (Grants for Rent and Ownership). These are given as a means of achieving the regeneration of areas of housing and social disadvantage, and as a means of attracting the private sector into these areas. The four Urban Partnership areas are designated as priority areas for the allocation of these grants.

Local facilities and environment

It has already been seen that the provision of better social and community facilities was a key demand from residents long before the Partnership came about. Improvements to the area are apparent in terms of local play areas, landscaping and the removal of some of the excessive parking areas. There is a continuing programme to achieve this in all of the area's neighbourhoods. However, some of the larger schemes that the Partnership itself has identified as being desirable are still in the planning stage. These include an ice rink, a new social club and leisure centre, improved sports facilities and a sports stadium and, perhaps most important of all in terms of both usefulness and image, the redevelopment and expansion of the shopping centre. This scheme would include a new library, bingo hall and cinema. At the time of writing it was hoped that phase 1 of the scheme – involving redevelopment of the shopping and the provision of a library – would be agreed very soon. The next stage, which may include offices, will have to wait for more funding. The Representative Council feel that Lothian and Edinburgh Enterprise Ltd should provide funding for this phase.

Publicity

The existence of problems in an area leading to a poor public perception of that area can turn into a self-reinforcing spiral. Poor image leads to lack of investment by business and a desire on the part of residents to leave, and the effects of these decisions themselves lead to a worsening of the image. It is not surprising, therefore, that one of the main strands of the Partnership's work lies in the creation of a better image for Wester Hailes. This work started at the beginning of the Partnership period. A positive slogan was adopted – "Wester Hailes – Full of Potential" – and full use was made of events such as the visit of Prince Charles to the area in 1988. The Scottish Office stresses the need to ensure that it is the image of the area that is being promoted rather than the image of the Partnership initiative.

The approaches adopted in this part of the strategy are varied. Poster campaigns have been employed to inform residents of Partnership campaigns, such as those on health and training. Efforts have been made to promote more positive reports about the area in the media, and opportunities have been taken to promote the area through events. There is, in addition, a wider image to create. Wester Hailes is, in population terms, the size of a town such as Galashiels. Yet it is looked upon as one homogeneous peripheral housing estate. Part of the work of the Partnership lies in reinforcing resident's perceptions that it is a series of neighbourhoods and the external perception that it is a small town. However, despite these varied approaches, the 1994 Partnership Progress Report states that a recent study of local perceptions of the area found that these were still largely negative.

It is obvious that a public relations strategy cannot in itself change perceptions. This must come about through improvements in housing, in the local environment and in access to jobs.

Employment, training and education

Wester Hailes itself contains few jobs. Those people with jobs will usually have to travel either to Edinburgh or to the large new industrial and retail areas at South Gyle and Maybury Park. Of those with jobs, 13.3 per cent work in Wester Hailes and 55.1 per cent travel to Edinburgh. Of greater immediate importance is the high level of unemployment on the Estate. In April 1989 there were 1116 registered unemployed people, with 250 additional people not registered but looking for work; the unemployment rate was 19.6 per cent. Of those unemployed, 44 per cent had been out of work for more than a year and 27 per cent for more than two years. Youth unemployed counted for a fifth of the total and 37.1 per cent of the unemployed were unskilled or semi-skilled manual workers. By July 1993, the unemployment rate had risen to 22.6 per cent.

The Education, Training and Employment Subgroup agreed its own strategy

168

for the remainder of the period of Partnership in 1993. This identifies five target groups: short-term, long-term and young unemployed people, women and employed people. The strategy's approach for all these groups involves a mix between further research into both current local initiatives and approaches tried elsewhere, devising ways of targeting the groups for better training and provision of information, building up knowledge about these groups, and studying barriers to change.

There was a degree of success in the first five years of the partnership. Nevertheless, the aim of halving the gap between Wester Hailes unemployment rates over five years remains elusive. There are several reasons for this. One of the most important is that those who do find jobs often move out of the area and, thus, may even be counted within any improvement in Edinburgh's total employment rate. The Partnership is concerned enough about the discrepancy between apparent success and the "statistical" outcome that it has commissioned a study on the phenomenon known as "labour market churning". This involves not only people with jobs leaving the estate, but those without jobs moving in and it involves people progressing through placements and training schemes, whereas they do not show up on the statistics of the unemployed.

It is a usual characteristic of partnerships that the private sector would play the major part in implementing a training and employment strategy. Wester Hailes does not follow this pattern. The Scottish Office agrees that Wester Hailes is different from the other Scottish initiatives in the degree to which the private sector is expected to be involved. There is a Business Support Group. However, the "goals" set out in their 1994 Updated Mission Statement appear limited. In employment, these range from providing access to local business training programmes to ensuring that member firms' job advertisements appear in the local Job Centre, and from interviewing "all suitable Wester Hailes job applicants" for vacancies in member firms to encouraging work placement and work shadowing schemes. They also promote a Compact Scheme with the local high school, and maintain links with the primary schools. One of the wider tasks is to break down barriers between industry, commerce and the local community (Wester Hailes Partnership Business Support Group 1994).

Social policy

The goal of the Social Policy Subgroup – to increase average household income in real terms – appears not to encompass the range of concerns about lack of facilities, opportunities and activities that has characterized many of the community campaigns in the past. The provision of more facilities, such as play areas and meeting rooms, is the responsibility of the Environment and Local Facilities Subgroup, but, even given this, the remit of the Partnership has excluded some social issues that are encompassed neither by other groups nor by the focus on household income. Although the 1989 Partnership Strategy for Wester Hailes contains chapters relating to the work of the other four subgroups, it does not devote a specific section to social policy. In 1990, the Wester Hailes Representative Council published *Moving forward: a social policy for Wester Hailes*, stating that "a concern has been expressed that, since the adoption of the partnership strategy for Wester Hailes, several social aspects of community life have been overlooked" (Wester Hailes Representative Council 1990). It was this concern that led the representative Council to publish its own social strategy. That document highlighted areas not covered adequately by the Partnership: education, health, leisure and recreation, and social welfare; in addition, it focused on four different groups in the community: under-twelves, families, youth, single people and the elderly.

The Partnership has now started to focus on some of these issues, notably education and health. It has been meeting local head-teachers and has commissioned research. Its health campaign has focused on healthy eating for school-age children and on encouraging the establishment of clinics in the area to reduce the expense of having to travel into Edinburgh.

The emphasis on increasing household income – and thus opportunity and choice – is understandable. This has centred on a benefits campaign that has involved delivering to every house leaflets on specific allowances, briefing community workers and training local people, and providing advice on such issues as the Child Support Agency. It also involves actions to promote energy efficiency in the home and, thus, to save on fuel bills. Such actions can be overwhelmed by decisions far beyond the control of the Partnership – such as the imposition of VAT on fuel.

The final objective of the Partnership not dealt with as yet is "to give the community a stake in the new assets to be created locally and a share in the process of their creation". It is worth noting that the local community were already trying to work towards this before the Partnership came into being through the Land and Property Trust. This started to use Urban Programme funding to buy land and buildings, either for the community's own developments, such as workshops, or to enable other schemes, such as the more recent nursery project to go ahead. The Trust has failed to make the necessary profits to enable it to become self-financing, although some within the Representative Council still look to it as a model of what could have been achieved, even without Partnership.

One final initiative needs to be mentioned under this heading. The Partnership has started a service-quality project. This will look at the delivery of a whole range of services, from refuse collection to housing management, and examines ways in which these might be improved. At present, it is concentrating on environmental services, including lighting, landscape maintenance and street sweeping. This is included under the heading of "ownership of assets" because, at the time of writing, the improvements to services that were starting to flow from this project were being seen by the Resource Team as one of the few tangible lasting benefits that Partnership had brought and which would not have happened without it.

170

Conclusions

There are some key questions that need to be considered when looking at this model of partnership, led by central government. The first must concern why this particular model of partnership was chosen. This is not totally clear. Michael Cunliffe (at the Scottish Office) stated in an interview simply that the four Partnerships were set up to see whether the model would work. However, he stresses the need to seek voluntary commitment, and points to the Glasgow Eastern Area Renewal (GEAR) project where, he feels, local people were being bypassed. Thus, one of the prime considerations in deciding on the structure and approach was the desire to ensure that the local community were as involved as possible and that partnership was not merely between tiers of government and service providers. This is shown by the fact that, according to Dave Lochhead, Head of Strategic Development in the City of Edinburgh District Council's Strategic Services Department, there was very limited dialogue at all between the Scottish Office and the District and Regional Councils, but the focus in the early days was firmly on the residents of the area and, in particular, local community organizations.

This leads on to the question as to who forms this partnership. First, it has already been seen that the private sector does not play as large a role in this partnership as in others studied and, therefore, although it is part of the Partnership, it is not a key player in it. Secondly, if it is true that this partnership was set up partly to develop means of including local communities in area renewal, then the easy answer to this question would be that the partnership is between government and the local community. However, the research undertaken showed that neither of these partners felt that this was really the case.

The interviews were designed to enable the researchers to hear both sides of the same point being stated with equal force. If perceptions of complex situations can be encapsulated in a few sentences, the viewpoints of the participants appears to be as follows. Those who might be termed to be on the "official" side (including local government and the service providers) feel that they have demonstrated their commitment to partnership by providing significant amounts of resources, not least in terms of staff hours, including those spent at meetings. They are starting to feel that this commitment is not appreciated by the community representatives, who seek more resources still and who are not afraid to voice their criticisms vociferously at meetings. Words such as "aggressive" and "confrontational" are used to describe the approach taken by the community spokespersons. They feel that, articulate as the community is, its members do not fully realize the constraints under which the public sector must operate. The community, it is felt, should move on from a confrontational stance to one where truer partnership exists through an acknowledgement of the points of view of others.

The corollary of this is predictable. The community representatives feel that the "government" side comes with its large budgets and expects the community to be grateful for such largesse. The community feels that its commitment to

171

partnership is shown not only explicitly in the time spent consulting on proposals and then preparing for and attending meetings, but also in a far wider way by living in the area and knowing that they and their successors will have to live with the results of partnership, long after the formal structures have been dismantled and the resource team has departed. They feel that they bring a knowledge and experience to partnership that the other side cannot have, and yet they feel that officials talk down to them or try to hide behind jargon. If they are confrontational, it is only because they are trying to get straight answers out of the "official" side.

A further issue relates to the role of the resource team. This has been discussed above, but it is worth pointing out here that the Representative Council has its own staff. This may be the most effective way of achieving their own priorities, but it does reflect a feeling that the resource team is directed too much by the Scottish Office. The people of the community feel that they should have some say in the staffing and budget of the team. Even one of the local-government partners felt that the team had turned too much of its budget into highly paid jobs. The community representatives also felt that the team had too much power in choosing which issues to carry forward. Sorrel Brookes sees it as the role of the team to push matters forward, to "harden up" the broad goals, and to keep things moving.

As this case study was being written, in 1994, there were some real doubts being expressed as to whether the Partnership would run its full course. If the characterizations of opposing positions described above are true, then it may be understandable why the "partners" are drifting apart and, therefore, why the Partnership is in "crisis" (a word used by a key participant in it).

The situation described can easily lead to the conclusion that Partnership in Wester Hailes is between various levels of government and between the formal service providers such as Scottish Homes, the Health Board and the local enterprise bodies. However, it is apparent that even within the "official" side there is a greater commitment to the Partnership from some members than others. Some participants have cited Lothian and Edinburgh Enterprise Ltd's apparent distancing from the project. This case study has already described the limited role played by the private sector, and it is apparent that there are varying levels of input by different local authority services. Benefits have and will flow from such a partnership, but it is not what appears to have been originally intended.

Having set up a longer-term, fairly complex and resource-intensive model of partnership, it is worth considering what has been achieved that would not have been achieved without the Partnership having been established. The corollary to this is what may have been stifled by the imposition of the Partnership methodology.

In the interviews, this specific question was put to a variety of participants. It is interesting how widely the responses differ. Sorrel Brookes cites only the housing improvement as possibly happening without the Partnership. Many more changes would not have happened, including environmental improvements, the shopping centre redevelopment, the 75-place nursery school, the service-quality project, the focus on employment and training, the development of neighbourhood councils, a greater understanding between the different players, and the dedicated urban programme.

David Jack, Depute Director of Planning for Lothian Regional Council, had a different view, asserting that generally everything that has happened in Wester Hailes would have happened, but at a slower rate.

The Representative Council also appears hard pressed to identify clear benefits stemming directly from partnership. Lynne Main (the Chairperson) points to increased funding for the area from some of the partners, but not all. However, she questions whether such a benefit is either worth the time and the effort that the community put in or is reflected in any dramatic improvements in unemployment rates or in social and community developments. Others are not even as generous as this. According to Jack McNeill, Partnership Committee representative and town centre spokesperson, no benefits come directly from the Partnership. However, he feels that benefits can be seen in the Urban Aid regime, which is speedier, involves joint decision-making and the Scottish Office is now more flexible as to how the money is spent. There is thought to be very little added value. The cost of the Partnership now is more than was previously allocated to projects, he says. The community puts time, energy and local knowledge into the Partnership, but the public sector can only put in resources. He also feels that Partnership has helped to stifle projects and he refers to the Land and Property Trust, which, he states, turned an initial turnover of £80 000 a year into a £2 million annual profit. It must be stressed that all these views were put forward at a time when the Partnership still had five years to run, officially, and at a time when the "official" and the community sides were questioning the effectiveness of the whole project.

Sorrel Brookes is concerned that the structure and the processes of this Partnership may have stifled the independence of the local community. This echoes Dave Lochhead's concerns about the "depoliticization" of the issues in the area. It certainly appears that the members of the Representative Council spend a great deal of time involved in the process of partnership and, although the Chairperson still feels that it is worthwhile, this view is not unequivocal.

How, then, is success to be measured when the Partnership does come to an end? The simple answer is to state that the project is being monitored both in-house and by external researchers. The Scottish Office has commissioned household surveys and some of the overall aims quoted earlier in this case study – notably that relating to the environment – contain indications of how success will be measured. However, it is difficult to arrive at a dispassionate assessment of such matters as community involvement. As David Jack points out, physical improvements can be measured, but the economic and the social side are more difficult to assess.

It is even more difficult when there does not appear to be full agreement as to what can be changed during the period of the Partnership and, in particular, what can be changed in the remaining five years. The community representatives feel that the original aims were too ambitious and were based on optimism for the economic future of the area. They see the need for a clearer dialogue within the partners of what can be achieved in reality.

Finally, it should be borne in mind that even apparently sound indicators of improvement can be called into question. The 1994 Progress Report states that "between 1990 and 1992 the number of crimes reported by the police in Wester Hailes had fallen significantly . . ." (Wester Hailes Partnership 1994b: 15). However, the local community point to the fact that there are no public telephones in the housing areas at all and that telephone ownership in the area is very low. They feel that this fact must impact on the number of incidents reported.

As well as change within the area, one success may be that the partners themselves have changed their approach, policies or practices. It is worth considering whether the Partnership has had any effects on the partners, as well as on the area. The most apparent "cross-over" between the Partnership and more general practice can be found in the City of Edinburgh District Council. The locally based partnership approach adopted in Wester Hailes reflects, and is reflected in, the District Council's decentralization strategy. Dave Lochhead felt that the Partnership has forced the District to examine its own practices in greater depth than before, including the way in which it prioritizes its Urban Programme. The City has established nine area boards that will both co-ordinate the delivery of council services locally and will feed into the budget-setting process with bids on an area basis. This should mean that service delivery is not focused solely on the existing remits of individual departments but that new ways of working emanate from the new focus on areas. Such a strategy may have been implemented anyway, but in an interview Dave Lochhead said that he felt that the Wester Hailes experience has highlighted the Council's difficulty in being responsive to locally determined priorities and has informed the decision-making on which structure to adopt.

The work in Wester Hailes has also led to a better dialogue with Lothian Regional Council, but Lochhead senses an unwillingness by some Regional departments to enter into partnership – notably Social Work and Education. He also feels that partnership has introduced a new language – the world of goals, objectives and performance indicators – that "depoliticizes" issues. On the other hand, the period of Partnership can be seen to be building up the capacities of the local community for continuing involvement and action when the formal structure has been dismantled. David Jack too feels that the community role is becoming progressively more representative. However, he feels that this project does not examine the role of the community enough and he cites the EU poverty programme projects as fulfilling this role to a greater extent.

The final two questions that need examining are interrelated but obvious. What successes can be claimed thus far and what will be left of lasting value. The first of these is perhaps easier to answer. Mike Cunliffe at the Scottish Office points to a range of successes, including major progress on the housing front, the initiation of training programmes, the creation of local employment, environmental improvements (including a community park), the provision of community facilities, and a new focus on education. Sorrel Brookes agrees that environmental and physical changes are apparent, but admits that there is not much to show in terms of really basic change in the area. This is echoed by Lynne Main, Chairperson of the Representative Council, who points particularly to the demolition of high-rise housing as the greatest physical indicator of change. However, she also looks to continuing high unemployment and continuing poverty as an indicator that the underlying problems remain.

As this book is being written, the projected ten-year period of the project is only half way through. As this case study has shown, much has been achieved and learnt, but much more remains to be done. It is too early to determine what lasting effect this project may have, either on Wester Hailes itself or on urban policy and practices in Scotland. Indications can be gained, however, by looking at the exit strategy of the partners. The Scottish Office is quite clear about this. Their exit strategy is based on the perception that the Scottish Office is the only partner that will withdraw after the project runs its course. The exit strategy must, therefore, concentrate on continuing the best working practices and relationships among the members of the Partnership. This outcome is desired by the community as well as by government. If this can be achieved, then this – coupled with the improvements in housing, facilities and the environment – may be all the can be hoped for in the long term. Alternatively, if the local community feels alienated from the process at this stage, and there are wide and growing variations in the commitment of the other partners, then even this new way of working may be too much to hope for.

However, we should end on a forward-thinking note. *Progress in partnership* concludes that "the Government believes that the experience of the Partnership approach has confirmed the wisdom of involving local communities fully in regeneration plans for their areas" (Scottish Office 1993: 24). Dave Lochhead feels that this indicates that partnerships such as Wester Hailes are not a "flash in the pan", but it will continue to be a feature of local government. The hope is that whatever is learnt from the experiences of the Wester Hailes Partnership will be used to improve the ways in which partnerships are set up, resourced and run in future.

CHAPTER 9

The Woodlands Community Development Trust

The Woodlands area

The Woodlands area of Glasgow is a relatively discrete neighbourhood lying about 1.6 km to the west of the city centre, with a population of about 5500. The area is densely developed, with the traditional pattern of Glasgow tenements, although the main streets have shops and restaurants on the ground floors. Woodlands is divided into two, both socially and in terms of housing conditions. The western side is largely occupied by a majority of middle-class owner-occupiers where housing conditions are generally of a high standard. By contrast, the eastern side has a high proportion of multi-occupied and privately rented accommodation with an above-average proportion of flats being overcrowded and lacking basic amenities. The majority of members of ethnic minorities live in this eastern section. Until 1985 the city council's approach had been the comprehensive clearance of substandard housing, although, while some sites had been cleared, little redevelopment had taken place. The population of Woodlands is relatively young, cosmopolitan and transient, and because of the relatively low cost of housing and its proximity to the city centre, it has attracted both students and ethnic minorities. Indeed, it is now one of the largest centres for ethnic minorities in Scotland. Approximately 27 per cent of the population of the East Woodlands area is non-White with about 80 per cent coming from the Indian subcontinent. In the 1970s, Woodlands was also gaining a reputation as a "red light" area, and kerb-crawling in the narrow streets off the Woodlands Road was a growing problem to residents.

Throughout the 1970s, several community organizations were established to represent different interest groups in the area or to press for improvements to the housing and community facilities. These often came into conflict with each other and the city council. As local-authority funding went into a decline, the City Housing Department found it impossible to complete the comprehensive redevelopment of the eastern section of Woodlands, and increasingly looked to community-based housing associations.

The Woodlands Residents Association was the main representative body of the owner-occupiers in the west end of Woodlands and one of its main priorities was to promote housing renovation with improvement grants and the stone-cleaning of their tenement blocks. At least two members of the Association resigned in order to form a more broadly based Community Council to represent the whole area. They were subsequently involved in setting up the Trust.

A second group, the Parkwood Community Development Association, was also set up at about the same time to promote the greater integration of the different ethnic groups through the provision of a community centre. The Charing Cross Housing Association was the main housing agency in the area, which at this time set about cementing closer links with all local organizations in the area.

Thus, by the early 1980s considerable uncertainty existed about how the housing and related problems of the Woodlands area could best be tackled. It was clear that the Housing Department lacked the resources to execute a comprehensive improvement strategy. Meanwhile, residents organizations were pressing for a social, economic and physical strategy to improve the area. The idea of setting up a community development trust emerged from several different sources and was soon adopted by some councillors, a member of the city planning department and local activists. The planning officer had been involved in the setting up of the Bridgegate Trust to renovate the former fish market near the River Clyde. A planning student from Oxford Polytechnic had also suggested the idea, after doing a project in the area, and others had been influenced by emerging literature on the subject. In the end it was the City Council that was most committed to the concept of a trust; it was an opportunity to illustrate its commitment to greater public participation in urban renewal and to involve other agencies in sharing the financial burden. Local residents were initially suspicious, given the Council's record in the area, but key interests were eventually won over to the idea of setting up a trust.

Formation

At the time, the idea of setting up a community development trust to promote the regeneration of an entire neighbourhood was novel in Glasgow. The City Council had always prided itself on its ability to provide for all the housing needs of the city, and at the time it was the largest public sector landlord in the UK. The establishment of a trust could involve the transfer of council-owned land to a voluntary organization, with the possibility that some of this could be sold on to housing associations or private developers, and all sites could be developed according to an integrated plan. This had not been done before on such a scale in Scotland. The underlying rationale was that, by carrying out a comprehensive development package, the Trust could ensure that local housing needs were met, the local environment was upgraded and, most important, proceeds from the development could be recycled in the area, to the benefit of all sections of the community. Initially, funding was made available by the Council to carry out a feasibility study into the potential for success of the Trust proposal. Martin Hilland was recruited from the Charing Cross Housing Association to carry out this task.

In August 1984 a public meeting was called to report back on the study and to consider setting up a steering committee for the proposed Trust. This attracted about a hundred interested people. A steering committee was set up to take the idea of the Trust forward by drawing up a constitution, negotiating funding with public and private bodies, and preparing a strategy for the future activities of the Trust. A local councillor, John Ross, agreed to chair the steering committee until the Trust was formally launched.

Woodlands Community Development Trust (WCDT) was formally established on 21 February 1985 after two years of preparatory work by the local authority and local organizations. The main objective of the Trust was:

. . . to co-ordinate the regeneration of East Woodlands. It aims to attract private and public capital to the area to develop it in the interests of the local community. This involves building new houses but also repairing existing houses, improving the environment and building a community centre and a new traffic system. The Trust recognises that this area and the rest of Woodlands have considerable problems and that regeneration will involve more that construction work. In that principle the Trust is willing to support and take on itself any project that will benefit the area and strengthen the community. (WCDT 1988)

Organization

Part of the feasibility study involved researching alternative constitutional structures and at the time there were few models available. The eventual outcome was to register the Trust as a company limited by guarantee, with charitable status. Membership is available to any local resident for an annual fee of £1, and, at the discretion of the committee, people living outside the area who have an interest in Woodlands can also become members. The Trust's members become shareholders, but with a limited liability of £1. The Trust had a Committee of 11 or 12 members, made up primarily of people living or working in the area, and committee meetings are held on a monthly basis. Bob Shaw, who had previously been involved in setting up the Community Council in Woodlands in the 1970s, was elected as the first convener of the Trust. The committee was initially made up of three constituencies: individuals, local voluntary groups and the local authority, and decisions were taken forward only when there was a majority in all three constituencies. Particular attention was paid to ensuring that the constitution was structured in such a way that no one interest group could dominate the organization. Thus, a third of the committee stand down each year and membership fees must be paid up well in advance to prevent a "take-over" by any one faction. In recent years, commitment has begun to fall off, and by 1994 membership of the board is made up of six representatives, one of whom is nominated by the Parkwood Community Council.

- Iain Urquhart (acting Chair)
- Sue Kinn (Treasurer)
- Simon Berry
- Stewart Leighton
- Sandra Lindsay (Parkwood Community Council)
- Tom Mulholland

The Trust now employs six staff, including the director, a post that Martin Hilland filled from the launch of the Trust until the end of 1992, when Douglas Harrison was recruited. The other staff are a business manager, an administrator, two clerical workers and a community arts worker. Core funding has been obtained from several sources since 1985, including the Urban Programme, Strathclyde Regional Council's community business management grant and funding linked to Glasgow's designation as "City of Culture" in 1990.

WCDT has three wholly owned subsidiary companies managed through the committee of the Trust. These companies operate as separate commercial entities, but any profits made by the subsidiaries are covenanted to WCDT. The subsidiary companies are Woodlands Community Factoring Ltd, now called Common Factor Ltd, Woodlands Community Maintenance Ltd and Woodlands Community Developments Ltd.

Funding

Core funding was provided from the Urban Programme until September 1992, when the local authority agreed to provide a loan of £75 000. This is repayable from income generated from the sale of the Trust's housing developments. The Trust is aiming for self-sufficiency and, by 1992, 70 per cent of WCDT funds were generated from commercial sources. As well as providing the running costs, at no cost Glasgow District Council also transferred to the Trust all its landholdings in the area on ten sites. This transfer was subject to a condition that development should take place on the sites according to an agreed timetable. The Council reserved the right to take back the land if the development programme was not maintained without good cause. An officer each from the Planning and Estates Departments were nominated to monitor the work of the Trust and to report quarterly to the North West Management Committee.

The Trust has also received capital funding from other sources, including Scottish Enterprise (formerly the Scottish Development Agency), which provided in particular LEGUP and Land Engineering grants, Strathclyde Regional

179

Council (Employment Grants scheme), European Social Fund (Strathclyde Community Business management grant and the Job Training scheme), the Scottish Arts Council, City of Culture grants, Scottish Homes (housing association finance and streetscape schemes), and the Clydesdale Bank (bridging finance and mortgages).

Projects

The development of East Woodlands

One of the original concerns that led to the setting up of the Trust was the amount of vacant land in the area and the threat of further demolition. Therefore, the physical development of the area was the primary objective. The steering committee set up prior to the launch of the Trust had begun to look at how best to set about regenerating the East Woodlands area. The first year was spent consulting the local community in order to produce a development plan for the area that would be responsive to the wishes of local people. It was decided that the best way forward was to hold an architectural competition in which Scottish architects were invited to submit letters of interest to the Trust. From these, five practices were selected and invited to submit detailed proposals for the development of East Woodlands. In particular, the brief specified that plans should be readily understandable to local people. The outcome of the competition was that the design submitted by the Glasgow firm of McGurn, Logan, Duncan and Opfer was selected by a panel made up of the WCDT committee, local people and professional assessors.

The winning scheme proposed the construction of slightly over 200 new homes and the repair of 560, as well as provision of a community centre, a park, and a new traffic management system. This development plan was then presented to potential developers and financiers, and was also used to build the confidence of residents that the redevelopment of the East Woodlands area was both possible and realistic. Housing associations were invited to consider developing some of the sites for affordable rented accommodation, public sector funding was sought, and private sector financial institutions were approached. At the same time, the District Council and housing associations in the area began to undertake a programme of repairs, which also helped to build confidence in the plan.

The local housing associations also became involved in the WCDT renewal strategy by agreeing to build houses for rent on some of the development sites in the East Woodlands area. The WCDT annual report for 1988 records that the Charing Cross Housing Association agreed to build houses on three sites: family housing on West End Park Street and Canarvon Street, and sheltered housing on Arlington Street; the Margaret Blackwood Housing Association proposed housing for disabled people in a scheme that would link up to the proposed new community centre; and the Fourwalls Housing Cooperative was also committed to building new rented accommodation in the area.

The proposed new community centre included in the development plan has been an issue in Woodlands since the early 1980s, and had been advocated by various local residents, including the Parkwood Community Development Association. The development plan showed the community centre as a multi-cultural and sports centre with a meeting room, reading room, café, and a hall with a capacity of 250 people. The centre – to be located on the corners of Arlington Street, Grant Street, and Ashley Street – was estimated to cost £1 million. However, this project has now been postponed, since it proved impossible to achieve a consensus between different sections of the community on how the centre could be used to the benefit of all interests.

A new traffic-management scheme was designed primarily to deter kerb-crawling, but the agreement of all parties was difficult to achieve. After three public meetings, the issue was finally resolved, with a proposal for partial road closures and the introduction of some one-way streets, different road surfaces to slow vehicle speeds, parking restrictions for non-residents, and some pedestrian-only areas. One unintended outcome of this proposal was that it further accentuated the physical division between the ethnic minority and White communities.

Woodlands Community Developments Ltd

The Woodlands Community Developments Ltd is one of the three subsidiary companies of the Trust. It holds all the Trust's land originally given by the City Council. The company also acts as a development company to construct houses for sale. These are initially offered to past and present residents of the area and, if any remain unsold, they are then put on the open market. Woodlands Community Developments Ltd received LEGUP and Land Engineering grants from the SDA, and the Clydesdale Bank provided bridging finance and a mortgage. The company is particularly concerned to provide good-quality and well insulated housing, built to a high standard and in sympathy with the surroundings. Surplus from the sale of the housing is covenanted back to the Trust and can be used to finance other projects. Woodlands Community Developments Ltd also acts as the overall co-ordinator of the East Woodlands development plan, in conjunction with the East Woodlands Group, a co-ordinating body made up of officers, councillors and community representatives.

A community-based repairs and factoring service

Woodlands Community Factoring Ltd was set up as a result of dissatisfaction with the existing property management and repair services provided by most private landlords in the area. It aims to provide an efficient and high-quality service at a reasonable price. The service is offered to the owners of tenements and the company has about 1200 clients in Woodlands and throughout the Strathclyde region. Financial support has come from Strathclyde Regional Council's Community Business Management grant, although this was restricted to assistance with book-keeping and accountancy. The company has faced some opposition from commercial companies, which have lost business, and some difficulties have been experienced in debt-collecting in an area of significant poverty.

Economic, training and employment initiatives

Economic, training and employment initiatives were not an initial concern of the WCDT, since it was primarily involved with the physical regeneration of East Woodlands. However, by 1990 the Trust was increasingly looking at the training needs within the area and it launched two courses targeted at women in the ethnic minorities. The courses attracted about 30 people and aimed to equip the women with the skills to enter the city centre office job market (Glasgow has the largest concentration of offices north of Manchester). Women from the ethnic minorities are particularly disadvantaged in the employment market in Glasgow and at least 60 per cent of families in the ethnic minorities are sustained by family-run businesses. Very few of these have had any management training and it was becoming clear that the mainstream training programmes on offer were not relevant to, or attracting, this section of the population. As a result, a sum of £19 000 was obtained from Scottish Enterprise in 1993 to set up a pilot project for women. Places on the course were oversubscribed, but some women faced objections from their families and some were the wives of foreign students who were unlikely to remain in the area for very long.

The training programme is aimed primarily at the ethnic minority community, reflecting the multi-cultural nature of the Woodlands population. Women are targeted, as they are seen to be most disadvantaged in entering the job market but they need employment to maintain household income. The training initiatives of WCDT have received funding from the European Social Fund, Strathclyde Regional Council and Strathclyde Community Business.

Early on in the project, the Trust created temporary employment for some unemployed local residents through the Manpower Services Commission's Community Programme. It was able to provide 36 jobs for one year in order to landscape vacant sites in the East Woodlands area. In 1994 the Trust had a training programme totalling over £200 000 involving 50–75 local people.

In the longer term, the Trust is aiming to provide training and employment initiatives with the Ethnic Minority Enterprise Centre, which covers the whole of Glasgow. This is now being funded by the Glasgow Development Agency, the City Council and Strathclyde Region, and will provide training and business advice services to ethnic minorities throughout the city. It is managed by representatives of ethnic minorities and was launched in 1994.

Arts and cultural development

Since 1989 WCDT has employed a community artist (Sean Taylor) as a full-time member of staff. He works with community groups and schools in Woodlands and other parts of Glasgow on a programme of cultural events. He has also instigated a programme of public art in association with recent housing developments in the area and he works closely with the Woodlands Festival Committee.

Progressing the development plan

A revised capital programme for the ten sites in the Trusts's ownership is set out in Table 9.1. This identifies the proposed development agency, the number of units created, the cost, and the years in which development is planned. Site 1 was completed by the Charing Cross Housing Association in 1991. Site 8, the first to be completed by the Trust in 1992, at Carnarvon Street and Ashley Street involved a development for sale. This was funded jointly by Woodlands Community Developments Ltd, the former SDA, and a bank, producing 24 units at a cost of £1.6 million. By 1994 all the sites had been completed or were under construction, apart from sites 2 and 4 and the Trust's final development at site 6. These are likely to begin construction by 1996. Figure 9.1 illustrates the location of the ten sites in Woodlands.

Table 9.1 East Woodlands capital programme at April 1994.

Site	Agency	Units	Cost (million)	Date constructed	Tenure
1	Charing Cross HA	43	£1.6	1991	For rent
2	Charing Cross HA, Scottish Homes	21	£1.2	1994	For rent, sheltered
3	WCD, GDA, bank	24	£1.8	1994	For sale
4	CCHA, M. Blackwood HA, SH, GDA	42	£4.2	1994–6	For rent
5	WCD, GDA, bank	20	£1.4	1994	For sale
6	WCD, GDA, bank	67	£1.9	1994–6	Student accom.
7	CCHA, SH	50	£2.8	1992	For rent, shared ownership
8	WCD, SDA, bank	23	£1.6	1992	For rent
9	CCHA	23	£1.3	1992	For rent
10	Fourwalls Co-op, SH	11	£0.6	1993	For rent
		324	£18.4		

The new-build programme is expected to create a total of 324 new units, of which 44 will be owner-occupied, 23 in shared-ownership, 169 for rent and 144 for special needs purposes. A capital programme of repairs was also proposed in 1991 for four tenement blocks owned by the City Council. The intention was that approximately £6 million would be spent on renovating 112 housing units.

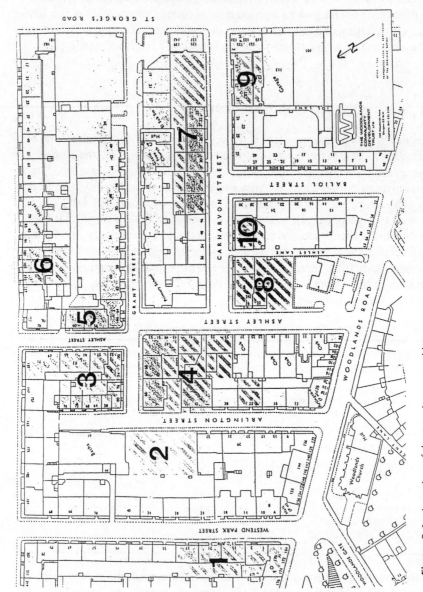

Figure 9.1 Location of the ten sites owned by WCDT.

In addition, in 1991 it was estimated that £1.5 million would be needed for street-scape improvements and £350 000 for the new park.

A total expenditure of about £25 million was planned for East Woodlands, but the Trust has faced difficulties, particularly in raising finance and in co-ordinating the development plans of housing associations. In the first instance, the Trust was hoping to attract private companies to develop the vacant sites and was using the development plan to generate interest. As the recession deepened, the private sector became increasingly unwilling to risk investment in an area such as Woodlands, where there had been little new private housebuilding in recent years. The Trust therefore set up its own development company, Woodlands Community Developments Ltd, to provide a vehicle to carry out development. The Trust also claims that agencies such as the former Scottish Development Agency were slow to provide matching funding and may have delayed some developments by up to two years. Similar delays have occurred in negotiations with the Glasgow Development Agency over funding of about £0.5 million for sites 3 and 5. The absence of public sector support may well have made banks and building societies more wary of committing resources to the area.

Confidence in the area was not helped by the decline in housing finance available to the Council for new development and repairs to its own stock. Lack of Council funding also proved a problem for the development of a new park that had been proposed in the original development plan and for which prospects looked bleak in 1994. However, the Trust hoped to use about £250 000 of its surplus derived from its first housing development for sale for the construction of the park. Finally, delays occurred on the sites allocated to housing associations, as a result of financial restraints imposed by the funding body, Scottish Homes. Scottish Homes also raised objections to the streetscape proposals that had been agreed by Strathclyde Regional Council, Glasgow District Council and WCDT after extensive local consultation.

The delay in raising finance for the Trust's development projects meant that the vacant land which had been transferred to the Trust was not developed within the agreed programme. After extensive negotiations and in the light of the difficult market conditions and uncertainties over public sector funding, it was agreed that the programme could be extended.

Conclusions

When the Woodlands Trust was launched in 1985, it had a relatively clear set of objectives and had the full backing of the Council in taking over the ten vacant sites in the area. Its primary task was to generate a community-based approach to urban regeneration, by which the transferred sites would be developed according to an integrated strategy and the proceeds would be ploughed back into the area to provide much-needed community facilities and environmental improvements. From this perspective, the Woodlands Trust was similar to several other community-based development organizations in other parts of the country. At the time it was argued that the Woodlands community could unite around an agreed set of objectives involving the provision of both owner-occupied housing (for those who could afford it) and rented and special needs units to be provided by housing associations. The Council would also contribute to the plan by renovating its own stock in the area. The Trust was launched in a spirit of enthusiasm and was broadly supported by existing organizations, although those willing to play a leading role in managing it tended to be drawn from the White and more affluent sections of the local community.

Over the past ten years some problems have arisen, many of which were beyond the control of the Trust, such that some of those closely involved have questioned whether in retrospect a Trust was the best vehicle for the task. One of the main problems was the economic recession and the cut-back in public sector resources that severely affected the Trust's development programme from the late 1980s onwards. The funding of the Trust was predicated on the ability to raise finance from public and private sources to develop owner-occupied housing for sale, such that a surplus would be created to be applied to other social and community objectives. In reality, the eastern side of Woodlands was a high-risk location for investment in a recession and it proved very difficult to raise matching funding from public and private sources. Likewise, because housing was not being constructed, the Trust was unable to fund the park, streetworks and the community centre, which might have made the area more attractive to investors and house-purchasers. At the same time, housing associations found it difficult to meet their commitments to the strategy, because of uncertainties and constraints on their own funding.

Some observers have also questioned whether the Trust was launched in the right way; early successes are often important in building confidence and commitment. Instead the Trust set up an extensive consultation programme to find out what people wanted, and promoted an architectural competition that absorbed at least a year. The first housing development was completed only in 1991. Although compact and self-contained, the Woodlands area is clearly a heterogeneous community. It is divided both racially and socially between the east and west ends, as well as containing considerable proportions of unemployed households living in poverty and a forceful middle-class element primarily concerned with conservation and environmental issues. Some Trust members now feel that more should have been done in the early years to build a consensus between the disparate sections of the community and to promote the Trust as a vehicle for bringing benefits to the whole area. As it is, some take the view that the Trust is simply an arm of the council and others see it as what one interviewee described as "a rather patronising White agenda sort of organization".

If the Trust was accepted by some parts of the community, it may have been because it was independent of both central and local government. As Bob Shaw, the Trust's first convener, describes its origins:

186

If the Woodlands Trust had been invented by central government and imposed on the City of Glasgow it would have been fought, denounced and treated as a cancer from Whitehall. Instead it grew organically locally and people accepted it. However, they accepted it as much because it was seen as a local set of solutions for a local set of problems. The ethos and thinking behind it wasn't properly accepted so the practicalities were put through the local authority. A lot of assumptions were made because at the beginning there was no global structure and there was a failure in the structure about funding and speed. That led to the current position where we have gone through a period where we went around telling people we had power. Now we realize we only have "permission" to seek funding or to deal with social problems. (Interview with Bob Shaw, March 1993.)

Thus, because the Trust was not part of a national "top-down" strategy with guidelines and funding attached, it had to develop a "bottom-up" approach where essentially its role was to persuade others to do things without raising too many expectations. This also created problems for the Trust in an area with a fractured community structure. It was necessary to encourage active involvement in the Trust, when apathy and cynicism were common reactions, and at the same time to ensure that as far as possible the Trust bridged the different and often conflicting interest groups in the community. The latter was never really achieved and several observers point to the low proportion of ethnic minorities and women on the committee. In periodic reviews the Trust attempted to recruit active members of other community organizations, but they were often already overcommitted, and support dwindled. As a result, the Trust has yet to develop a broad consensus beyond the existing (mainly White and middle-class) active members, and now accepts that more could have been done to promote and publicize its work. The underlying fear seems to be that significant changes to the composition or approach of the management structure could enable factional interests to launch a "take-over". This became particularly apparent in the dispute about how the proposed community centre would be used by the various local interest groups.

There are also mixed feelings about the role of lay-people in community-based organizations. Clearly, a considerable commitment is needed to take part in an organization such as a trust. Regular committee meetings must be attended and complex decisions, often involving large sums of money, have to be taken. In the Woodlands experience, certain professionals also take advantage of inexperienced lay-committees whose members do not have the skills to issue contracts and to monitor those working on a fee basis.

What has the Trust achieved to date? Despite the difficulties already outlined, the two council officers appointed to monitor the performance of the Trust are broadly satisfied that it has done the best it was able to do in the circumstances. It has produced plans for a range of housing developments and tenures, which so far have been constructed to a high specification and design standard. It is debatable whether the provision of a proportion of owner-occupied housing, which so far has been slow to sell, was appropriate in an area of high unemployment and relatively low incomes, or was included largely to generate a surplus for the Trust. However, the housing associations have provided high-quality rented accommodation for a variety of general and specific needs. The delays in the building programme have so far most notably postponed the provision of the park and streetscape improvements, as well as preventing the Trust from becoming financially self-sufficient, as was originally intended.

Whether similar developments would have occurred on the gap sites without the intervention of the Trust is also open to speculation. The wholly owned trading companies, such as Common Factor Ltd, have provided a high-quality service in the area, and may well continue beyond the life of the Trust. Some experience has been gained in the training field, but the recent launch of the Ethnic Minority Enterprise Centre for Glasgow as a whole may limit the growth of this area of work. Alternatively, the Trust could focus on local economic development by becoming part of a larger organization covering a wider area.

As a model for urban regeneration, a community development trust has both strengths and weaknesses. In areas with a relatively stable community and with organizations with relatively appropriate skills and experience, trusts are often able to develop and co-ordinate local interests to carry out significant development programmes. In this context, a trust is able to access public and private resources and to ensure that surpluses are channelled into social and community objectives. In areas such as Woodlands, with complex and often conflicting community interests, a different approach may be needed. One Glasgow Council officer was convinced that a trust was not the best vehicle for regeneration. He argued that "involving the community is almost directly contrary to achieving regeneration in an expedient manner", but if this approach is taken "what is needed is goodwill and trust between partners". It was his view that the council should have retained responsibility for implementing the development programme, whereas the Trust provided a co-ordinating role. This was an approach adopted in 1990 in the Crown Street Regeneration Project in the Gorbals district of Glasgow, with the Glasgow Development Agency owning the land and working closely with public agencies and private developers. A residents' steering group acts as a sounding board for local opinion (Galloway 1993).

This case study clearly illustrates some of the problems that can arise in working in partnership. Although the Trust had the advantage of taking on the City Council's land portfolio and could prepare its own plans for redevelopment, it had no additional funds to finance development. In an adverse economic and public sector funding climate, it could only resort to powers of persuasion and negotiation. And in doing this, it was in a relatively weak position. Delays in obtaining funding approval from statutory agencies also illustrate the limited powers of co-ordination at the Trust's disposal. In addition, many of the elements of the plan that residents would perceive as real benefits were dependent on the construction and sale of private housing and have yet to be achieved.

Moreover, the Trust had the added task of developing a consensus among factional elements of the community in order to represent their views with a single voice to the statutory agencies. For the reasons already cited, this proved very difficult.

Although the initial optimism in the Woodlands Trust may have been tempered by the difficulties experienced in achieving its development objectives, several options exist for the future. The Trust could continue in its present form, but tensions within the community could further weaken its effectiveness. Alternatively, it could confront these tensions and draw in a wider spectrum of interests to play a more direct role in running the Trust, and focus on existing strengths such as training. A third option might be to transform the organization into a co-ordinating body, within which residents are one segment of a wider coalition of local interests and development agencies.

The Woodlands examples illustrates particularly clearly both the practical difficulties of achieving an effective community-based approach to urban regeneration and the importance of achieving a consensus among the community interests represented in the regeneration agency.

CHAPTER 10
An evaluation of alternative approaches to partnership

> I am certain that we must, in the future, tap more than ever two resources that have contributed in the past, but have a lot more to offer. The resources are at the opposite end of the spectrum – the European Community and local initiative and enterprise. I do not see these in opposition or competition to each other, but working together in partnership. *David Hunt MP, Secretary of State for Wales, 25 January 1993*

In the concluding chapters we hope to draw out some of the specific and broader themes associated with the concept of partnership, arising from both the case studies and the earlier chapters on theoretical explanations and the historical development of the idea. At best, the evaluation of something as complex as urban policy is an inexact science, and our approach has been to examine not just the outcomes in terms of jobs created, houses renovated or the number of training places provided. We are particularly concerned about the processes at the national and local levels that have given rise to coalition building, the way resources of all kinds have been deployed, and the extent to which the capacity of local communities to contribute to, and in some cases manage, regeneration programmes has been developed. Perhaps most important, we are explicitly adopting the position of Stone (1987; Stone et al. 1991) and Keating (1991), quoted in Chapter 2, who suggest that urban regimes are "constellations of public and private power within a structurally defined context . . . with the composition of each and the balance between (economic and political power) varying among cities" (Keating 1991: 7–8). From this starting point it is necessary to examine empirically which interests are involved, how resources are allocated, which stakeholders are gaining and which losing, and whether outcomes suggest that the organization's own objectives are being achieved.

The six case studies have been researched and written up in a narrative form, which makes clear the origins, development, internal and external relationships, and actions of the six examples. In carrying out the study, we have drawn on the concept of pluralistic evaluation, whereby research must not only evaluate "success" but must also "explore and explain the institution . . . and its services" (Smith & Cantley 1985: 12). Our approach has therefore been to develop an understanding of the roles of the different stakeholders and interest groups in each case, as well as exploring how the agency has been influenced by the social, economic and policy context in which it is operating. From detailed interviews with key actors, attendance at formal and informal meetings, documentation produced by the agency, and other sources, a composite picture can be built up, which gives a rounded view of the agency operating within its institutional context.

Our intention is to approach the evaluation in two stages, in order to explore different aspects of the concept of partnership in urban regeneration. The first stage will involve an internal evaluation according to five different criteria, in order to see how far there is common experience between the six case studies. This will focus particularly on the origins, internal structure, decision-making processes and outcomes. The second stage will be an external evaluation of the contribution of these partnerships to a wider understanding of urban regeneration and urban policy. Questions will be raised concerning the place of the agency in the wider policy context, the extent to which both physical and redistributive strategies can be achieved, as well as issues concerning transparency, accountability and the likely long-term impact on urban problems. Perhaps most important, if partnership is to continue to be an essential ingredient of urban policy, how can the State create a policy framework that provides positive support and what kinds of partnerships should be actively promoted?

Internal evaluation

In taking the idea of the urban regime as a starting point, it will be necessary to explore the origins of each partnership, the ways in which the interested parties came together to define a set of common objectives, and the resources it was able to generate or exert an influence over. The analysis then moves on to review the processes by which decisions are made and action taken, and finally attention is paid to the outputs, impacts and outcomes resulting from the direct deployment of resources and the indirect influence on other actors in the target area. The approach will be to review each of these criteria in turn to see how far common experiences emerge.

Origins

Partnerships arise through the mobilization of different interests in response to a combination of structural factors, government initiatives and local circumstances. The initial starting point is normally a concern that action needs to be taken to tackle economic, social and environmental issues that are perceived locally as being a growing threat to economic prosperity and social cohesion. The lead is often taken by a significant interest, such as central government, the local authority, chamber of commerce or community organizations, which then mobilizes others to join in a coalition of agencies. A strategy is then prepared and organizational arrangements devised in order to achieve agreed objectives. At the same time, a target area is identified. The initial mobilization process may be launched in response to local perceptions of need, although more often government policy may be the trigger. Government policy may be seen as both a threat – in that some unwanted initiative, such as an urban development corporation, might be imposed on the area – or be perceived as an opportunity, where additional resources might be made available to an appropriate delivery mechanism. The involvement of different local interests, and the balance of power between them, may at least in part reflect conditions imposed by government on the nature of agencies most likely to receive preferential funding from central sources.

All of the case studies examined here emerged in the late 1980s. The areas, which range from the very local to the city-wide, were suffering from growing unemployment and all were experiencing the adverse consequences of economic restructuring that caused a decline in manufacturing industry and a boom in the service sector. Local authorities had experienced a decline in statutory powers and finance for at least a decade, and central government was both transferring powers to unelected quangos and promoting the involvement of the corporate sector in urban regeneration. Thus, while debate continued at the national level about the advantages of the Single European Market and the globalization of capital, business, State and local elites were searching for new ways to promote growth and attract inward investment in an increasingly competitive market. In some cases the emphasis was more on the condition of housing in the area, linked to other aspects of urban deprivation, such as unemployment and dependency on welfare payments.

In both Birmingham and Greenwich the initial trigger for partnership formation was the threat of the imposition of a government-controlled urban development corporation. Birmingham had experienced a succession of government policy initiatives, including being designated one of the first Inner City Partnerships. Its Labour administration had also developed a pragmatic approach to working with the private sector on joint ventures such as the city centre and National Exhibition Centre. In addition, after the 1984 local election, regular meetings had been instituted between Albert Bore, Chair of the Economic Development Committee, and major local companies. It was John Douglas, Managing Director of R. M. Douglas, a local firm of developers, who had first promoted the idea to the City Action Team of a regeneration initiative led by the private sector. The idea was soon adopted by the city's Chamber of Commerce and Industry, and was discussed at the regular liaison meetings with the City Council.

The initial proposal that emerged in 1987 was for an urban development agency to be controlled by the City Council, but with minority private sector involvement. Funding was to be sought from central government. After the 1987 general election, Nicholas Ridley, the new Secretary of State for the Environment, was committed to promoting a new generation of UDCs and, in principle, Birmingham was a suitable candidate. When approached by Birmingham City Council, strongly supported by the private sector, he agreed to accept a locally controlled regeneration agency, but on condition that the private sector would be in the majority, that no central funding was provided and that the area be designated a Simplified Planning Zone. Thus, when Birmingham Heartlands (BHL) was established in 1988, it differed substantially from the original proposal. The majority of shares were held by the private sector and there was no additional funding provided. Initially, the intention was that the company itself would be the primary developer, but legal difficulties concerning potential conflicts of interest resulted in a further change. BHL would promote a series of development frameworks for different sites, and implementation would be monitored through working parties. The City Council would remain responsible for its own housing in the area and for planning matters.

A further pragmatic response to local circumstances occurred in the early 1990s when it became clear that the severe economic recession was likely to bring a halt to development in Birmingham Heartlands. The initial response was to submit a bid for the first round of City Challenge in 1991. When this was rejected, BHL had little alternative but to negotiate terms for UDC status. The outcome was a guarantee of funding over five years and the retention of some of the positive features of BHL, such as the City Council's nominating half the places on the board, the retention of BHL's strategy and a continuing role for the Council's planning department in advising on all planning matters. In the Birmingham case, negotiations surrounding BHL and the UDC were largely carried out between the City Council, the private sector and central government. The voluntary sector appears to have largely been excluded from the debate and there was little pressure from the locality to play a representative role on the boards of either organization.

In the case of the Greenwich Waterfront, the original circumstances were similar to those in Birmingham. Deindustrialization and economic restructuring throughout the 1980s were producing high levels of unemployment and increasing amounts of vacant and derelict land. By 1988, at the height of the property boom, the London Borough of Greenwich became concerned that sites would be developed in a piecemeal fashion and that the private sector organization, British Urban Development, was investigating the development of the British Gas site at Port Greenwich. In addition, there was also a local concern that the government was considering the designation of a further set of UDCs or an extension of the LDDC's boundaries. Initially, these growing pressures led Greenwich to consider preparing a development brief for the Waterfront area. It soon became clear that, given the current levels of unemployment and deprivation, a much broader corporate strategy was needed. Greenwich was also strongly committed to the principle of public consultation and its membership of the Docklands Consultative Committee (DCC) led it to take the view that any strategy for the area should be based on public participation and community involvement. The DCC was therefore commissioned to carry out a detailed public consultation exercise, whereas the Civic Trust Regeneration Unit was invited to prepare a strategy for the Waterfront. Although there were some locally dependent corporate interests in the area, such as British Gas and the Woolwich Building Society, there was no strong lobby for greater private sector involvement at this stage. Thus, the agency that emerged was firmly directed by the local authority, although it later incorporated community and business forums and was managed by a complex representative structure.

The Newcastle Initiative emerged in a similar economic and political climate, but through a very different process. In this case it was a local and national business elite that took the lead. The late 1980s marked the high point of the government's attempts to involve business leadership in urban regeneration with organizations such as the Confederation of British Industry (CBI) claiming a leading role in the field. The influential CBI report, *Initiatives beyond charity* (CBI 1988), set out guidelines for the formation of business leadership teams in major cities. This was reinforced by the formation of the Business in the Cities Forum in December 1988 to provide a support network for business leadership teams.

Newcastle provided an appropriate location for the establishment of the first pilot project. Its economic structure was heavily weighted towards the declining manufacturing and heavy engineering sectors, despite having attracted significant amounts of office-based and service industries into the city centre from the 1960s onwards. It also had a closely knit business elite, which, like the City Council, was concerned to promote the city as a thriving regional capital of the North East. As Shaw (1993) notes, economic decline over at least 60 years had generated a series of alliances between public and private sectors, leading to the formation of non-elected development and promotional agencies operating regional and local growth strategies. It was therefore fertile ground for a further development of this process such as The Newcastle Initiative (TNI), not least because two members of the CBI task force came from Newcastle.

The CBI task force's core team began to promote the idea in Newcastle from January 1988 through a series of presentations and dinners for senior business executives. Clearly drawing on the US growth coalition tradition, the core team set about (according to the management jargon of the time) "securing leadership commitment", "establishing change agents", and "identifying flagship projects" in order to "build momentum". Initially, the intention was to identify ten private sector representatives for the board, together with four senior public sector figures with no voting rights. An executive office was staffed by a small team of secondees, with a budget of approximately £110 000. TNI is thus a non-elected promotional agency that implements its strategy through informal mechanisms of influence, promotion and negotiation. TNI also recruits senior managers of key local agencies, who in turn can exert influence through interlocking membership of the region's governmental and business infrastructure. It emerged at a juncture in national politics when business leadership was strongly supported by government, and was broadly welcomed when Newcastle was suggested for a pilot project.

The Woodlands Community Development Trust (WCDT) and Brownlow Community Trust (BCT) represent community initiatives operating in very different urban contexts. The Woodlands example emerged in a highly developed, heterogeneous community on the fringes of the central area of Glasgow in the mid-1980s. Glasgow City Council's faltering housing programme had left several gap sites in the East Woodlands area, and growing evidence of deprivation and an increasing proportion of ethnic minorities caused both the City Council and the more affluent owner-occupiers to the west to consider alternative approaches to regeneration. The boundaries of Woodlands were clearly defined by both the perceptions of residents and City Council, which had already established a community council for the area.

The idea of setting up a development trust arose among councillors and officers and key activists in the area. It was attractive in that the Council's ownership and responsibility for ten vacant sites could be transferred to a non-profit company, and the local community could take on responsibility for how those sites were developed and how any surpluses arising could be ploughed back into social, economic and environmental projects. Although the housing and planning departments supported this option, it now appears that the Estates Department favoured retention of the sites. Among the residents, a small and articulate proportion broadly favoured the proposal, a second group saw the Trust as a front for the local authority, while a third group remained sceptical or apathetic. At least two years was spent in preparatory consultation and in carrying out a council-sponsored feasibility study into the proposal, before the Trust was formally established in February 1985 as a company limited by guarantee. At least a further year was spent in holding an architectural competition and in preparing the development plan. After extensive delays in programming and raising sufficient capital from public and private sources, the first housing association development was completed in 1991 and the Trust's first development for sale in 1992.

In contrast, in Brownlow, the formation of the Trust emerged from both the relatively unique historical origins of the Craigavon New Town and the need to respond to the availability of funding. Brownlow is the only completed section of the proposed New Town of Craigavon, which was designed in the 1960s to relieve overcrowding in Belfast and to provide a focus for economic development in Northern Ireland. The few jobs that were created had largely disappeared by the mid-1970s, with the result that the worsening economic and political conditions created a population with high levels of unemployment, poverty, ill health and social exclusion in a partially completed new town. From the beginning, despite these adverse conditions, community organizations promoted a series of plans to improve living conditions and reduce poverty.

195

From 1969, the Brownlow Community Council had been established by residents and the Development Commission to meet the needs of those moving into the area, until the latter was disbanded in 1973. By the mid-1980s a full review of the needs of the area was carried out by residents and the statutory agencies. The Greater Brownlow Review led to the setting up of a non-sectarian community organization called the Brownlow Community Development Association (BCDA). This produced its own strategy for the future, Brownlow 2000, which identified in particular the need for economic development to create jobs. At the same time the BCDA persuaded the DoE to appoint consultants to prepare an economic strategy for the town. One of the major recommendations was that the town itself should form a community company to promote a new village centre. This was later established as Brownlow Ltd.

While discussions were proceeding between the BCDA, Brownlow Ltd and the statutory agencies, about how a strategy might be advanced, the Southern Health and Social Services Board received information about the third European Poverty Programme. This offered matching funding in order to set up several model action projects across Europe to develop "transferable methods and models of good practice in combating exclusion" (BCT 1992), linked to a major transnational evaluation programme. A steering group of residents and other voluntary and statutory bodies was hastily assembled and the DoE consultants were retained to advise on the submission. The strategy that was eventually submitted to Brussels was based on the principles of participation, partnership and an integrated approach, and it identified as the target groups women, children, the long-term unemployed and the young unemployed. Once funding had been approved, the steering group became a company limited by guarantee and a charity to be known as Brownlow Community Trust. Under the terms of the grant, the Trust was required to run social and community programmes in close collaboration with the statutory agencies; the acquisition of land or buildings was precluded. Brownlow Ltd, which was represented on the Trust, continued to pursue its economic and training remit.

In Scotland a review of urban policy in the late 1980s, carried out by the Scottish Office, led to the launch of the Wester Hailes Partnership as one of four demonstration projects. For two decades, urban regeneration had concentrated on the inner areas of west and central Scotland through partnership arrangements between local authorities, the Scottish Development Agency, community-based housing associations and a wide variety of statutory agencies. The SDA in particular had supported and encouraged private sector involvement and the voluntary sector had received significant funding through the Urban Programme. *New life for urban Scotland* (Scottish Office 1988) noted the significant achievements in the inner city, but found that the peripheral housing estates on the fringes of the main conurbations were displaying growing concentrations of unemployment, worsening housing conditions and the absences of social amenities and commercial facilities that other areas took for granted. The report proposed a shift in resources towards these areas by applying the principles of partnership, co-ordination and targeting learned elsewhere. In particular, the four areas chosen – Castlemilk (Glasgow), Ferguslie Park (Paisley), Wester Hailes (Edinburgh) and Whitfield (Dundee) – would be managed by partnerships under Scottish Office leadership. The three key principles to be applied were to be an integrated approach to economic, social and physical regeneration, the inclusion of the private sector, and the full involvement of the local community "to allow local people to take responsibility for their areas" (Scottish Office 1993: 6).

Little is known about how the four areas were selected, except that the Scottish Office sought an even distribution across central Scotland, based on indices of deprivation and other geographical and political factors. In Wester Hailes a management board of 17 was established in 1989 to be chaired by a representative of the Scottish Office. Members were drawn from local authorities, statutory agencies, a business support group and a residents' organization known as the Representative Council, itself funded through the Urban Programme. A resource team of 12 staff, directed by a secondee from the Scottish Office, provided administrative support and co-ordinates the strategy, which has an expected life of ten years.

From the foregoing discussion of the origins of the six case studies, it is apparent that local circumstances, the perceptions and actions of particular local interests and agencies, and the national policy context at the time – came together to produce a complex framework from which particular partnership arrangements emerge. In all cases an uneven balance of power exists between public, private and voluntary sectors and it is the way these interests interact at a particular conjuncture that broadly determines the outcome. In Greenwich, and to a lesser extent in Birmingham, the local authority was the dominant interest, whereas in Woodlands and Brownlow it was local community representatives and, particularly in the latter, the statutory agencies. In Newcastle the TNI was largely a creation of the private sector in response to a CBI initiative, where the local authority provided passive approval, and local community interests were hardly involved. In Wester Hailes and Brownlow, national and European policy developments provided the primary motivation for coalition formation. In most cases, the definition of the target area proved relatively uncontentious.

Constitution

The constitution of partnerships tends to reflect several competing pressures. The initiators normally wish to attract a wide range of local interests in order to increase the political impact of the agency in the locality, while ensuring that the dominant interests can retain influence over the strategy and objectives. Where national policy impinges on the purpose or funding of the agency, the distribution of partners may be predetermined.

In the case of Birmingham Heartlands, the City Council originally proposed a structure where it was the dominant partner, the private sector was in the minority, and the voluntary sector was unrepresented. This was rejected by the DOE, which favoured an agency led by the private sector, with the City Council in the minority. The outcome was that DOE approval was given for 65 per cent of the shares to be owned by five companies (Douglas, Galliford, Tarmac, Wimpey and Bryant), 35 per cent to be in the control of the City Council, and one share was to be retained by the Chamber of Commerce and Industry. In the transition to the UDC, DOE approval was given for half the places on the board to be nominated by the Council and the other half to be appointed by the Secretary of State. Sir Reginald Eyre held the post of Chairman in both organizations. Since the objectives of BHL and BHDC were predominantly development orientated, representation of local residents on the board was dismissed at an early stage in favour of public consultation measures and the establishment of the Heartlands Trust. BHL and BHDC appear to have operated effectively as decision-making bodies. A total of £297 million was invested or committed from all sources by May 1993, and further expenditure by BHDC of between £5 million and £9million per year was projected over the next five years. Several innovative consultation methods had been initiated, such as "planning for real", and there is broad support for the work of the UDC among residents, local interest groups and the City Council.

In Greenwich Waterfront the Borough Council has invested much time in mobilizing different interests in the area to play their full part in the partnership. In the early stages, both the Docklands Consultative Group and the Civic Trust Regeneration Unit carried out extensive consultation exercises with local residents and voluntary organizations. In addition, Coopers & Lybrand seconded a member of their staff to the Partnership to assist in setting up a Business Forum. By October 1992 over 120 local businesses were affiliated. In June 1992 a steering group was set up with the long-term objective of registering as an independent company limited by guarantee. Five places have been allocated to the London Borough of Greenwich, five to representatives elected by the business forum, and five to representatives of the community forum. In addition, there is a place for one representative of Thamesmead Town Ltd. Council influence is maintained through membership of the steering group and through the Waterfront team leader, who works half time as the Director of Leisure for Greenwich. The co-ordinator was also seconded from Greenwich Planning Department. The balance of power is broadly weighted in the council's favour, although the business and community forums can have considerable influence on specific policy issues. Several representatives have commented on the bureaucratic nature of the agency and the relative lack of evidence of progress on the ground.

In Brownlow and Woodlands there is a considerable emphasis on community involvement and community management of the projects. How far the two examples give rise to community control or empowerment is debatable. In Brownlow the Trust board is made up of 23 members, of whom nine come from statutory agencies, two (councillors) from the borough council, four from Brownlow Community Development Association, four from other community projects in the area, and four community representatives elected annually. Since the beginning of the project, the board has been chaired by the unit general manager of the Southern Health and Social Services Board. There are no private sector companies represented on the board, because there are few located in Brownlow and their involvement was not a condition of EU funding. From the interviews carried out with participants, it became clear that in the early stages the board was largely dominated by the representatives of the statutory agencies. It was they who had the most experience of working through committees and who understood the complex interrelationships between the statutory and voluntary sectors in Northern Ireland. The community representatives, on the other hand, were sceptical of the project in the early stages and took some time to build confidence and to exert greater influence over proceedings. As the board became more familiar with their role, community representatives were more willing to intervene or to express dissent. The decisions of the board were almost always unanimous, and votes were very rarely needed.

In Woodlands the Trust was broadly conceived as a partnership between the local community and Glasgow City Council. In the early years the committee was made up of 11 or 12 members drawn from individuals living in the area, local community groups and the local authority. This has now decreased to six, who are almost entirely local residents, of whom one is nominated by the Park Community Council. The City Council also nominated two officers to monitor the Trust's activities. Interviews with key participants suggest that apathy and divisions between sections of the community have adversely affected the work of the Trust. Membership of the board requires significant management skills and regular attendance at meetings over an extended period. Those willing to take on such a role have tended to come from the White, middle-class section of the community, and this has caused those sections not represented to raise doubts about the role and purpose of the Trust. In addition, delays caused by the difficulties of raising capital finance from public and private sources have severely undermined the ability of the Trust to meet its development programme and to build confidence in the area, through the provision of facilities and improvements to the environment. The Trust is itself aware of its failure fully to explain its role in the early years and to build support across all sections of the community, yet not to raise expectations that a quick solution to the areas's problems could be achieved.

The Newcastle Initiative took a very different approach. The principle behind it was that business should be seen to be taking a lead in regenerating the city. It therefore set about setting up a small and lean management structure, involving ten of the most senior business executives; representatives of the public sector were invited as observers but did not have voting rights. The board does not have executive powers, but it initiates concerted action through promotional activities, influence and membership of other organizations and agencies. Although TNI has selected the Cruddas Park Development Trust as one of its projects, it does not consider that community representation on its board is appropriate. In order to maintain flexibility, the Chief Executive and an assistant are seconded for a maximum of two years each. By 1994 the membership of the board had increased to 19, drawn from national and multinational companies, local and national government departments, the City Council, the Newcastle universities and the local newspaper. The current Chair is the Chief Executive of English Estates. Board members are selected according to the size and importance of the company or organization, and influence is brought to bear through informal contacts, dinners, promotional activities and, perhaps most important, interlocking membership of development agencies, such as TECs, City Challenge and the UDC.

The constitution of the Wester Hailes Partnership was predetermined by the Scottish Office, which had one representative on the board in addition to the Chair. Two representatives each were appointed by Lothian Regional Council and Edinburgh District Council. The LEC, the Employment Service, Scottish Homes, the Health Board, Capital Enterprise Trust and the business support group each appointed one, whereas the Representative Council has five spokespersons with voting rights at any one meeting. The board meets about seven times a year.

Objectives

Partnership objectives are often relatively unclear in the early stages of a project although the initiating agency attempts to create an agenda through the co-option of other interests and in the way the partnership is structured. Some partnerships appoint consultants to prepare a strategy, or do so themselves, and government policy and funding regimes can also be a significant influence. In most cases considerable flexibility is built into the strategy, so that pragmatic responses can be made to new opportunities as they arise. These might include political or economic changes at the local level, or potential access to funding from central government or the European Union. The extent to which the partnership's strategy creates a feasible and achievable set of targets for the area can be of crucial importance to a successful partnership, as is the influence it can bring to bear on the implementation of its objectives.

In the run up to the launch of Birmingham Heartlands, a development strategy was commissioned from Roger Tym & Partners in 1987. This was then made the subject of public consultation and was subsequently revised by Birmingham City Council. The strategy reviewed the social, economic and physical characteristics of the target area, as well as identifying opportunities and constraints. It proposed the joint aims of attracting new economic activity and jobs, and improving living conditions for the existing residents. These were to be achieved through a physical development strategy, a marketing strategy and measures to ensure that those living in the area benefited directly. Proposals were included for six subareas, such as the new urban village at Bordesley, the redevelopment and improvement of some industrial sites, and major infrastructural projects such as the spine road and the Midland Metro. In all, the consultants estimated that 200 ha could be developed for residential, business and industrial uses over a ten-year period. Both BHL and BHDC have remained broadly committed to the original strategy, although the priority and phasing of different elements has fluctuated. A balance between property-led and redistributive objectives has also been maintained. The UDC tends to apply a property-led approach to the development of industrial and new housing sites and the provision of infrastructure, while redistributive objectives are applied in the improvement of existing housing, where the City Council plays a primary role, and the provision of training, child-care and the support of the Heartlands Trust. The development of Bordesley urban village suggests a dual approach involving the promotion of private house-building and the provision of affordable housing, social facilities and environmental improvements. The 1993–4 corporate plan estimated that 21 000 new jobs would be created in 8.3 million sq. ft (770 000 m^2) of new floorspace, and that 570 new homes would be constructed and 400 refurbished in the lifetime of the agency.

In Greenwich there was a more extensive period of consultation before a strategy emerged. From 1988 until early 1991, the Borough Council commissioned several studies of the area, set up interdepartmental working parties and consulted local organizations on the needs of the area. The strategy that emerged in 1991 (London Borough of Greenwich 1991) was produced jointly by the Planning Department and the Civic Trust Regeneration Unit, and included development guidelines, an urban design framework, targets for community provision and a framework for implementation. Because of the size of the area and the uncertainty surrounding some key sites, its primary aim was to establish a set of principles to which all sectors could subscribe. A complex organizational structure was proposed, made up of a board to oversee the strategy, some agencies to implement the strategy in defined areas, and a community forum to encourage the greater involvement of local groups. The strategy was launched at a public meeting attended by local interests, business and practitioners.

The Waterfront strategy represented a reasonably clear vision of how the Borough saw the area developing, although some of those involved later suggested that perhaps too much time had been spent in consultation and that the proposed organizational framework was too complex. Council officers argued that time was needed in order to establish confidence and to integrate the views of all concerned. This was primarily because in the early 1980s a sense of mistrust had developed between the private sector and the Council, which many perceived as being hostile and uncaring. The local community was also fragmented and suspicious that it would be bypassed by an alliance between the council and local businesses. Moreover, blight had been caused in the Waterfront area by uncertainties relating to a series of major road proposals and the possibility of extensions to the Docklands light railway and the Jubilee line. On top of this, restructuring in the local economy, and the changing perceptions about the role of the area in relation to the wider London property market, meant that major strategic decisions were essential before development could take place on any scale.

Thus, although the London Borough of Greenwich had assembled a reasonably well balanced coalition of local interests in a complex set of organizational structures, it was difficult to maintain the momentum until strategic decisions were made largely outside the area. The partnership therefore focused on small-scale improvements in the town centres of Woolwich and Greenwich, on promoting the advantages of the area, and in lobbying central government and Brussels for additional resources and ensuring that advantageous decisions were made on infrastructural investment. Thus, as the partnership developed, its objectives tended to be determined by opportunities arising from national and European policies; for example, bids were submitted to City Challenge, the Urban Partnership Fund, the Millennium Fund and the KONVER initiative.

In Brownlow the objectives of the Trust were clearly laid down by the European Poverty 3 programme. Six principles had been established to which all bids had to conform. These stressed the need for partnership, the involvement of all agencies, a multidimensional approach to poverty, the integration of economic and social policies, additionality and the direct participation of the target groups. In preparing its bid, the Trust identified the causes of poverty in Brownlow, proposed to target the unemployed, lone-parent families and children, and set out a series of objectives. These included building community cohesion, decreasing dependency, enhancing enterprise and the quality of life, and to improve services, and to promote co-ordination and the integration of service delivery. The outcome was that the Trust obtained £2.2 million in funding, with just under half coming from the EU. The remainder was to come from the statutory agencies. The objectives remained relatively fixed throughout the life of the project, although the target group of lone-parent families was subsequently revised to include all women. In addition, the operational principles were simplified to participation, partnership and an integrated approach.

Much of the work of the Trust has been concerned with allocating resources to social and community projects designed to meet the needs of the target groups and the wider community, as well as achieving a closer integration of the services of the statutory agencies. Priority has been given to meeting social needs such as training, childcare, education, healthcare and cultural activities. Apart from preparing an economic strategy, the Trust has not become directly involved in economic development or in attracting inward investment.

In Woodlands the objectives of the Trust emerged from discussions with the City Council. In the early 1980s the main problems as perceived by Council officers and some of the community groups were poor housing conditions, a deteriorating environment, and social problems such as kerb-crawling. The objectives that emerged from discussions between the Council and leading members of the local community council involved the transfer at no cost of ten sites in East Woodlands to a newly formed community-based development trust. By developing the sites the trust could both create high-quality housing for sale and involve housing associations in the provision of rented accommodation. The resulting financial surplus could be used to improve social facilities, to run training programmes and to upgrade the environment. After running an architectural competition, and after extensive public consultation, a development plan was prepared for the ten sites. This was a condition of the transfer of ownership from the Housing Department. Some of the difficulties that emerged later arose from the problems the trust experienced in raising capital finance from public and private sources.

The objectives of The Newcastle Initiative arose from a CBI report (CBI 1988), which set out to demonstrate the need for the corporate sector to play a leading role in urban regeneration, on the grounds that this created prosperity for all. The CBI report argued that a common process could be adopted in which the key elements were physical development, the creation of employment opportunities, community involvement and working in partnership. During the formation of TNI, discussions took place about which projects could most usefully be pursued. Five were eventually selected, derived from the interests of key members and an assessment of where TNI could have the maximum impact. They tended to be largely promotional and advisory in nature, since the organization had few resources and no direct powers of implementation. The Grey Street Renaissance and the Theatre Village were both about the refurbishment and attraction of business investment to parts of the central area, Japanese Links and publicity were promotional and marketing campaigns, and business action in the community involved providing business advice to the Cruddas Park Development Trust and later to the West End Partnership. After the appointment of a new Chief Executive in 1992, these were revised: the Grey Street Initiative was enlarged to include the whole of Grainger Town, the Theatre Village was dropped because it had been superseded by the West End Partnership, and the Japanese Links campaign was dropped. While retaining an interest in Cruddas Park and City Challenge, TNI has now adopted as two major objectives the promotion of the arts and Newcastle upon Tyne as a city of higher education.

Soon after the Wester Hailes Partnership was launched, it produced a strategy document setting out goals for housing, the environment, employment, social policy, local facilities and image. These were then developed into detailed programmes of action. In the early stages, housing and training were the main priorities, but, as the programme developed, all objectives were given equal attention. More recently, seven interdependent objectives were identified, covering, housing, unemployment, household income, facilities and the environment, economic activity, the development of new assets by the community, and image enhancement. Five subgroups of the Partnership board oversee progress in key policy areas. The underlying principle of the partnership appears to be to increase household incomes, improve service delivery and to develop the range of services and facilities available in order to integrate Wester Hailes more fully into the wider urban economy and society.

Resources

A primary aim of all partnerships is to mobilize additional resources in order to implement the agreed strategy. The financial environment in which partnerships operate is becoming increasingly complex. Central government and the EU are increasingly allocating capital and revenue resources on a competitive basis and are requiring evidence of other additional funding and private sector leverage. Partnerships are proving increasingly adept at lobbying for resources on this basis and are involving those partners that offer increased credibility in the eyes of funders. In addition, partnerships are working closely with government agencies, such as Task Forces, TECs and LECs, which themselves can contribute matching funding for projects that meet their funding criteria. Thus, partnerships are working at the local, national and European levels to access additional resources for their area.

The experience of Birmingham Heartlands Ltd indicated that a partnership between the local authority and private sector interests was insufficient to generate adequate resources during an economic recession. The failure of its first-round City Challenge bid led to negotiations for UDC status and an allocation of £26.4 million in the first four years. In addition, substantial additional resources have been agreed by the Department of Transport for the spine road, and negotiations are continuing for the funding of the Midland Metro. A further £4–9 million is expected in the coming years from European sources. The City Council has also used the Urban Programme for schemes such as the construction of the Kingston day nursery and has an Estate Action programme in the Heartlands area. The Task Force and TEC have also assisted with the provision of an Enterprise Centre and training schemes such as Just for Starters. Over the lifetime of the UDC, it is anticipated that £305 million of public resources will be spent, generating private sector investment of £957 million.

Greenwich Waterfront is less fortunate than Birmingham Heartlands in that it has no direct source of funding and is dependent on its members for implementing the strategy. It has therefore focused on influencing the spending decisions of the local authority, the TEC and, as far as possible, major landowners such as British Gas, the Ministry of Defence and Thamesmead Town. In addition, the partnership has submitted bids for City Challenge, the Urban Partnership Fund, Derelict Land Grant, City Grant and the Millennium Fund. Additional benefits will arise from English Heritage's Conservation Area Partnership scheme and the successful bid for the EU's KONVER programme for the Royal Arsenal site. For the future, indirect benefits will arise from the extensions to the DLR and Jubilee line, and from the potential involvement of English Partnerships in the area.

The Brownlow Community Trust receives revenue funding from the EU and the statutory agencies, which is then used for core and project funding according to its objectives. It is not permitted to fund capital projects, but has influenced investment decisions by agencies such as the Housing Executive and Southern Health and Social Services Board.

The Woodlands Trust was originally funded through the Urban Programme until 1992 when it received a loan of £75 000 from the Glasgow City Council. Capital funding for housing development has been raised from both the Scottish Development Agency (subsequently the Glasgow Development Agency) and from commercial sources.

The Newcastle Initiative operates on a revenue budget of about £200 000, more than half of which comes from the secondment of staff and donations in kind. It has no capital finance, but operates in a promotional role in attracting additional public and private investment to the city.

Wester Hailes Partnership has an annual budget of about £0.5 million from the Scottish Office to cover the salaries of the resource team and other running costs. In addition, it has an Urban Programme allocation, which has risen from £1.9 million in 1991–2 to £2.46 million in 1993–4. Scottish Homes has an additional allocation for the four New Life areas, and in 1993–4 spent £5.7 million in Wester Hailes. All other agencies are encouraged to bend their mainstream programmes in favour of Wester Hailes. The Partnership is unable to disaggregate budgetary figures to identify additional expenditure.

Outputs, impacts and outcomes

The assessment of the achievements of a partnership is surrounded by methodological difficulties that make a quantitative evaluation almost impossible. In the first place, it is not possible to assess what might have happened in an area if a regeneration agency had not existed. This is the "policy off" problem. Would investment have taken place anyway through the agency of the local authority or other organizations? Secondly, there is the problem of timing. At what point in the development of a partnership is it appropriate to carry out an evaluation? Is an assessment carried out in the early stages realistic and meaningful? Thirdly, there is the problem of assessing additionality. If new public and private resources are attracted to an area, are they genuinely additional or would the investment have occurred anyway? Fourthly, against what criteria should judgements be made? Some would argue that an evaluation can be made only against the objectives set by the organization itself; others might suggest that wider criteria are more relevant, such as economic prosperity, job creation, environmental improvement and social wellbeing. This gives rise to a further problem of evaluation. How meaningful is it to look at a defined geographical area without taking account of fluctuations in the regional or national economy and changes in government policy?

The approach taken here is to review both the structure and the processes of partnerships as urban regimes operating at different scales, and to assess their impact in both qualitative and quantitative terms against the original objectives. In this chapter we assess the case studies primarily in terms of the internal processes and outputs. A later section will attempt a wider evaluation of partnerships as an approach to urban policy, to assess how far they are an effective response to economic restructuring and urban deprivation.

In attempting an evaluation of the case studies, we are focusing on three main questions:

- Is the way the partnership was conceived and structured an adequate response to its task?
- How successful is the agency as a process for achieving urban regeneration?
- What qualitative and quantitative impact has it had on its target area to date?

Birmingham Heartlands

BHL began in 1988 as an experimental urban regeneration agency, conceived by the private sector, but fully supported by Birmingham City Council. It was established in a period when central government was promoting the idea of business leadership as a means of bypassing local authorities, and its original structure was largely the outcome of a deal struck with Nicholas Ridley, then Secretary of State for the Environment. The development strategy prepared by consultants was an important early influence that effectively identified the problems of the area and a realistic strategy by which they might be tackled.

By the early 1990s, BHL was at a turning point. The extent of investment in commercial property in areas such as Waterlinks, private and housing association development at Bordesley Village, and council housing improvement in Nechells and Bloomsbury – all indicated that BHL had been able to effectively co-ordinate the various agencies involved. However, the worsening economic recession was causing further industrial restructuring and plant closure, and leading many developers to freeze their investment plans. In the transition to development corporation status, many of the positive features of BHL were retained. In particular, there was continuity of staff between the two organizations, together with the direct involvement of leading councillors on both boards. In addition, the streamlined decision-making procedures between BHL and the city council were maintained, so that expenditure programmes and planning procedures could be effectively dovetailed.

As a model for achieving urban regeneration, the experience in Birmingham Heartlands must be considered positive. First, it has been able to remain flexible and to adapt to changing economic conditions and central government policy-making, while adhering closely to its purpose and objectives as set out in the development strategy. Secondly, it has been able to generate and retain a broad spectrum of support, most notably from the private sector, the City Council and local residents. Latterly, it has also achieved recognition for its achievements from central government. Thirdly, it has been able to integrate a property-led and promotional role effectively with – as far as government policy allows – an emphasis on redistributive strategies and community participation. This has been aided by division of the area into recognisable zones for which different types of strategy have been devised. For the areas of substandard industrial building and dereliction, a positive marketing strategy has been adopted, which uses infrastructural investment to attract private investment. In contrast, in such residential areas as Nechells, Bloomsbury and Duddeston, emphasis has been placed on improving living conditions and providing health and social facilities for existing residents. Throughout the area there is a general commitment to environmental improvement and the provision of training, childcare, education and health facilities for all. Overall, value for money has been achieved by BHDC using its limited resources to maximum effect by "acting on the margin – intervening in the market place only where it is necessary and cost-effective, co-ordinating available resources from public and private sectors, and empowering local people to participate in the mainstream rather than developing an alternative one" (BHDC 1993b: 1).

BHDC may be effective in technical and organizational terms, but how transparent are its decision-making procedures and to whom is it accountable? On this score the Birmingham Heartlands experience is less good. Neither BHL nor BHDC had local residents or community representatives on the board, but instead relies on public consultation arrangements such as exhibitions, public meetings and "planning for real" exercises. Consideration has been given recently to setting up a community forum, but to date this idea has not been taken forward. The Heartlands Trust has not sought any intermediate representative role between residents and the agency. Like other UDCs, the public are not permitted to attend board meetings; however, an element of indirect public accountability could be said to exist through the six local authority members. Within the main housing estates, BHL worked with the City Council in setting up the Nechells working party to devise a development strategy for the future, and in Bloomsbury an estate management board has devolved management powers and operates a revenue budget. The overall approach might best be described as one of encouraging community participation at the street level, but permitting little direct involvement in determining strategy or resource allocation.

The economic and social impact of urban regeneration in the Heartlands is more difficult to assess. BHL did not have, and BHDC currently does not operate, a rigorous monitoring system of impacts and outcomes, but prefer to measure achievements in terms of gross public and private expenditure in the area. The census figures (see Table 4.1, p. 84) suggest that by 1991 – three years after the formation of BHL – the population had declined by 21 per cent, but that housing conditions had significantly improved and that the proportion of owner-occupied housing had increased by almost 45 per cent. The proportion of unemployed residents, however, had increased from 29 per cent in 1981 to 32 per cent in 1991.

The first published review of expenditure in the area records that by May 1993 approximately £300 million of public and private investment was completed or committed (see Table 4.3, p. 91). The largest items included £100 million from the Department of Transport for the spine road, £52 million of private investment with City Grant in the Waterlinks development, £44 million towards housing improvement in Nechells, £37.5 million in the Heartlands Industrial area, £36 million in Bordesley Village, and the remainder on a variety of industrial, environmental and training projects.

The BHDC corporate plan for 1993–4 did not identify specific targets for the year but instead identified key outputs for the plan period of 1992–7 and the total lifetime for the corporation (see Table 4.5, p. 96). Outputs for the plan period include 2.7 million sq. ft (750 000 m²) of business floorspace, 5000 new jobs, 493 new houses and 90 ha of reclaimed or developed land. This would be achieved through public expenditure of £258 million, matched by private sector investment of £234 million, a ratio of just less than 1:1. Over the total lifetime of BHDC, the estimate is that public and private expenditure will be in the ratio of 1:3. This reflects growing levels of private sector investment arising from the construction of the spine road and the Midland Metro.

In carrying out an evaluation of this kind, it is almost impossible to determine how far this level of expenditure is additional, that is, expenditure that would not have happened without the presence of BHDC, and to what extent this investment is creating net benefits for residents.

Greenwich Waterfront

The Greenwich Waterfront Development Partnership is more difficult to evaluate, because it does not maintain systematic records of expenditure or impact. It was established in 1992 as a co-ordinating and facilitating agency to take a strategic approach to the area and to create a consensus between government, landowners, businesses and the local community. It has no additional budget over and above the resources of the partners, and therefore had no option but to adopt a promotional and pragmatic stance in order to attract additional public expenditure in order to attract finance from existing and inward investors.

As a process for achieving urban regeneration, this approach clearly has its limitations. The Greenwich Waterfront has considerable development potential resulting largely from the rapid decline of the local economy in the 1980s. At least 324 ha are vacant or derelict, including the 121 ha of the Greenwich Peninsula site and the 31 ha of the Royal Arsenal. However, the area also has strategic importance, in that it is directly south of the London Docklands area and is increasingly seen as a "point of entry" to the recently designated Thames Gateway. In addition, decisions relating to the location of stations on the Jubilee line extension and the route of a third crossing at Blackwall Tunnel remained unresolved in 1994. The Waterfront Partnership has lobbied the Department of Transport to achieve the maximum benefits for the area, and has also sought the involvement of English Partnerships in redeveloping the Royal Arsenal. A submission has been made to the Millennium Fund for the Peninsula site.

Given that these strategic matters have yet to be resolved, the partnership has largely concentrated on smaller-scale activities, such as setting up agencies in Woolwich and Greenwich town centres and in working closely with Thamesmead Town Ltd. Some notable successes have been achieved, such as the designation of Greenwich as one of the first of English Heritage's Conservation Area Partnership schemes and the award of a KONVER grant from the EU. But however successful the partnership is in bringing together local interests, its impact and effectiveness will be restricted until key decisions are made in arenas over which the partnership can exert only limited influence.

Brownlow

As a model action programme funded by the EU, the Brownlow Community Trust aims to establish "transferable methods and models of good practice in combating exclusion . . . to inform social policy at local and European levels" (BCT 1992). It approached this task by drawing together representatives of statutory agencies and the local community in order to plan and implement a series of social programmes. The programme expenditure of £2.2 million over five years has largely been allocated to community initiatives orientated towards the target groups to provide support and assistance in the fields of training, advice, healthcare, community action and the environment.

An important element of the programme has been the encouragement of a partnership approach towards the delivery of services. The Trust board has brought together officers from departments responsible for health, social services, education, housing, planning and the local authority. Direct and indirect benefits have arisen from the closer co-ordination of service providers, although in a period when budgets have been under pressure there is little evidence of new initiatives or additional expenditure that would not otherwise have occurred. For example, the Housing Executive worked closely with tenants in devising an improvement strategy for the Edenbeg Estate, whereas reorganization in the Executive may lead to the closure of the local office. Moreover, the extent to which the statutory agencies have changed their service delivery mechanisms or bent their budgets in favour of Brownlow is doubtful. This is largely because the agencies send representatives to meetings of what they perceive as a "community project". It was less successful in altering policies or working practices of the statutory agencies themselves.

The core problems in Brownlow are poverty, unemployment and a very high dependency on welfare payments. Thus, what the area needs most is an increase in employment opportunities and training to enable residents to compete effectively. The Trust is able to fund only revenue projects and thus is dependent on statutory agencies and Brownlow Ltd to increase the amount of economic activity and to increase skill levels. Unemployment has gradually increased over the project period and is officially recorded at 28 per cent, although residents claim that in reality this figure is much higher. This trend is leading to out-migration and a growing demoralization of the remaining population.

Thus, although the Trust has achieved some important successes in bringing together the statutory agencies and in initiating community projects, regeneration of the area will take place only when the underlying economic circumstances are tackled. The closer involvement of those government agencies with an economic

209

remit in the Province, and a specific budget for capital and revenue expenditure, are needed to launch a social, economic and environmental strategy for Brownlow. The Trust has played an important role in demonstrating what can be achieved within a limited budget. This now needs to be built on through a strategy more akin to City Challenge in England or the Wester Hailes example in Scotland.

Woodlands

The Woodlands Community Development Trust was conceived as a mechanism by which the local community might take on the task of co-ordinating the process of regenerating the Woodlands area through the agency of a development trust. This involved establishing a committee that reflected local interests and preparing a development plan that drew on the resources of the local authority, housing associations, Scottish Homes, Scottish Enterprise and the private sector. At an early stage it was agreed that ten vacant sites in the eastern half of the area would be transferred at nil cost to the Trust from the City Council. The surplus arising from the developments would be used to provide facilities and to enhance the local environment, as well as covering the running costs of the Trust.

As a mechanism for urban regeneration, the Trust had considerable potential, but experienced some difficulties that weakened its impact and threatened its long-term future. First, it experienced significant delays in getting the commitment of housing associations and in funding its own developments for sale. It was unfortunate that, when the Trust was ready to begin development, the local housing market was in recession and there was a squeeze on the budgets of housing associations. Secondly, the Woodlands area is made up of a variety of social and ethnic groups with very different perspectives on the needs and priorities in the area. The Trust has tended to reflect the interests of the White, middle-class elements, and some observers now argue that more could have been done to involve the marginalized groups, such as Asian residents and business owners. The burden of managing the Trust increasingly fell on a diminishing number of activists who largely represented one social group in the area. Thirdly, the Trust may have been over optimistic about what could be achieved, and thus tended to raise local expectations that could not be met. Moreover, the surpluses arising from the Trust's own developments have so far not been sufficient to provide other benefits in the area or to cover running costs. However, some success has been achieved in the provision of training schemes and through the wholly owned subsidiary companies, such as Common Factor Ltd.

The development programme is likely to be completed by 1997 and consideration will need to be given to what the future role of the Trust is to be. In total, approximately 324 housing units will be created at a total cost of £17 million, and a further 112 units will be renovated largely by the Housing Department. Further expenditure is planned on streetscape improvements and a new park. This will clearly bring real benefits to local people, but the question has been raised as to whether the same outcomes might have been achieved more quickly if carried out by the City Council in the first place. Alternative scenarios might include the housing department acting as the lead agency in developing the sites itself, or selling some on to housing associations or private developers, or a consortium of development agencies being established, as has happened in the Crown Street area of the Gorbals. It is also arguable whether the presence of the Trust has made the development process more accountable to local people than if carried out by the local authority.

The Trust represents an imaginative attempt to ensure that residents have a significant influence over the regeneration of their area and that the financial benefits are channelled to meet social and community needs. Over the past ten years, much has been learnt about the process of launching and sustaining a community-based development programme that can be applied elsewhere.

Newcastle

TNI emerged at a time when both central government and organizations such as the CBI wished to see the private sector playing a leading role in urban regeneration. This was to be achieved partly through representation on agencies such as UDCs and TECs and also through the establishment of initiatives such as business leadership teams and Business in the Community. TNI was one of the first outcomes of the CBI's report, Initiatives Beyond Charity (CBI 1988), and was designed to demonstrate how the private sector could promote regeneration and economic growth in a city through a shared vision based on flagship projects.

In Newcastle TNI fitted into a long tradition of multisectoral growth coalitions that developed between central government, the local State as well as organizations representing capital and labour. The thinking behind TNI was that by bringing together the leading companies in the region in order to fund a small executive office, a series of demonstration projects could be established that would promote a growth-orientated strategy that would provide a vision for others to follow. The initial intention was that TNI would have a board made up of the ten leading companies with four representatives of the public sector having observer status. This has gradually expanded into a board of 19, on which local quangos, development agencies and the two city universities are particularly well represented (see Table 7.2, p. 145).

TNI's approach has been to develop a limited number of initiatives in the city, which are largely concerned with promoting development and investment in the city centre through projects concerned with conservation, environmental improvement, the arts, higher education and, largely through personal contacts, support for Cruddas Park and two City Challenge agencies. TNI has very limited resources of its own and these are largely raised through corporate sponsorship. However, it is able to exert considerable influence through interlocking membership of boards, quangos and development agencies operating in the city and region. It is therefore important to see TNI as part of a complex network in a crowded arena, which is able to exert considerable influence on both the public and private sectors. In this respect it is comparable to the American concept of the growth coalition (Logan & Molotch 1987).

As a model for urban regeneration it has significant limitations. Although promoting the idea of regeneration through a shared vision, and claiming to promote projects in the interest of the city as whole, it excludes significant local interests, such as small businesses, residents and trade unions. Membership of the board is limited by invitation only to a narrow group of large companies and employers, and is therefore both unrepresentative and unaccountable to the city as a whole. Its primary motive is to generate a pro-growth, post-industrial approach to restructuring the city's economy. Other significant local interests, such as the City Council and trade unions, may find themselves out-manoeuvred or persuaded to accept such an approach by the lure of inward investment and jobs. Moreover, because of the bias in representation in favour of large companies, small and medium-size enterprises may also find their interests displaced in favour of those of the national and multinational companies.

It is also doubtful how far TNI has had a significant impact on the projects it has adopted as its own. Because of its limited resources for implementation, it has had to select projects where there is no apparent champion, but where resources are likely to be forthcoming to achieve an impact. It has therefore become involved in projects where success is ultimately dependent on public funding becoming available. The Grey Street Renaissance, the Grainger Town Initiative, Cruddas Park, City Challenge and the environmental initiative have all required public action and investment to enable them to happen. The Theatre Village and Chinatown project was subsequently dropped when the area was taken over by the West End Partnership.

In conclusion, TNI may at best be seen as a useful forum where senior executives from the corporate and public sectors can develop a shared concept of how the public and private sectors might work more closely together. It remains unrepresentative, unaccountable to wider interests in the city, such as residents and small businesses, and extremely opaque in its decision-making and how its influence is brought to bear.

Wester Hailes

The four New Life partnerships set up by the Scottish Office in 1989 represented a response to growing levels of deprivation in Scotland's peripheral estates and an opportunity to apply the lessons learned in earlier approaches to urban regeneration. The GEAR project and other initiatives promoted by the SDA had brought about substantial redevelopment and improvements in housing conditions, but had only a marginal impact on unemployment (Donnison & Middleton 1987). The selection of Wester Hailes as one of four demonstration projects provided an opportunity for some of these earlier faults to be put right over a ten-year period. The Scottish Office itself would chair the partnership, contribute addition Urban Programme funding, bring together all the relevant statutory agencies and the private sector, and for the first time give residents themselves a major role in planning and implementing an appropriate urban regeneration strategy. In contrast to the UDCs in England, considerable flexibility was built into the

Scottish approach to allow all local interests to play a full part in developing an appropriate strategy that could integrate and co-ordinate previously compartmentalized policy areas. In this respect the approach is similar to City Challenge in England.

After five years of activity, it is already apparent that progress is being made in several policy areas. A holistic view is being taken towards the needs of the area and several innovatory approaches are being adopted. A service-quality assessment has been carried out, and improvements in childcare, community safety and reducing household safety have been instigated. The redevelopment of the shopping centre should bring a wide range of local services and additional facilities, such as a library. Significant inroads have also been made into the housing problems on the estate. By 1994, ten high-rise blocks had been demolished, 248 new houses built for rent by housing associations, and 249 housing units had been renovated by the District Council and housing associations. In addition, targets have been set to increase tenure diversification, and environmental improvements have been carried out to include the provision of play facilities.

Unemployment has been a far more difficult issue to deal with and, despite several targeted measures, the unemployment rate in Wester Hailes has increased since mid-1990 in line with that of Edinburgh as a whole. In April 1989, 20 per cent of the Wester Hailes population was unemployed, compared to 14 per cent in the city as a whole. By April 1993 the figures were 24 per cent and 18 per cent respectively (Wester Hailes Partnership 1994b: 7). The proportion of long-term unemployed people in Wester Hailes is now roughly comparable to that in Edinburgh. Research carried out for the Partnership suggests there are several reasons for the lack of impact of training and other policy measures. First, there is the lack of new jobs becoming available in the wider area, so that two thirds of those completing training programmes remain unemployed after completion. Secondly, three quarters of those completing training programmes are women who are less likely to be recorded as unemployed. Thirdly, there is evidence of labour market churning, whereby the relatively high turnover of residents to the estate is likely to draw in a higher proportion of those unemployed. Residents who gain employment are more likely to move out. Overall, the additional impact of the Partnership is almost impossible to measure, because of the difficulty of measuring net additional expenditure by the agencies involved.

As a mechanism for regeneration, Wester Hailes does have the advantage of involving all the relevant local agencies, local residents and the business support group. Thus, unlike Brownlow, it is possible to integrate development-orientated and redistributive strategies. However, after five years, some tensions have arisen. First, there is some uncertainty about the continuing role of the Scottish Office as lead agency. Because of the difficulties of increasing economic activity, it may be that the Scottish Office will attempt to distance itself by handing over this responsibility to the local authority or LEC. Secondly, tensions have arisen over whether the resource team is responsible and accountable to the Partnership board, as residents argue it should be, or to the Scottish Office, as is the current position. The resource team feels that the representative council is too confrontational, whereas the representative council takes the view that the resource team is more concerned with its relationship with the Scottish Office than in being genuinely accountable to the Partnership board. Thirdly, there is evidence of different levels of commitment from the partners towards agreed objectives. Interviewees expressed concern that some of the less accountable organizations, such as the LEC and Scottish Homes, resisted being fully associated with the Partnership and in committing resources to it.

Thus, after five years, there is some evidence that improvements have resulted from the partnership in terms of housing provision, the service-quality assessment, environmental improvements, nursery provision, training and community involvement in particular. But much remains to be done, particularly in increasing household incomes and economic activity. It may be that the wrong kind of area was selected for a project of this kind. Since Wester Hailes, with a population of 11 000 almost entirely in council-owned accommodation, has a high residential turnover and few opportunities for economic development, it may be that the area was the right size to achieve housing and social objectives but inappropriate for economic ones. Given the way the housing allocation system works, substantial improvements would need to be achieved to change the residents' perceptions of the area before those gaining employment can be persuaded to stay. As it is, the relatively low status of the area, associated with its lack of commercial and social facilities, will continue to encourage those fortunate enough to get jobs to move out. The effect of the training and employment initiatives may also be to create displacement, whereby a job gained by a Wester Hailes resident is at the cost of someone else in Edinburgh becoming unemployed.

Conclusions

Partnerships examined here represent an attempt by locally dependent interests to form collaborative organizations in order to promote strategies for local regeneration. They have emerged both through the availability of central government and European funding sources and as a response to the declining influence of local authorities. Although local government is a major actor and the prime mover in several cases, the initiative to establish partnerships comes as likely as not from the private or community sectors, or as a response to changes in government policy. Partnerships are primarily concerned with the generation of additional capital and revenue funding and will adopt a pragmatic and promotional role in order to increase the opportunities available. Those that are able to interact with local, regional, national and European funding mechanisms tend to maximize additional funding sources. Alliances will be struck with other elements of the local State in order to ensure that overall levels of expenditure are maximized in the target area. Although innovative approaches to project initiation are adopted, links are also maintained with statutory planning and funding procedures carried out by local government. The outputs and impact of partnerships will be dependent on the extent to which public sources of funding can be utilized to achieve the circumstances in which private sector investment can take place. The constitution and membership structure of a partnership broadly determines the extent to which it is open or closed to influence by local political interests. Although in some cases membership is open to local representation, in practice public accountability is relatively limited in all cases. Table 10.1 summarizes the characteristics of each of the case studies.

External evaluation

In this section we explore some of the broader issues relating to the role of partnerships in urban policy. Are there common practices and processes emerging from the case studies and elsewhere, which might be applied more generally, for example through the Single Regeneration Budget and City Challenge? What conclusions can be drawn about the way partnerships encourage the development of an agreed strategy through the integration and co-ordination of local agencies and interests, and how far are requirements for participation, consultation and the involvement of all sectors being met? Are these agencies having a real impact on urban problems in a manner that makes them open and accountable to a wider constituency? Finally, suggestions will be made about how the effectiveness of partnerships might be increased in future through reforms to their constitution and the relationship with government funding mechanisms.

Good practice in urban regeneration

Although there is considerable variation in the areas, context, constitution and strategies of the six case studies we have examined, some common themes are emerging. From this comparative analysis it is possible to identify elements of good practice that might be replicable elsewhere.

One of the first conclusions to emerge is that urban regeneration is a term that itself is full of ambiguity and is defined differently in different locations and contexts. As has been noted in the case studies, the partnerships have adopted different sets of objectives, which have tended to emerge gradually, partly as a reflection of the power relations between partners and partly in response to opportunities arising as the role of the partnership has developed. Most of the case studies began with a relatively clear analysis of the problems and opportunities of their area, together with targets to be achieved over the lifetime of the project. However, these targets often involved the development of sites, improv-

Table 10.1 Characteristics of six partnership case studies.

Partnership	Year of formation	Designated area/population	Representation on board	Objectives	Budget
Birmingham Heartlands Ltd/ Birmingham Heartlands Development Corporation	1988	East Birmingham 1000ha 10000	6 private sector 6 city councillors	Regenerate the area by increasing investment, retaining & increasing jobs, reclaim land, improve infra-structure, improve & develop housing	£37.5m over 5 years
Greenwich Waterfront Development Partnership	1992	LB Greenwich 1012ha 70000	5 council 5 business forum 5 community forum 1 Thamesmead Town	• Co-ordination of development • Economic & social regeneration • Involvement of all sectors	Revenue from LB Greenwich & secondments No capital.
Wester Hailes Partnership	1989	Wester Hailes estate, Edinburgh 12000	17 from central & local government, employment, health & housing organizations, local community & business support group	• Integrated approach • Involvement of private sector • Community participation	£0.5m for revenue. £2.5m p.a. urban programme over 10 years. Mainstream budgets of partners
Brownlow Community Trust	1989	Brownlow estate, Craigavon 8500	9 statutory agencies 2 councillors 4 BCDA 4 local agencies 4 community reps	To develop transferable methods to combat social exclusion through participation, partnership and an integrated approach	£2.2m revenue from EU & match funding from statutory agencies over 5 years
Woodlands Community Development Trust	1985	Woodlands, Glasgow 5500	6 residents	Co-ordination of development & improvement of Woodlands	UP and £75,000 loan from city council. 10 sites transferred at nil cost.
The Newcastle Initiative	1988	Newcastle upon Tyne 283000	19 private sector & public sector managers	Promotion of business activity through flagship projects	£200,000 p.a. revenue from sponsorship

ing co-ordination between agencies and improving housing and social conditions, but lacked quantifiable measures of achievement. In the case of Birmingham Heartlands, measurable targets were established with the setting up of the development corporation, and the Wester Hailes Partnership clarified its objectives in 1994. Others identified objectives and target groups, but, because of uncertainty relating to timing and funding, did not produce quantifiable measures. It appears that those partnerships that had dedicated resources at their disposal tended to be more precise, whereas those that had broadly promotional objectives, or were dependent on others for funding or implementation, relied on imprecise targets. The development strategy prepared by Roger Tym & Partners in 1988 for BHL has proved to be a very effective analysis of the problems and needs of the area, with a clear set of strategies as to how they might be met. This provided sufficient guidance to the partners, without being overprescriptive, and it remains the basis for implementation by BHDC.

The implementation of strategies takes place through several complex mechanisms. Partnerships need to be able to command their own resources and to influence the spending programmes of others directly. In the cases of BHL, Greenwich, Woodlands and Brownlow, serious problems arose, because these partnerships were almost entirely dependent on persuading others to invest in the area. TNI was established as an exclusively promotional organization, and largely uses its members' influence to achieve results. Close links with other agencies, such as a local authority, are clearly not enough, and access to a dedicated budget is essential to maximize the influence of the agency and to increase leverage over other public and private funding sources. In this respect, BHDC and, to a lesser extent Wester Hailes, were able to achieve the greatest impact. As leverage becomes an increasingly common approach to project funding, it is essential for partnerships to be able to commit their own resources in order to attract others.

All the case studies except Brownlow and TNI have adopted both property-led and redistributive policies towards their areas. Some commentators have pointed to the inequalities arising from the government's commitment to property-led urban regeneration, which emerged in the mid-1980s (for example Healey et al. 1992, Turok 1992, Imrie & Thomas 1993a). Our research suggests that most partnerships have now adopted various interpretations of a "holistic" approach where a range of strategies are designed to achieve both property-related and social and economic objectives. These are understood to include both the physical improvement and partial redevelopment of an area, as well as the reduction of unemployment, improved housing opportunities and provision of community facilities. However, there are clearly limitations to the extent to which social equity can be achieved between the target area and the urban or regional context. National legislation and fiscal policies make this extremely difficult. Examples are many but include the reduction of local authority autonomy, changes to welfare payments and housing benefits and the introduction of VAT on domestic fuel, which is extremely regressive in its impact on the poor and those living in the North and Scotland. Legislative changes have also prevented local authorities setting up enterprise boards or developing interventionist economic development strategies through planning agreements and contract compliance. In some circumstances a strategy towards property development can be combined with socially orientated programmes, such as training, preferential access to employment and the provision of community facilities. But as was noted in the case of Brownlow, a focus entirely on social factors is unlikely to have a lasting impact if this is not closely linked to development opportunities. As Stone et al. (1991) suggest, a human resource approach is more demanding because it requires both the mobilization of the local elite and the full participation of those who stand to benefit. In the UK it is almost impossible to pursue redistributive objectives because of the legislative and financial context in which all State agencies operate.

The definition of target areas in urban regeneration is a continuing subject of debate. Although government and development agencies prefer to select a relatively small target area so that improvements are easily visible and the co-ordination and integration of the partners is facilitated, several commentators have pointed to the contradictions that may result (Deakin & Edwards 1993). On the one hand, an area may be defined geographically because it contains a concentration of derelict land or high levels of unemployment, or socially because it is perceived as a recognisable community, but on the other there are limits to the extent to which redistributive objectives can be achieved in a narrowly defined area. As noted in Wester Hailes, job markets operate at the urban or increasingly regional scale and jobs created in a locality cannot be offered exclusively to local residents. Likewise, increasing the ability of residents in the target area to compete for employment through training may well result in reduced opportunities for others elsewhere who will remain or become unemployed. As has been discovered in Wester Hailes, levels of unemployment in the target area tend to remain constant either because the new jobs are going to non-residents or because residents who get jobs then move elsewhere. In addition, if there is an overall lack of job opportunities, supply-side measures such as training will have little impact and merely create the phenomenon of labour market churning where the same or new residents pass through training programmes with few tangible benefits in terms of reduced unemployment.

Integration, co-ordination and representation

A fundamental characteristic of partnerships is the need to build a coalition of local interests in order to pursue a regeneration strategy and to co-ordinate the individual and collective efforts of the constituent members. The case studies illustrate a range of different models in this respect. Examples range from Wester Hailes, which is a Scottish Office-led agency with other local State, business and community representation, to agencies with strong local authority representation such as Greenwich and Birmingham, to other combinations as

218

displayed by Brownlow, Woodlands and TNI. All the examples aim for integration and co-ordination through the partnership itself and by influencing the separate resource allocation decisions of constituent members, central government, the EU and private sector investors. Whereas those agencies with their own budgets tend to determine spending plans in advance, those at the promotional end of the spectrum tend to operate on a more pragmatic basis.

Membership is a crucial variable in the constitution of partnerships. It is essential that all the significant development agencies are involved as well as the local authority. The Birmingham case illustrates clearly how close officer and member contacts can streamline decision making and integrate the relevant planning, housing and financial powers of local government within the partnership strategy. Likewise, close links need to be maintained with TECs and LECs, housing associations and other public sector agencies. The private sector needs to be involved where it is a major stakeholder in the area although except in the case of TNI and the business forum in Greenwich there are relatively few local businesses directly involved in the case study examples. Wester Hailes has a business support group and in Birmingham none of the contractors on the BHL board have been reappointed to BHDC. The conclusion here seems to be that business involvement is not essential to the management of partnerships but that locally dependent companies should be consulted through a representative forum. Partnerships do, however, seek to create an organizational, economic and physical environment that is attractive to inward investment in accordance with the agreed strategy.

Most of the case studies accept the need for local community involvement in both the management of the organization and in consultation relating to the strategy. In Wester Hailes, Woodlands, Brownlow, and Greenwich there is significant community representation in management. In all these cases there are complex arrangements for selecting representatives from different constituencies who are able to exert differing amounts of influence over the partnership. In the Wester Hailes example it was noted that tensions existed because of uncertainties about whether the resource team was accountable to the partnership board or the Scottish Office. In Birmingham there is no community representation although there is considerable evidence that residents are effectively consulted on major planning and investment decisions. Only in TNI is there no community representation or involvement of residents as an interest group.

Evidence from Woodlands and Brownlow suggests that the impact of partnerships is seriously weakened if they do not incorporate those agencies with a primary responsibility for land ownership and economic development and which also have dedicated resources to be applied in the area. The ownership of problems and solutions by the public sector agencies with responsibility for them is an essential element of a local coalition and onto this core should be grafted other local stakeholders who can assist with regeneration. Community participation in management and implementation is also essential. In most of the case studies there appeared to be differing interpretations of whether regeneration was to take

219

place primarily in the interests of local residents or whether they were merely bringing local knowledge, commitment and ownership to a strategy that emerged from a wider debate or even as a series of technocratic solutions to problems. In practice, most community representatives remained broadly critical of the partnerships of which they were members and the extent to which policy co-ordination and integration was being achieved. This may have been because their expectations had been unduly raised in the early stages or because they had gained an insight into the complexities of collaborative action, which they might otherwise not have had. In this respect the need for time and resources to build the capacity of community representatives to participate fully is essential, as was noted by Macfarlane & Mabbott (1993) in relation to City Challenge.

This leads on to the broader questions of representation, accountability and which interests benefit from partnerships. Our findings suggest that they represent relatively closed institutions by which dominant local stakeholders collaborate in order to achieve partial definitions of the public interest. These definitions are largely determined by technocratic rather than democratic processes where dominant interests (which in some cases might include the local authority and sections of the local community) structure the boundaries of the debate in their own interests. In addition, some examples will use innovative mechanisms of local consultation, such as business or community fora or innovative methods of public consultation, which are in general an improvement on those used by local authorities or UDCs. Thus, partnerships can be seen as both relatively closed to external political influence and relatively unaccountable to a wider constituency. However, comparisons need to be made not only with a notional, ideal and fully participative model but also with the generally elitist and technocratic solutions to urban renewal employed by both public and private sectors in the past.

Of all the examples of partnership examined here only BHDC is managed by six private sector representatives appointed through the patronage of the Secretary of State for the Environment and these are balanced by six councillors from the city council. In all other cases the management boards are made up of local residents, officers from public sector agencies or executives from the private sector who are largely self-selected. Although it is possible to question how far any members of management boards are representative of wider interests, this did not seem to be a matter of concern to our interviewees. Recent criticism of patronage in the press seems to have been confined to the extent of political appointments to statutory agencies, such as TECs, LECs, UDCs and the Welsh Development Agency, because of the narrow strata of society from which appointees are drawn and suspicions concerning their political allegiance (see for example, *The Guardian*, 19 November 1993). There was no evidence that private sector representatives were significantly influencing the priorities or spending decisions of any of the partnerships except possibly in the case of TNI where influence was brought to bear on development agencies such as UDCs and City Challenge agencies.

The impact on urban problems

Because of methodological difficulties it is almost impossible to achieve a quantifiable assessment of the impact of partnership programmes. Many partnerships do not set measurable objectives, local State agencies do not always maintain accurate data on expenditure by discrete areas and it is difficult to separate *additional* expenditure from what might have occurred in the normal course of events. Thus, most partnerships focus on involving stakeholders and integrating and co-ordinating their separate contributions within the framework of more or less clearly specified objectives. This emphasis on process and strategic objectives is preferable to that adopted by City Challenge agencies that tend to be locked into a tight set of quantifiable performance indicators and suffer from annuality – the need to spend a fixed amount within the limitations of the financial year.

The broad conclusions from the case studies is that urban regeneration is a difficult process that takes time and great amounts of effort to achieve relatively small gains. Impact tends to be easier to achieve on physical targets such as housing and environmental improvements. Marginal improvements can be made to improving local wellbeing through measures such as the provision of healthcare, nursery facilties, public safety and the funding of voluntary organizations. With sufficient resources, supply-side improvements can be made to the skills and training of those seeking employment and through educational compacts and preferential interviews. The most difficult objectives involve increasing the numbers of available jobs for target groups, increasing household incomes and reducing welfare dependency. In this respect the availability of work will depend far more on national, regional and urban economic trends than on any influence a local development agency may have. A major conclusion from this study is that the local economic conditions in a defined area with a high level of deprivation cannot be isolated from wider processes of economic restructuring and disinvestment. All that it can hope to do is to contribute to protecting or marginally increasing the net jobs available in the local labour market through supply-side measures.

The implications for an effective urban policy

The launch of the City Challenge initiative in 1991 marked an important development in the partnership approach to urban problems. Criticisms of its scale, underfunding and the problem of annuality apart, it marked an important recognition by central government that solutions are more appropriately devised at the local level and with the maximum involvement of all sectors. It revealed the extent of synergy that emerged between locally dependent interests that hitherto had not been apparent in the Inner City Partnerships or UDCs. Yet, as the examples covered in this book have shown, some localities had been developing similar approaches since the mid-1980s. In many of these cases it was the local authority that had played an important role in promoting and implementing innovative solutions. In Scotland and Wales these were linked to integrated urban regeneration and economic development strategies promoted by development agencies.

After two rounds of City Challenge the government announced the Single Regeneration Budget (SRB) to be allocated by integrated regional offices in England responsible to a ministerial committee on regeneration. The SRBs will be allocated to partnerships covering wide areas, local strategies or pilot initiatives. The guidance on effective partnerships (DoE 1994: 31) broadly follows the City Challenge model but notes that local authorities or TECs would play a leading role in co-ordination and financial management of public funding. In Scotland and Wales existing arrangements will continue because of the financial and policy integration achieved by the Scottish and Welsh Offices and the presence of respective development agencies. In Scotland and Wales the Urban Programme is likely to be used increasingly to promote and fund new partnership arrangements.

It is too early to say how effective the SRBs will be and current indications suggest that bids for 1995–6 will far exceed the available resources. However, the new approach is a positive one in that it will encourage the integration and co-ordination of the policies and funding regimes of the four government departments concerned, which was one of the major recommendations of the Audit Commission in 1989. It will also draw on the energies and resources of the raft of government agencies and local initiatives currently operating in relative isolation in many areas. As has already been demonstrated in many City Challenge areas, it will enable innovative policy solutions that cross policy boundaries to be effectively promoted. Nevertheless, major concerns remain about the total level of funding available after top-slicing has taken place, the lack of integration with other government departments, such as the Departments of Health, Social Security and Education, which will be exposed, and what will happen to the many projects that lose out in this increasingly competitive environment. As political preferences will inevitably be a factor in the selection process, how will competing bids between regional and national priorities be resolved and will bids from the voluntary sector be as favourably received as those from business-dominated coalitions? At present there is no guidance on the criteria for the selection of bids (one of several procedural issues discussed by Stewart 1994).

Assuming the regional offices take on an increasingly important strategic role in urban regeneration, pressure will grow for greater democratic accountability at the regional level. This will be further exacerbated by the growing importance of integrating European structural funds with national, regional and local grant regimes. The extent to which the UK will adapt its constitutional framework to a European federal model based on subsidiarity remains highly contentious. However, evidence suggests, and the government already appears to accept some of the arguments, that effective urban regeneration requires a strategic framework that harnesses the resources of all levels of the State.

Interesting comparisons can be drawn between the British model of the competitive allocation of resources for urban regeneration, where there is an inevitable waste of resources in preparing unsuccessful bids, and the contract model adopted in France. Here the primary mechanisms of urban policy are the *Contrat de Ville*, a form of partnership between central and local government at the local or urban level, and the *Charte d'Objectif*, a similar initiative to City Pride where urban areas or subregions enter into contracts to enable them to compete more effectively within the European hierarchy of cities.

The *Contrat de Ville* system was introduced into the highly complex structure of public administration in France in 1988 and led to the establishment of an interministerial delegation (DIV) to co-ordinate the inputs of the central ministries. Areas invited to participate are initially selected on the basis of a statistical analysis of levels of deprivation. In the experimental phase 13 areas were selected ranging from one small town, seven cities, four major urban conurbations and one *departement*. Through a series of negotiations co-ordinated by the *Préfet*, a strategy emerges first at the local level but which is then modified through discussions with central government. The State provides up to 50 per cent of the funding for programmes that can cross all policy areas and involve innovative approaches. As Le Gales & Mawson (1994) describe the process:

> The Contrat de Ville, as it emerged, was not a general development plan, rather its purpose was to tackle specific social and economic problems in urban areas through an agreed inter-agency strategy designed to encourage coherence between the plans of the various ministries and local authorities. The Contrat can be interpreted as a form of partnership in which the State, by offering greater influence over its programmes and some limited additional funding, demands of the local authority that it is representing the interests of all sections of its population, and engages in collaborative action with neighbouring local authorities to tackle urban problems straddling local authority boundaries. The local authority, in turn, requires of the State the delivery of high-quality services either, directly, or by providing the means to do so through the local authority or other relevant bodies (Le Gales & Mawson 1994: 23)

In the case of Lille the contract is valued at a total of FF1500 million to be spent over three years in 86 communes. It is supervised by an assembly of partners, representing the State ministries, the prefecture, the communes and the region. Day to day decisions are taken by the steering committee and there are 12 working groups, supported by a technical group, organized around the 80 programmes. In contrast to Britain, the contracts are largely between central and local government, although in the case of Lille an external advisory body from the local community, business, trade unions and technical advisors was planned but had not been constituted by 1993 (Le Gales & Mawson 1994: 60).

Although simple comparisons between different political and administrative systems are often misleading and the French contract model has not been without its problems, it may be that some elements are transferable. The French approach has the advantage of being relatively open and formalized, permits a dialogue between central and local government based on the latter's preferred strategy, and sets out a programme potentially involving all State agencies with the resulting advantages of integration and co-ordination. The British system is *ad hoc* and competitive, requiring the regional offices to select bids on the basis of unspecified criteria. Although guidance is available on the type of partnerships and bids that are likely to succeed, the contribution of non-participating departments and "Next Steps" agencies remains uncertain. The implication is that local government has an enabling or leadership role in formulating bids but a dialogue with the regional offices over the content of each bid can be entertained only once the initial selection has been made.

In 1992 the French Government announced that over 150 *Contrats de Ville* would be commissioned but in future they would incorporate other programmes and would be fully integrated with the XIth National Plan with a total urban policy budget of FF7200 million Francs in 1993. As Le Gales & Mawson conclude:

> The new round of Contrat de Ville can be seen as the final stage in the evolution of French urban policy from an administratively fragmented and small-scale programme of initiatives designed to tackle the problems of suburban estates to a comprehensive all embracing national policy. In political and administrative terms, there is now just one urban policy initiative that, in turn, is fully integrated in the State planning cycle. (Le Gales & Mawson 1994: 68).

A similar approach can be envisaged in England, whereby the regional offices enter into a dialogue with single or groups of local authorities selected on the basis of deprivation indices and economic need. The local authorities would co-ordinate a programme of expenditure involving contributions from all sectors at the local level in return for additional funding from central government and Europe. These local contracts would then be fully integrated into the annual cycle of government expenditure planning across all central departments. Reforms along these lines would remove the need for competitive bidding for resources, would favour those areas in greatest need, would enable a dialogue between central government and local agencies to take place and would fully integrate urban policy objectives into expenditure planning at the national level. It would also provide a means for effectively linking European structural funds with local delivery mechanisms.

In Chapter 11 the changing policy context in which the concept of partnership has developed in the UK is reviewed and the theoretical debates in Chapter 3 are revisited.

CHAPTER 11
Conclusions

British urban policy over the past 25 years can best be characterized as the search for appropriate responses to political opposition and social unrest resulting from rapid economic restructuring at the local level. The increasing trend towards the globalization of capital has brought successive waves of restructuring, disinvestment and reinvestment, which have impacted most significantly on the major urban conurbations. The State has responded by devising policy measures to revitalize sectors of the economy, attract inward investment, and to ameliorate or modify adverse impacts through largely supply-side measures. However, within this broad thrust there have been significant fluctuations in the underlying philosophy and purpose of policy. This book has charted some of these variations by examining the concept of partnership in the wider context of urban policy in general.

The model of partnership between central and local government set out in the 1977 White Paper (DoE 1977d) represented the final attempt to seal the post-war consensus, by which urban change could be managed through improved co-ordination between the two tiers of government and the channelling of additional resources to areas of greatest need. Although the mechanism for funding Inner City Partnership areas was retained by the then incoming Conservative Government, these were broadly sidelined in favour of the new political project of promoting the enterprise culture.

The enterprise culture at its simplest involved, in Michael Heseltine's words, "redefining the frontier between the public and private sector" (*Hansard*, 13 September 1979) in favour of the latter. It replaced the former alliance between central and local government with one between central government and the private sector. This in turn, in contradiction to the philosophy of neoliberalism, required central government to become more interventionist and policy-making more centralized in underpinning the private sector. Hence, by the mid- to late-1980s the local implementation of urban policy was largely controlled by State-funded quangos managed by private sector representatives appointed through government patronage. The inner cities achieved national policy significance after Mrs Thatcher's third general election victory in 1987, with the appointment of Kenneth Clarke as Minister with special responsibility for the inner cities. Both *Action for cities* (Cabinet Office 1988) and *Initiatives beyond charity* (CBI

1988) were published soon after Clarke's appointment. By 1989 the government's own Audit Commission was effectively undermining the facade of a well co-ordinated inner-city policy by advocating greater devolution of decision-making and powers of co-ordination to the local level (Audit Commission 1989). At the same time, as the case studies in this book have shown, a policy vacuum was developing at the local level, which a variety of local interests sought to fill through collaborative mechanisms.

A third phase of policy was ushered in by the return of Michael Heseltine to the Department of Environment and the launch of City Challenge in 1991. Although many of the previous initiatives were retained and the broad commitment to the enterprise culture was reinforced, City Challenge was at least partially welcomed for its flexibility towards locally determined policies, its commitment to partnership between all sectors, and the lead role given to local authorities. It is very unlikely that further rounds of City Challenge will be announced, but many of the characteristics of City Challenge agencies, and the associated financial and administrative arrangements, have been set out in the *Bidding guidance* (DOE 1994) for the Single Regeneration Budget.

The concept of partnership has therefore been of growing importance to policy-making in relation to urban policy for two decades. By the early 1990s there was a consensus developing between all the main political parties that a closer involvement between the public and private sectors, together with the direct participation of local communities and the ability to cut across traditional policy boundaries, are all essential elements of an effective urban regeneration strategy. Moreover, experience gained during the recent recession indicates that strategies based on the property-led approach, "trickle-down" and partnerships dominated by the private sector, bring few benefits and merely accentuate the peaks and troughs of economic cycles.

In addition, there appears to be a growing realization that some flexibility in the construction of partnerships is essential at the local level and that it is the primary task of central government to provide an effective policy framework without undue interference at the local level. However, much remains to be done to create the strategic linkages between locally based partnerships, central government budgets and, of increasing importance, access to European structural funds. The extent to which the UK can and should adapt its constitutional framework to achieve a system of elected regional authorities remains at present highly politically contested.

The political dimension of urban regeneration

Throughout this book we have argued that a new accommodation has emerged between advocates of the free-market and interventionist approaches to urban regeneration. Paradoxically, the launch of the SRB and related reforms suggest

226

that central government is promoting a corporatist or "modified market" approach at the local level, while retaining many of the neo-liberal tenets of the enterprise culture at the national level. How far the two political stances can be accommodated remains uncertain, particularly as policy at the European level is increasingly orientated towards the social market concept.

We therefore conclude that the rise of the partnership approach can best be seen as a response to both economic restructuring and a complex series of political responses over time. In economic terms, capital is increasingly operating at a global level, whereby competitive advantage is often achieved by shifting investment between locations and across regional and national boundaries. At the same time, governments have responded by offering incentives to investment in less favoured areas through leverage mechanisms and by reducing the legal constraints that can legitimately be placed on the private sector. In addition, the nature of public policy itself has been changed by inducing the corporate sector to assist in managing adverse economic circumstances through patronage, privatization and partnership arrangements. Therefore, it appears that, whereas at the local level central government has broadly shifted its position from the New Right free-market model to the centrist social market, many of the more interventionist-inclined urban authorities have, voluntarily or under duress, moved from an interventionist stance to the centre. The three models are set out in Table 11.1.

The impact of urban policy

How far urban policy is able to improve the economic and social wellbeing of localities and to reduce urban deprivation remains at best uncertain and at worst requires a negative conclusion. Recent surveys provide depressing reading. Willmott & Hutchison (1992: 82) conclude that:

> After 15 years, and many new initiatives, surprisingly little has been achieved. Given the record so far, it is difficult to have much confidence in more of the same or to feel at all hopeful about the future prospects for deprived urban areas.

Likewise, research funded by the Joseph Rowntree Foundation indicates that in 1991 more than 11 million people were living under the poverty line of half the national average income, far exceeding the all-time low of 3 million living under this threshold during the Labour Government's administration in 1977 (Goodman & Webb 1994).

The DOE-sponsored study of urban policy (Robson et al. 1994) also produced evidence of the uneven effects of inner-city expenditure "suggesting a process of increasing polarization (of unemployment) . . . in which the most deprived areas have seen their socio-economic problems grow increasingly severe" (Robson et

227

Table 11.1 Three models of urban regeneration.

	Free-market enterprise model	Social market model	Interventionist model
Role of central government	To attract inward investment through incentives and minimal social costs, e.g. on employment	To promote joint public–private intervention, to encourage partnership arrangements through financial incentives	To provide legislative powers and finance to direct private sector investment decisions
Role of local state agencies	To promote a property-led approach through local incentives, land reclamation and infrastructure	To encourage local partnerships linking social and economic objectives, e.g. through leverage and targeting of areas and groups in need	To direct and control investment decisions through planning agreements and equity investment
Role of private sector	To advocate the advantages of a free-market approach at all levels of government	To participate in policy-making and implementation	To respond to directions from the public sector
Policy objectives	To maximize private sector investment	To maximize local economic activity to achieve economic, social and environmental objectives	To plan for economic growth, job creation and redistribution of benefits to workforce and wider community
Policy instruments	Financial incentives and to minimize legislative controls	Partnership organizations, mixed funding, policy innovation, place marketing	Planning agreements, enterprise boards, social and fiscal policies
Political ideology	Neo-liberalism, privatism	Social democratic, mixed market	Interventionist, municipal socialism

Source: Adapted from Moore & Richardson (1989: 100).

al. 1994: x). Although the overall conditions in the inner areas of large cities had in many cases worsened, surrounding areas had benefited. The study found that 18 of the 57 urban priority areas have mainly positive outcomes, 18 have mixed outcomes and 21 have poor outcomes. Only 9 UPAs had high inputs and poor outcomes in relation to five key indicators (ibid.). In addition, there was widespread agreement among the private sector and policy experts that central government policy was fragmented, compartmentalized and short-term, and that, together with financial restrictions on local authorities, this had inhibited the formation of partnerships in the 1980s.

The implications of evidence such as this must be that urban policy initiatives have a negligible impact on the overall level of economic activity or household income at the national level, but may have the effect of displacing jobs from one group of relatively deprived residents to another. Other non-measurable benefits may arise from the improvement of housing conditions, the provision of social facilities and environmental improvements, but again benefits may be reallocated between areas so that one gains at the expense of another if the total amount of resources is not increased. The overriding conclusion that may be drawn is that cities need to be seen as an important element of the national economy and that the growth, redevelopment and improvement of these assets can and should be linked with redistributive welfare policies as part of a strategic and comprehensive national economic policy driven by the public sector. Evidence from our case studies, and other reviews of community businesses in what has become known as the third sector, suggests that a significantly different policy context and accounting procedures would need to be established to enable this sector to make a significant contribution to urban regeneration (McArthur 1993).

Towards an urban politics of collaboration and influence

In Chapter 2 we reviewed the main influences giving rise to the partnership approach, of which economic restructuring, the centralization of power, the fragmentation of policy and the urban leadership vacuum were the most significant. It was noted that changes in the philosophy and outlook of the public, private and voluntary sectors were producing circumstances in which closer collaboration was advantageous. Several theoretical statements provided signposts to explaining the growing significance of partnerships.

Logan & Molotch's (1987) description of urban growth coalitions proved a relevant starting point, but differences in the administrative context between the USA and the UK suggested that the model is of limited relevance to the UK. The fundamental differences seems to be that growth coalitions in the USA are in effect delegated powers and responsibilities for urban renewal, whereas in the UK the involvement of pro-growth interests tends to be grafted onto public sector agencies. The Newcastle Initiative, perhaps the example that best relates to the

American model, works more through the local authority and government-funded development agencies, rather than independently. In addition, like Harding (1991), we found little direct involvement by private property interests, except in the case of Birmingham Heartlands Ltd, where the five founding companies were later disqualified from membership of the UDC.

Cox & Mair (1989) argue that it is local dependence, not an interest in land-rent, that is the necessary condition for local business coalitions. We found considerable evidence of this from both the public and private sectors. In all our case studies it was those agencies that had a local economic or social remit that were most committed to coalition building, together with institutions such as large landowners and universities, which are increasingly required to operate on the basis of market principles. In Greenwich it was companies such as British Gas, with a major landholding in the area, and the Woolwich Building Society that were locally dependent. By definition, local residents and voluntary organizations fall into the same category.

Boyle (1993) and Shaw (1993) develop the concept of local dependence by exploring partnership formation in Scotland and the North East respectively. Both note that this was not a new phenomenon, but that examples in both cases could be traced back at least to the 1930s. Shaw stresses that "it is the continuity in structures, personalities and policies that need to be explained as well as the changes" (Shaw 1993: 258). Others, such as King (1985), have noted how agencies such as local chambers of commerce have extended their role from the narrow one of protecting members' interests to playing a more active part in the realm of public policy, and that in many cases they have been encouraged to do so by local authorities.

Thus, as the autonomy of local government was substantially reduced throughout the 1980s and as other interests and agencies sought the means to exert greater influence in the policy vacuum created by the fragmentation and centralization of government policy, new mechanisms for partnership and collaboration were devised. As central government became aware of these changes, its response was to encourage the trend by building in the competitive allocation of resources based on leverage – previously only open to a few local authority budgets – to almost all spending programmes.

Whether these trends can be explained best as a new urban corporatism (Dunleavy & King 1990), it is clear that a new order is developing in which the urban regime (Keating 1991, Stone et al. 1991) is the primary agency for promoting both economic and physical regeneration. However, rather than being free-ranging private-sector dominated agencies, they are increasingly being integrated into an entrepreneurial form of public policy process. Stewart (1994: 143) describes the procedural changes towards SRBs and the increased powers of the regional offices as "competitive localism . . . involving the decentralization of administration as opposed to the devolution of power and influence". Moore & Richardson (1989: 143) define partnership agencies as policy entrepreneurs and argue in the context of their study of local enterprise agencies that they need to be located in a context of "system-maintaining behaviour". Moore & Richardson (ibid.) also refer to a study of corporate social responsibility by Beesley & Evans (1978) in which the latter argue that both the market system and the public choice system (i.e. the political process) have limitations in handling social problems. An emerging third system is what they call "societal self-regulation", of which corporate social responsibility would be an important element. This third approach would require cultural and procedural changes in both government and the corporate sector leading to "mutual dependency and dual legitimacy" (Moore & Richardson 1989: 142) through new co-operative organizational frameworks. Evidence to date suggests that most companies that adopt corporate social responsibility objectives adhere to them so long as they do not conflict with the company's financial and market objectives, and perceive relatively clear distinctions between their (often limited) commitment to social responsibility and what are the proper concerns of the public sector.

Urban policy has been in a state of flux over the past 25 years, but, contrary to the predictions of Michael Heseltine, we have not simply witnessed the rolling back of the boundaries of the State to release the competitive drive of the free market. Neither has there been the convergence of UK and USA urban policy towards privatism, as suggested by Barnekov et al. (1989: 1), whereby the private sector becomes "the principal agent of urban change". Instead, we have witnessed the transformation of the public sector through the incorporation of many of the tenets, practices and procedures of the enterprise culture.

While the traditional boundaries between the public and private sectors have fluctuated back and forth, policy space has been created for a series of innovative experiments in urban governance, perhaps best described by the politically neutral term of "urban regimes". Harvey (1989) and others argue that in a post-industrial society the nature of urban governance changes from managerialism to entrepreneurialism, in which local authority powers are integrated with commercial interests. The evidence from our research suggests this trend is well advanced, whereas the consequent changes in role required and the new skills needed, particularly in the public and voluntary sectors, have yet to be fully appreciated.

Cochrane (1993) notes that for the future it will be necessary for local government to perform the role of catalyst in building complex intersectoral urban regimes, while campaigning for transparency, accountability and democratic legitimacy. It seems that urban politics will increasingly be characterized by competition for resources and investment, collaboration between those with mutual interests, a comprehensive approach to urban problems and local corporatism, in the sense that co-operation between sectors will be the primary mechanism for decision-making and action. The challenge for the future is perhaps to accept that urban regeneration agencies will be facilitators, enablers and policy entrepreneurs, but to devise ways in which they can also be democratically controlled and politically accountable.

231

References and bibliography

Abel-Smith, B. & P. Townsend 1965. *The poor and the poorest*. London: Bell & Hyman.

Amin, A. & J. Tomaney 1991. Creating an enterprise culture in the North East? The impact of urban and regional policies of the 1980s. *Regional Studies* **25**(4), 479–87.

Anon. 1993. *The case for East London: objective 2 status for the Lee Valley and East Thames Corridor* (a joint submission by 12 London boroughs, August). London: Borough of Newham.

Archbishop of Canterbury's Commission on Urban Priority Areas 1985. *Faith in the city: a call for action by church and nation*. London: Church House Publishing.

Atkinson, R. & G. Moon 1994. The City Challenge initiative: an overview and preliminary assessment. *Regional Studies* **28**(1), 94–7.

— 1994. *Urban policy in Britain: the city, the state and the market*. Basingstoke: Macmillan.

Audit Commission 1989. *Urban regeneration and economic development: the local government dimension*. London: HMSO.

— 1991. *The urban regeneration experience: observations from local value for money audits* [Occasional Papers 17]. London: Audit Commission.

Bailey, N. 1994 Towards a research agenda for public–private partnerships in the 1990s. *Local Economy* **8**(4), 292–306.

Bailey, N. & A. Barker (eds) 1992. *City Challenge and local regeneration partnerships: conference proceedings*. London: School of Urban Development and Planning, Polytechnic of Central London.

Bailey, N. & K. MacDonald 1992. Community development trusts: riding the recession? *Town and Country Planning* **61**(6), 169–76.

Bailey, N., A. Barker, K. MacDonald 1993. Picking partners for regeneration. *Town and Country Planning* **62**(6), 136–45.

Barker, A. & N. Bailey (eds) 1992. *City Challenge and local regeneration partnerships: Second conference proceedings*. London: School of Urban Development and Planning, University of Westminster.

Barnekov, T., R. Boyle, D. Rich 1990. *Privatism and urban policy in Britain and the USA*. Oxford: Oxford University Press.

BCT 1992. *Progress through partnership*. Brownlow: Brownlow Community Trust.

— 1993a. *Brownlow – inside lives*. Brownlow: BCT.

— 1993b. *Working towards a Europe of solidarity – consolidating the partnership*. Brownlow: BCT.

Beecham, J. 1993. A sceptical view. *Policy Studies* **14**(2), 14–18.

Beesley, M. & T. Evans 1978. *Corporate social responsibility*. London: Croom Helm.

Benington, J. 1975. *Local government becomes big business*. London: CDP Information and Intelligence Unit.

Bennett, R., G. Krebs, H. Zimmermann (eds) 1990. *Local economic development in Britain and Germany*. London: Anglo-German Foundation.

Bennett, R. & G. Krebs 1991. *Local economic development: public–private partnership initiation in Britain and Germany*. London: Pinter (Belhaven).

Bennett, R., P. Wicks, A. McCoshan 1994. *Local empowerment and business services*. London: UCL Press.

Berger, R. 1989. *Against all odds: the achievements of community-based development organizations*. Washington: National Congress for Community Economic Development.

Berry, J., J. McGreal, B. Deddis 1993. *Urban regeneration: property investment and development*. London: Spon.

Bianchini, F., J. Dawson, R. Evans 1992. Flagship projects in urban regeneration. In *Rebuilding the city: property-led urban regeneration*. London: Spon.

BHDC 1993a. *Birmingham Heartlands Development Corporation*. Birmingham: BHDC.

— 1993b. *Corporate plan 1993-94, final draft*. Birmingham: Birmingham Heartlands Development Corporation.

Birmingham, City of 1992. Birmingham Heartlands: a unique story of success. *The Planner* **78**(11), 15–19.

BHL nd. *Waterlinks development framework*. Birmingham: Birmingham Heartlands Ltd.

— nd. *Bordesley development framework*. Birmingham: BHL.

— 1991a. *Birmingham Heartlands Ltd – an urban development agency*. Birmingham: BHL.

— 1991b. *Birmingham Heartlands: development progress*. Birmingham: BHL.

— 1992. *Birmingham Heartlands Ltd: progress over four years*. Birmingham: BHL.

Boyle, R. 1989. Partnership in practice: an assessment of public-private collaboration in urban regeneration – a case study of Glasgow Action. *Local Government Studies* March/April, 17–28.

— 1990. Regeneration in Glasgow: Stability, collaboration, and inequality. In *Leadership and urban regeneration*, D. Judd & M. Parkinson (eds), 109–132. London: Sage.

— 1993. Changing partners: the experience of urban economic policy in west central Scotland 1980–90. *Urban Studies* **30**(2), 309–324.

Brindley, T. & G. Stoker 1988. Partnership in inner-city urban renewal – a critical analysis. *Local Government Policy-making* **15**(2), 3–12.

Brindley, T., Y. Rydin, G. Stoker 1989. *Remaking planning: the politics of urban change in the Thatcher years*. London: Unwin Hyman.

British Business 1987. Inner cities: the challenges and the policies. *British Business* (23 October).

Brownlow Ltd 1993. *A global approach to community development: annual report*. Brownlow: Brownlow Ltd.

Business in the Community 1990. *Leadership in the community*. London: Coopers & Lybrand.

Cabinet Office 1988. *Action for cities*. London: Cabinet Office.

Carley, M. 1991. Business in urban regeneration partnerships: a case study in Birmingham. *Local Economy* **6**(2), 100–115.

CBI 1988. *Initiatives beyond charity: Report of the CBI task force on business and urban regeneration*. London: Confederation of British Industry.

Christie, I. 1991. *Profitable partnerships: an action guide for company investment in the community*. London: Policy Studies Institute.

Christie, I., M. Carley, M. Fogarty 1991. *Profitable partnerships: Report on company investment in the community*. London: Policy Studies Institute.

Christie, I. & H. Rolfe 1992. The TECs and inner city regeneration. *Policy Studies* **13**(1),

Civic Trust Regeneration Unit 1993. *Urban regeneration partnerships: an analysis of the knowledge, skills and attitudes needed by the managers of partnerships*. London: Civic Trust.

234

— 1993. *Greenwich town centre action plan*. London: Civic Trust.

Clavel, P. & N. Kleniewski 1990. Space for progressive local policy: examples from the United States and United Kingdom. In *Beyond the city limits*, J. Logan & T. Swanstrom (eds), 199–234. Philadelphia: Temple University Press.

Cochrane, A. 1993. *Whatever happened to local government?* Buckingham: Open University Press.

Cockburn, C. 1977. *The local state*. London: Pluto Press.

Colenutt, B. 1992. *Social regeneration: directions for urban policy in the 1990s*. Manchester: Centre for Local Economic Strategies.

Colenutt, B. & S. Tansley 1990. *Inner-city regeneration: a local authority perspective*. Manchester: Centre for Local Economic Strategies.

Comptroller and Auditor General 1990. *Regenerating the inner cities*. London: HMSO (National Audit Office).

Coulson, A. 1993. Urban development corporations, local authorities and patronage in urban policy. In *British urban policy and the urban development corporations*, R. Imrie & H. Thomas (eds), 27–37. London: Paul Chapman.

Cox, K. & A. Mair 1989. Urban growth machines and the politics of local economic development. *International Journal of Urban and Regional Research* **13**(1), 137–46.

Cruddas Park Community Trust 1992. *Cruddas Park Community Trust*. Newcastle.

Deakin, N. & J. Edwards 1993. *The enterprise culture and the inner city*. London: Routledge.

De Groot, L. 1992. City Challenge: Competing in the urban regeneration game. *Local Economy* **7**(3), 196–209.

DOE (Department of the Environment) 1977a. *Inner London: Policies for dispersal and balance – final report of the Lambeth inner area study*. London: HMSO.

— 1977b. *Unequal city – final report of the Birmingham inner area study*. London: HMSO.

— 1977c. *Change or decay – Final report of the Liverpool inner area study*. HMSO: London.

— 1977d. *White paper: Policy for the inner cities*. London: HMSO.

— 1979. *Inner cities policy: statement by Michael Heseltine, Secretary of State for the Environment* (press notice 390). London: DOE.

— 1985. *Urban programme ministerial guidelines*. London: DOE.

— 1989. *Progress in cities*. London: DOE.

— 1992a. *Annual report*. London: DOE.

— 1992b. Working partnerships: City Challenge implementing agencies – and advisory note. London: DOE.

— 1992c. *The urban regeneration agency: a consultation paper*. London: DOE.

— 1993a. *Annual report*. London: HMSO.

— 1993b. *Single regeneration budget: Note on principles*. London: HMSO.

— 1993c. *Estate action: annual report 1992–93*. London: HMSO.

— 1993d. *Task forces in action*. London: DOE.

— 1993e. *Working together: private finance and public money*. London: DOE.

— 1994. *Bidding guidance: a guide to funding from the single regeneration budget*. London: DOE.

Donnison, D. & A. Middleton 1987. *Regenerating the inner city: Glasgow's experience*. London: Routledge & Kegan Paul.

Dunleavy, P. & D. King 1990. Middle-level elites and control of urban policy-making in Britain in the 1990s. Paper presented to the Urban Politics Group, London School of Economics.

Edwards, J. & R. Batley 1978. *The politics of positive discrimination*. London: Tavistock.

235

Edwards, J. & N. Deakin 1992. Privatism and partnership in urban regeneration. *Public Administration* **70**, 359–68.

Emmerich, M. & J. Peck 1992. *Reforming the TECs*. Manchester: Centre for Local Economic Strategies.

English Heritage 1993. *Time for action. Greenwich town centre: a conservation strategy*. London: English Heritage.

Fox-Prezeworski, J., J. Goddard, M. de Jong (eds) 1991. *Urban regeneration in a changing economy: an international perspective*. Oxford: Oxford University Press.

Galloway, M. 1993. The Crown Street regeneration project. *Town and Country Planning* **62**(6), 140–41.

Gilchrist, J. 1985. *The Motherwell project: a study of agency intervention in urban renewal*. Strathclyde Papers on Planning, Department of Urban and Regional Planning, University of Strathclyde.

Gillespie, N. 1992. *Brownlow Community Trust: a draft historical account to September 1990*. Brownlow: BCT.

Gilloran, A. 1983. *Wester Hailes: ten years on*. Edinburgh: Wester Hailes Representative Council.

Glasgow City Council 1993. *Glasgow regeneration alliance: Shaping the future – A commitment to area regeneration*. Glasgow: Glasgow City Council.

Goldsmith, M. 1990. Local autonomy: theory and practice. In *Challenges to local government*, D. King & J. Pierre (eds), 15–36. London: Sage.

— 1992. Local government. *Urban Studies* **29**(3/4), 393–410.

Goodman, A. & S. Webb 1994. *For richer, for poorer*. London: Institute for Fiscal Studies.

Goodwin, M., S. Duncan, S. Halford 1993. Regulation theory, the local state and the transition of urban politics. *Environment and Planning* **11**, 67–88.

Gosling, P. 1993. *After the urban programme?* London: The Urban Programme Coalition.

GWDP 1992. *Brochure: Greenwich Waterfront Development Partnership*. London: Greenwich Waterfront Development Partnership.

— 1993. *Woolwich revival*. London: GWDP.

Griffiths, R. 1993. The politics of cultural policy in urban regeneration strategies. *Policy and Politics* **21**(1), 39–46.

Gulliver, S. 1984. The area projects of the Scottish Development Agency. *Town Planning Review* **55**(3), 322–34.

Gurr, R. & D. King 1987. *The state and the city*. London: Macmillan.

Hambleton, R. 1990. *Urban government in the 1990s: lessons from the USA*. Occasional Paper 35, School for Advanced Urban Studies, University of Bristol.

— 1991. *Another chance for cities: issues for urban policy in the 1990s*. Papers in Planning Research, Department of City and Regional Planning, University of Wales College of Cardiff.

— 1993. Issues for urban policy in the 1990s. *Town Planning Review* **64**(3), 313–28.

Hambleton, R. & M. Taylor (eds) 1993. *People in cities: a transatlantic policy exchange*. SAUS Study 11, School for Advanced Urban Studies, University of Bristol.

Harding, A. 1990. Local autonomy and urban economic development policies: the recent UK experience in perspective. In *Challenges to local government*, D. King & J. Pierre (eds), 79–100. London: Sage.

— 1990. Public–private sector partnerships in urban regeneration. In *Local economic policy*, M. Campbell (ed.), 108–127. London: Cassell.

236

— 1991. The rise of urban growth coalitions – UK style? *Environment and Planning C* **9**, 295–317.

Harvey, D. 1989. From managerialism to entrepreneurialism: the transformation in urban governance in late capitalism. *Geografiska Annaler* **71B**(1), 3–17.

Haughton, G. & D. Whitney 1989. Equal urban partners? *The Planner* **75**(34), 9–11.

Hayton, K. 1992. The decline of public-private partnerships: the fate of the Scottish enterprise trusts under Scottish Enterprise. *Regional Studies* **26**(7), 671–5.

— 1993. Progress in Partnership: the future of urban regeneration in Scotland. *Fraser of Allander Quarterly Economic Commentary* **19**(2), 51–6.

Hayton, K. & E. Mearns 1991. Progressing Scottish Enterprise. *Local Economy* **5**(4), 305–316.

Healey, P. 1991. Urban regeneration and the development industry. *Regional Studies* **25**(2), 97–110.

Healey, P., S. Davoudi, M. O'Toole, S. Tavsanoglu, D. Usher (eds) 1992. *Rebuilding the city: property-led urban regeneration*. London: Spon.

Heseltine, M. 1987. *Where there's a will*. London: Hutchinson.

Hood, N. 1991. The Scottish Development Agency in retrospect. *Royal Bank of Scotland Review* **171**, 3–21.

House of Commons Committee of Public Accounts 1986. *The urban programme* (House of Commons Paper 81, session 1985–6). London: HMSO.

Imrie, R. & H. Thomas 1992. The wrong side of the tracks: a case study of local economic regeneration in Britain. *Policy and Politics* **20**(3), 213–26.

— 1993a. The limits of property-led regeneration. *Environment and Planning C* **11**, 87–102.

— (eds) 1993b. *British urban policy and the urban development corporations*. London: Paul Chapman.

Industry Department for Scotland 1986. *Review of the Scottish Development Agency – summary*. Edinburgh: Scottish Office.

Jacobs, B. 1990. Business leadership in urban regeneration: towards a shared vision? In *Challenges to local government*, D. King & J. Pierre (eds), 195–211. London: Sage.

Judd, D. & M. Parkinson (eds) 1990. *Leadership and urban regeneration*. London: Sage.

Kearns, G. & C. Philo (eds) 1993. *Selling places: the city as cultural capital, past and present*. Oxford: Pergamon.

Keating, M. 1989. The disintegration of urban policy: Glasgow and the new Britain. *Urban Affairs Quarterly* **24**(4), 513–36.

— 1991. *Comparative urban politics: power and the city in the US, Canada, Britain and France*. Cheltenham: Edward Elgar.

— 1993. The politics of economic development. *Urban Affairs Quarterly* **28**(3), 373–96.

King, D. 1990. The new urban left and local economic initiatives: the Greater London Enterprise Board. In *Challenges to local government*, D. King & J. Pierre (eds), 101–121. London: Sage.

King, D. & J. Pierre (eds) 1990. *Challenges to local government*. London: Sage.

King, R. 1985. Corporatism and the local economy. In *Political economy of corporatism*, W. Grant (ed.), 202–228. London: Macmillan.

Law, C. 1988. Public-private partnerships in urban revitalisation in Britain. *Regional Studies* **22**(5), 446–51.

Lawless, P. 1989. *Britain's inner cities*, 2nd edn. London: Paul Chapman.

— 1990. Regeneration in Sheffield: from radical intervention to partnership. In *Leadership and urban regeneration*, D. Judd & M. Parkinson (eds), 133–51. London: Sage.

— 1991a. *Public–private sector partnerships in the United Kingdom.* Working Paper 16, Centre for Regional, Economic and Social Research, Sheffield City Polytechnic.

— 1991b. Urban policy in the Thatcher decade: English inner city policy, 1979–90. *Environment and Planning C* **9**, 15–30.

— 1994. Partnership in urban regeneration in the UK: the Sheffield Central Area Study. *Urban Studies*, **31**(8), 1303–324.

Le Gales, P. & J. Mawson 1994. *Management innovations in urban policy: lessons from France.* Luton: Local Government Management Board.

Leclerc, R. & D. Draffan 1984. The Glasgow Eastern Area Renewal Project. *Town Planning Review* **55**(3), 335–51.

Lewis, N. 1992. *Inner city regeneration: the demise of regional and local government.* Buckingham: Open University Press.

Lloyd, G. & D. Newlands 1988. The "growth coalition" and urban economic development. *Local Economy* **3**(1), 31–9.

— 1990. Business interests and planning initiatives: a case study of Aberdeen. In *Radical planning initiatives*, J. Montgomery & A. Thornley (eds), 49–58. Aldershot: Gower.

Loftman, P. & B. Nevin 1993. *Urban regeneration and social equity: a case study of Birmingham 1986–92.* Research Paper 8, Faculty of the Built Environment, University of Central England.

— 1994. Prestige project developments: Economic renaissance or economic myth? A case study of Birmingham. *Local Economy* **8**(4), 307–325.

Logan, J. & H. Molotch 1987. *Urban fortunes: the political economy of place.* Berkeley: University of California Press.

Logan, J. & T. Swanstrom (eds) 1990. *Beyond the city limits.* Philadelphia: Temple University Press.

London Borough of Greenwich 1991. *Greenwich Waterfront strategy.* London: LB Greenwich.

— 1992. *The Greenwich Waterfront City Challenge.* London: LB Greenwich.

— 1993. *Royal Arsenal development brief.* London: LB Greenwich (Department of Planning and Economic Development).

London Boroughs of Greenwich and Lewisham 1993. *Creekside strategy: a joint initiative for Deptford Creek.* London: LBs of Greenwich and Lewisham.

Mabbott, J. 1992. *Press release: action on urban programme.* London: National Council for Voluntary Organisations.

— 1993. The role of community involvement. *Policy Studies* **14**(2), 27–35.

MacDonald, K. 1993. The Wester Hailes Partnership. *Town and Country Planning* **62**(6), 144–5.

Macfarlane, R. & J. Mabbott 1993. *City Challenge: involving local communities.* London: National Council for Voluntary Organisations.

MacGregor, S. & B. Pimlott 1990. *Tackling the inner cities: the 1980s reviewed, prospects for the 1990s.* Oxford: Oxford University Press.

Mackintosh, M. 1992. Partnerships: Issues of policy and negotiation. *Local Economy* **7**(3), 210–24.

Marriott, O. 1989. *The property boom.* London: Abingdon Publishing.

McArthur, A. 1993. Community business and urban regeneration. *Urban Studies* **30**(4/5), 849–73.

McCrone, G. 1991. Urban renewal: the Scottish experience. *Urban Studies* **28**(6), 919–38.

McDonough, R. 1990. The Brownlow community and the Brownlow Community Trust. *TSB Business Outlook and Economic Review* **5**(3), 15–17.

— 1993. Brownlow Community Trust – A partnership in the making. *Town and country Planning* **62**(6), 143–4.

MHLG (Ministry of Housing and Local Government) 1962. *Town centres: approaches to renewal*. London: HMSO.

Milner Holland 1965. *Report of the committee on housing in Greater London* (Cmnd 2605). London: HMSO.

Molotch, H. 1976. The city as growth machine: towards a political economy of place. *American Journal of Sociology* **82**(2), 309–332.

Moore, C. 1990. Displacement, partnership and privatisation: local government and urban economic regeneration in the 1980s. In *Challenges to local government*, D. King & J. Pierre (eds), 55–78. London: Sage.

Moore, C. & J. Richardson 1989. *Local partnership and the unemployment crisis in Britain*. London: Unwin Hyman.

National Audit Office (NAO) 1990. *Regenerating the inner cities*. London: HMSO.

NCDP (National Community Development Project) 1974. *Inter-project report*. London: CDP Information and Intelligence Unit.

— 1975. *Forward planning*. London: CDP Information and Intelligence Unit.

Needham, R. 1990. The regeneration of Craigavon. *TSB Business Outlook and Economic Review* **5**(3), 22–5.

The Newcastle Initiative 1988. *Grey Street Renaissance*. Newcastle: Newcastle City Council, The Newcastle Initiative, Tyne & Wear Development Corporation.

— 1991. *The Newcastle environmental initiative*. Newcastle: TNI.

— 1994a. *The Newcastle Initiative*. Newcastle: TNI.

— 1994b. *The green business club*. Newcastle: TNI.

PA Cambridge Economic Consultants 1992. *An evaluation of the government's inner city task force initiative*, vol. 1: *main report*. London: Department of Environment.

Paddison, R. 1993. City marketing, image reconstruction and urban regeneration. *Urban Studies* **30**(2), 339–49.

Parkinson, M. 1988. Urban regeneration and development corporations: Liverpool style. *Local Economy* **3**(2), 5–13.

— 1991. The rise of the entrepreneurial European city: Strategic responses to economic changes in the 1980s. *Ekistics* **350/351**, 299–307.

— 1993. City Challenge: a new strategy for Britain's cities? *Policy Studies* **14**(2), 5–13.

Parkinson, M. & S. Wilks 1986. The politics of inner-city partnerships. In *New research in central–local relations*, M. Goldsmith (ed.), 290–307. Aldershot: Gower.

Pavitt, J. 1990. Urban renewal in Wales: the role of the WDA. *The Planner* (December), 70–74.

Pearce, J. 1993. *At the heart of the community economy*. London: Caloustie Gulbenkian Foundation.

Peck, J. 1993. The trouble with TECs . . . a critique of the Training and Enterprise Councils initiative. *Policy and Politics* **21**(4), 289–305.

Planning Week 1994. Urban development. Welsh focus: RTPI Conference, Cardiff. *Planning Week* **2**(21), 29–30.

Plowden, W. 1967. *Children and their primary schools*. London: HMSO.

Pollock, L. 1992. Europe's smart war on want. *The Guardian* (8 April).

Port Greenwich Ltd 1990. *Port Greenwich outline planning application*, vols 1–3. London: Llewelyn-Davies Planning.

— 1992. *Amended outline planning applications*, vols 1A–4A. London: Koetter, Kim and Associates International Ltd.

Public Sector Management Research Unit 1985. *Five-year review of the Birmingham inner-city partnership* (Inner Cities Research Programme 12). London: Department of Environment.

239

Rein, M. 1989. The social structure of institutions: neither public nor private. In *Privatization and the welfare state*, S. Kamerman & J. Kahn (eds). Princeton: Princeton University Press.

Richardson, J. 1983. *The development of corporate social responsibility in the UK*. Strathclyde Papers on Government and Politics 1, University of Strathclyde.

Rifkin, A. & L. Williams 1991. Greenwich waterfront takes waterfront initiative. *Planning* **927**(July), 18–19.

Robson, B. 1988. *Those inner cities: reconciling the social and economic aims of urban policy*. Oxford: Oxford University Press.

Robson, B. et al. 1994. *Assessing the impact of urban policy* (DoE Inner Cities Research Programme). London: HMSO.

Roger Tym & Partners 1988. *Birmingham Heartlands: development strategy for East Birmingham and technical appendices* [unpublished].

Scarman, Lord 1981. *The Brixton disorders, 10–12 April 1981. Report of an inquiry* (Cmnd 8427). London: HMSO.

Scottish Office 1988. *New life for urban Scotland*. Edinburgh: Scottish Office.

— 1989. *Realising the potential: the partnership strategy for Wester Hailes*. Edinburgh: Scottish Office.

— 1990. *Urban Scotland into the 90s*. Edinburgh: Scottish Office.

— 1993. *Progress in partnership: a consultation paper on the future of urban regeneration policy in Scotland*. Edinburgh: Scottish Office.

Seebohm, F. 1968. *Committee on local authority and allied social services* (Cmnd 3703). London: HMSO.

Shaw, K. 1993. The development of a new urban corporatism: the politics of urban regeneration in the North East of England. *Regional Studies* **27**(3), 251–9.

Shelter Neighbourhood Action Project 1972. *Another chance for cities*. London: Shelter.

Smith, B. 1993. *Profiting people – an economic strategy for Brownlow*. Brownlow: BCT.

Smith, G. & C. Cantley 1985. *Assessing health care: a study in organisational evaluation*. Milton Keynes: Open University Press.

Solesbury, W. 1993. Reframing urban policy. *Policy and Politics* **21**(1), 31–8.

Spencer, K. 1980. The genesis of Comprehensive Community Programmes. *Local Government Studies* **6**(5), 17–28.

— 1981. Comprehensive Community Programmes: the practical experience. *Local Government Studies* **7**(3), 31–49.

Squires, G. 1989. *Unequal partnerships: the political economy of urban redevelopment in postwar America*. New Brunswick, NJ: Rutgers University Press.

— 1991. Partnership and the pursuit of the private city. In *Urban life in transition*, M. Gottdiener & C. Pickvance (eds), 196–221. London: Sage.

Stephenson, M. 1991. Whither the public–private partnership: a critical overview. *Urban Affairs Quarterly* **27**(1), 109–127.

Stewart, J. 1989. The changing organisation and management of local authorities. In *The future of local government*, J. Stewart & G. Stoker (eds), 171–84. London: Macmillan.

Stewart, M. 1994. Between Whitehall and town hall: the realignment of urban regeneration policy in England. *Policy and Politics* **22**(2), 133–45.

Stoker, G. 1989. Creating a local government for a post-Fordist society: the Thatcher project? In *The future of local government*, J. Stewart & G. Stoker (eds), 141–70. London: Macmillan.

— 1990. Regulation theory, local government and the transition from Fordism. In *Challenges to local government*, D. King & J. Pierre (eds), 242–64. London: Sage.

Stone, C. 1987. The study of the politics of urban development. In *The politics of urban development*, C. Stone & H. Sanders (eds), 4–46. Lawrence: University of Kansas Press.

Stone, C., M. Orr, D. Imbroscio 1991. The reshaping of urban leadership in US cities: a regime analysis. In *Urban life in transition*, M. Gottdiener & C. Pickvance (eds), 222–39. London: Sage.

Sviridoff, M. 1989. The Local Initiatives Support Corporation: a private initiative for a public problem. In *Privatisation and the welfare state*, S. Kamerman & A. Kahn (eds), 207–233. Princeton: Princeton University Press.

Thake, S. & R. Staubach 1993. *Investing in people: rescuing communities from the margin*. York: Joseph Rowntree Foundation.

Thompson, R. 1993. Partnerships in extrovert and participative planning. *Town and Country Planning* **62**(4), 83–4.

Thornley, A. 1993. *Urban planning under Thatcherism: the challenge of the market*, 2nd edn. London: Routledge.

Tibbalds Colbourne Karski Williams 1990. Craigavon central area development study. *TSB Business Outlook and Economic Review* **5**(3), 18–21.

TNI: see (The) Newcastle Initiative

TCPA 1986. *Whose responsibility? Reclaiming the inner cities*. London: Town and Country Planning Association.

Turok, I. 1992. Property-led regeneration: Panacea or placebo? *Environment and Planning A* **24**(3), 361–80.

University of Newcastle upon Tyne 1992. *Newcastle's West End: monitoring the City Challenge initiative: a baseline report*. Department of Town and Country Planning, University of Newcastle upon Tyne.

Victor Hausner and Associates 1992. *Working partnerships – City Challenge implementing agencies: an advisory note*. London: Department of the Environment.

Wannop, U. & R. Leclerc 1987a. Urban renewal and the origins of GEAR. In *Regenerating the inner city: Glasgow's experience*, D. Donnison & A. Middleton (eds), 61–71. London: Routledge & Kegan Paul.

— 1987b. The management of GEAR. In *Regenerating the inner city: Glasgow's experience*, D. Donnison & A. Middleton (eds), 218–31. London: Routledge & Kegan Paul.

Wester Hailes Partnership 1992. *The role of the partnership resource team* (unpublished).

— 1993. *Unemployment and household income: Education, training and employment strategy*. Edinburgh: Wester Hailes Partnership.

— 1994a. *Wester Hailes housing strategy 1994–1999*. Edinburgh: Wester Hailes Partnership.

— 1994b. *Wester Hailes Partnership progress report*. Edinburgh: Wester Hailes Partnership.

Wester Hailes Partnership Business Support Group 1994. *Updated mission statement*. Wester Hailes Partnership Business Support Group (unpublished).

Wester Hailes Representative Council 1990. *Moving forward: a social policy for Wester Hailes*. Edinburgh: Wester Hailes Representative Council.

— 1994. *Annual Report 1994*. Edinburgh: Wester Hailes Representative Council.

White, W. 1990. Brownlow: a plan for regeneration. *TSB Business Outlook and Economic Review* **5**(3), 11–14.

Whitney, D. & G. Haughton 1990. Structures for development partnerships in the 1990s: practice in West Yorkshire. *The Planner* **76**(21), 15–19.

Wilkinson, S. 1992. Towards a new city? A case study of image improvement initiatives in Newcastle upon Tyne. In *Rebuilding the city: property-led urban regeneration*, P. Healey et al. (eds), 174–211. London: Spon.

Willmott, P. & R. Hutchison 1992. *Urban trends 1: a report on Britain's deprived urban areas*. London: Policy Studies Institute.

Winkler, J. 1977. The corporatist economy: theory and administration. In *Industrial society: class, cleavage and control*, R. Scase (ed.), 43–58. London: George Allen & Unwin.

Wood, C. 1994. Local urban regeneration initiatives: Birmingham Heartlands. *Cities* **11**(1), 48–58.

Wood, J. 1992. Community choice in economic renewal. *Town and Country Planning* **61**(6), 171–3.

WCDT 1991. *Director's report 1991*. Glasgow: Woodlands Community Development Trust.

WCDT 1991. *Annual report 1991*. Glasgow: Woodlands Community Development Trust.

INDEX